Creating the Fictional
Female Detective

Creating the Fictional Female Detective

The Sleuth Heroines of British Women Writers, 1890–1940

CARLA T. KUNGL

McFarland & Company, Inc., Publishers
Jefferson, North Carolina, and London

LIBRARY OF CONGRESS CATALOGUING-IN-PUBLICATION DATA

Kungl, Carla T.
   Creating the fictional female detective : the sleuth heroines of
British women writers, 1890–1940 / Carla T. Kungl.
      p.   cm.
   Includes bibliographical references and index.

   ISBN 0-7864-2528-8 (softcover : 50# alkaline paper)

   1. Detective and mystery stories, English—History and criticism.
2. Women detectives in literature.   3. English fiction—Women
authors—History and criticism.   4. Women—Employment—Great
Britain—History—20th century.   5. Women—Employment—
Great Britain—History—19th century.   6. English fiction—20th
century—History and criticism.   7. English fiction—19th century—
History and criticism.   I. Title.
PR888.D4K86 2006
823'.087209928709041—dc22   2006000010

British Library cataloguing data are available

On the cover: color art (inset) ©2006 Index Stock; background image
©2006 Clipart.com

Manufactured in the United States of America

McFarland & Company, Inc., Publishers
   Box 611, Jefferson, North Carolina 28640
      www.mcfarlandpub.com

For my husband and son, with much love

Acknowledgments

Much of this work was done at Case Western Reserve University in Cleveland, Ohio, with financial support from the Department of English, including an Arthur Adrian Fellowship and Andrew W. Mellon Fellowship. A trip to the British Library also helped fill in some background information on a few of these authors. Special thanks go to Mike Yeager from CWRU's Kelvin Smith Library, who managed to drum up some obscure texts on microfilm for me.

Many scholars read this manuscript at various stages and helped solidify its structure, including Angela Woollacott, Roger Salomon, and William Marling. Athena Vrettos spent far too many hours, I'm sure, providing careful and copious editing suggestions. I owe thanks most gratefully to Todd Crawley, Margaret Kocher, and Holly Roberts, for reading this manuscript in various stages and offering suggestions; and to Jennifer Waters, for putting my first Sayers novel into my hands. Sharon Harrow most recently gave suggestions for finalizing parts of project and in general served as an all-around cheerleader.

No words are sufficient to express the love and gratitude I wish to extend to my parents and siblings. They helped make me who I am, and thus made this book possible.

Contents

Preface

"Get a trained sleuth to do it," said Archie firmly. "That's what they're for. I can put you on to one if you like."

"A good man?"

"A sleuthess," said Archie impressively. "A perfect wonder—has old Sherlock boiled."

"A woman?"

"Well, a sleuthess. She's not exactly what you'd call a little bit of fluff, you know."

[...] "But who is she? And why drag in a sleuthess when there are lots of perfectly good sleuths?"

—Patricia Wentworth, *Grey Mask* (1928)

Charles Moray raises a good question, one that most certainly would still be raised in today's society: why, if one had the choice, would one hire a female sleuth instead of a male? What difference does it make? How can she possibly succeed?

In the above case, Miss Silver, one of the elderly spinster detectives that proliferated in the second half of the twentieth century, succeeds by employing strategies popular with many detectives from her time period: she is capable of following suspects without being seen, as no one notices elderly ladies much at all, and of getting a suspect's landlady to give her information without really being aware that she has done so.

But I would extend the above questions to the creators of female detectives as well: why, if one had the choice, would one create a female detective

instead of a male, especially in the 1890s, when Holmes-mania was sweeping across England? How could she possibly succeed?

Many standard and good answers are available. First and most obviously,
one created a female detective *because* Holmes-mania was sweeping the
nation, and detective-anything was guaranteed to sell. The popular magazines of the time, including *The Strand*, which had originally published
Doyle's work, as well as *Harmsworth's* and *Ludgate Monthly*, quickly published
such stories, and their audiences avidly read them. Add to this the fact that
the female detective was a highly unusual character—Fay Blake believes she
was created only to startle readers ("Lady Sleuths and Women Detectives,"
39)—and an early writer of detective fiction was bound to have success on
his (or her) hands.

The above parenthetical reference to the female writer of these stories
is perhaps misleading, because women writers of the late 19th and early 20th
centuries who created female detectives are the subject of this study. And
yet, just as most detectives were assumed to be men, the creators of these
detectives were also assumed to be men. What could a woman possibly know
about detective work? In what ways were women, whose knowledge of society was often considered appropriately domestic, suited to writing about
crime, murder, or logical deduction? Yet many of these early detectives—both
male and female—were created by women writers. Male writers, too, created
both male and female detectives. But I was intrigued by those early women
writers who chose to put a female in the starring role in their detective
fiction. Certainly popularity was a factor, but it seemed significant that,
being able to choose, they chose to place a female in the role of detective,
a role clearly designated masculine by late Victorian society. Why? What
were they trying to show? What might a female detective character allow
women writers to explore or express in their fiction that a male detective
could not?

In this study, I show the ways in which creating a female detective
allowed women writers to construct and to establish their professional
authority in the detective fiction genre. Employing certain narrative strategies within their fiction through the lens of a female detective's abilities and
adversities provided women writers with ways of expressing their fitness to
write in this particular genre and adapting it as a vehicle for women's writing. In doing so, they were also able to explore the contemporary tensions
between society's underlying domestic ideology and women's entrance into
the work force. The narrative strategies used by these women writers include
using domestic knowledge and female intuition as key crime-solving tools,
recuperating the despised spinster character, confronting the dilemma of
women writers and mass market writing, and engaging in the meta-fictional
technique of creating women writers of detective fiction to work as detectives

in their fiction. Writers from the 1930s such as Agatha Christie and Doro-thy L. Sayers were able to draw upon the authority achieved by their female predecessors in order to engage in self-conscious explorations not only of their society but of the detective fiction genre as well, changing the path the genre would take while continuing to create narratives with cultural reso-nance for women.

Scholarly studies of women's detective fiction are not uncommon, but most survey only half the terrain, focusing either on the women writers or on the female characters—never on both. Among recent collections that survey women writers of detective fiction are Kathleen Gregory Klein's *Great Women Mystery Writers: Classic to Contemporary* (1994) and Jean Swan-son and Dean James' *By a Woman's Hand: A Guide to Mystery Fiction by Women* (1994); however, these surveys cover both male and female detective creations. There are also studies that survey a variety of female detectives—Joseph Kestner's *Sherlock's Sisters* (2003) is the most recent example, one that also focuses specifically on the late 19th century—but there are others that include at least a chapter on early women detectives, including Klein's *The Woman Detective: Gender and Genre* (1995) and Patricia Craig and Mary Cadogan's *The Lady Investigates: Women Detectives and Spies in Fiction* (1981). These cover the female detective, but the author involved might be male or female.

There are no scholarly studies of this period that focus exclusively on the intersection of the woman writer and the female detective. This book offers a new reading that shows how these writers use detective fiction and the female detective to critique both society and genre, highlighting the specific cultural and gender issues that are raised by such a discussion. I use the detective story and female detective as created by women writers to explore the underlying social, sexual, and professional tensions in late Vic-torian through post-war England, re-examining the important and ever-shifting problems of women's roles in society, complicating traditional middle-class ideologies of womanhood, as their characters act within an accustomed sphere but in an unconventional profession.

This study examines the critical importance of early female detectives, both in their own right and as part of the larger genre of detective fiction. Many critics and editors have dismissed these early detectives as conven-tional and trite, when in fact the genre offers rich variety: fictional female detectives appear as both paid professionals and gifted amateurs; single, married, widowed; older spinsters and young adventurers; detecting for pleasure and to clear their own or a loved one's name. By using the logic and intelligence necessary to any detective, along with their own specialized knowledge, female detectives negotiated within societal strictures a specifi-cally female authority and professional identity. In choosing to create female detectives who were both varied and unusual, women writers confronted some of their own literary anxieties and ultimately were able to explore the ways they could create new routes to women's authority within a male-dominated culture and specifically in the detective fiction genre.

Introduction

I began this project from its conclusion; that is, with what now comprises the final chapter: Dorothy L. Sayers and her relationship to the character she created in four of her detective fiction novels, the writer-detective Harriet Vane. Harriet Vane was unlike any other female detective character I had encountered—interesting, intelligent, and well developed—and the obvious similarities between her and Sayers were intriguing. Yet she seemed curiously inept. Why was she never the "true" detective, responsible for solving crimes, but always in the position of helping Lord Peter Wimsey? Why create such an unconventional role model (introduced to readers in 1929 as she is on trial for the murder of her ex-lover) and then place her firmly in the traditional plot of the female romance novel: social complicity, then social aberration, then salvation through marriage, subjugation, and "happily ever after"? What happened to Harriet Vane?

From there I began to look more closely at other early fictional female detectives, assuming that their fates in fiction would be similar; this was, after all, popular formulaic fiction which usually demanded the standard conclusion, and for women this meant marriage at the end of the story. I was mistaken. Many were young, single, and anxious to find work—and this was in fiction from the 1890s. They often worked independently and remained outside of the bonds of the traditional marriage plot. Clearly there was something more going on in the female detective world than what had come down to us in the elderly, twittering Miss Marple stereotype. Critics had, for the most part, given the sub-genre merely a cursory glance. Performing basic plot analysis, feminist critics came to the conclusion that, despite their unconventional job, fictional female detectives did not work to expand roles for women. Female detectives stayed within the boundaries of stereotypical feminine behavior; they often got married in the end; or, if they remained single, they worked to promote the married happiness of others in the story, still upholding society's view of the proper role for women. Therefore, such criticism argues, time would be better spent looking at female detectives created in the past thirty years who more overtly challenged society's views of femininity; while studying these earlier characters might be a useful starting point, they can be dismissed from serious feminist critical attention.[1]

However, such a conclusion belied the astounding range of female detectives I had found in late nineteenth-century fiction. And although there were fairly equal numbers of female detectives created by men and by women, I was attracted to the women writers of these stories. It seemed significant that these writers chose to place a female in the role of detective, a role clearly designated masculine by late Victorian society. Why? What were they trying to show? What might a female detective character allow women writers to explore or express in their fiction that a male detective could not?

In seeking answers, I went back to Dorothy Sayers and her reasons for creating Harriet Vane. Sayers herself had written about the question, and her own accounts were illuminating. In her essay "Gaudy Night" (1937), she writes that though she had initially created Vane in *Strong Poison* to marry off Peter Wimsey, so as to put *his* detective career to rest, she found that when the time came she simply couldn't allow Harriet to accept Peter's marriage proposal at the end of the book without doing great injustice to what was supposed to be a purely functional character: "I could find no form of words in which she could accept him without loss of self-respect" (in Haycraft, *Art* 211). As often happens, the character took over and demanded different treatment than the author originally intended. It took two more lengthy books before Sayers could allow Harriet to accept Peter's marriage proposal. It could not occur until the characters were in a position of equality instead of one "false and degrading," until Sayers had made Peter a "human being" (211).

I saw the story anew. I saw that Harriet's "capitulation" to marriage (and Sayers' to the marriage plot) was of lesser importance than the much more forceful act of construction: the realization that through Harriet Vane (a female detective fiction writer) Sayers (a female detective fiction writer) was working through a professional knot. She was actively working to move her fiction from the puzzle-oriented plot that had come to prevail in the British strain of the detective fiction genre and return it to a more character-based, well-developed novel of manners, one which took into account cultural and social issues of her day. By casting Harriet in a situation similar to her own and showing her facing the same problems, as both a writer and as a woman, Sayers herself was exploring and developing her own goals as a writer, working to construct for herself a professional authority in the detective fiction genre.

My book seeks to develop this idea on a larger scale: to explore the ways that creating female detectives during the late nineteenth and early twentieth centuries helped women writers shape their own professional authority in the detective fiction genre. The largely male-dominated genre became stunningly popular during this time, and women writers who sought to make names for themselves in it needed to find ways of establishing their presence in this new market. Creating female detectives who were successful narratively—within the scope of the story they solved the crime and brought the narrative to its expected conclusion—helped women writers accomplish this task in many ways: they expanded roles for women in their fiction by placing a strong female character in a role which was not previously open to them; they sought to expand the existing ideology responsible for dictating those roles; they showed how stereotypically female traits, such as knowledge of the domestic sphere and innate curiosity, could be turned into functional crime-solving tools; they made money writing genre stories in periodicals and later as novels, giving them financial success and therefore expanding the economic and literary marketplace for women writers. By examining narrative strategies and biographical information, I look at what these authors accomplished through their female detective creations, adding new insights to the critical study of the genre and to the goals of women writers.

In examining the relationship of women writers to their female detectives, this book addresses a critical gap in scholarship. There have been no such studies focused solely on female detectives created by women writers of this time period.[2] As Craig and Cadogan write in their early study of female detectives, *The Lady Investigates*: "there is a strong tradition of women writers of detective fiction, which is not at all the same thing as the tradition of women detectives as characters in fiction, though sometimes the two overlap" (11). My study is the first to examine that overlap, female detectives created by women writers, as it explores the way these authors sought to establish their professional authority in the detective fiction genre.

Britain's Cultural History and Detective Fiction

Chronologically, this study moves from the 1890s, when the first female detectives created by women writers appeared, through the 1920s and 1930s "Golden Age" of detective fiction.[3] Within this time frame, significant changes took place not only in the detective fiction genre but also, more

in a stricter definition of the word. A household in which women did not have to perform any task to bring in an income came to be seen as a sign of class status and a social ideal.

Thus the image of the idle yet fulfilled domestic woman was born, crystallized in the designation "Angel in the House," a phrase taken from a popular mid-century poem by Coventry Patmore. As part of this ubiquitous philosophy, women were to be content with running a household, raising children, and engaging in light philanthropic work. Such a model of womanhood was perpetuated not only in the conduct and domestic advice books which flourished during this period (of which Sarah Stickney Ellis' *Women of England* is representative), but in novels and poetry as well. There was much literature written during the Victorian era that knowingly challenged this ideology, of course, especially towards the end of the century, but the model of the "ideal" woman—passive, self-sacrificing, and domestic—dominated.[10]

The converse of this model of successful womanhood was the unmarried woman, one who by her very existence signaled the failure of this ideal and who, as neither wife nor mother, was considered a failure herself. Beyond governessing or teaching, there were few jobs open to her, and because she had difficulty support herself—not only because of the social taboo against women working but because of the simple lack of jobs for middle-class women—she often had to rely on society's good graces for her survival. The literature of this time usually portrays the spinster as poverty-stricken, burdensome and often pathetic.[11]

Although many Victorian ideas about women's roles endured well into the Edwardian age, a society's ideologies are always fluid, as Mary Poovey makes clear. Those of the Victorian era which in retrospect seem implacable and eternal—ideals rooted in a system that was patriarchal, imperialist, bourgeois, and homosocial—were in fact "both contested and always under construction ... open to revision, dispute, and the emergence of oppositional formulations" (*Uneven* 3). Maintaining an idealized image of Victorian women, as a part of this cultural construction, was thus fraught with difficulty, and this ideal was consistently challenged, both overtly, through feminist and suffragist activities, and more subtly, through written texts that exposed its inherent inconsistencies. Thus, while women writers could not help but be influenced by stereotypical images of women, they could also express dissatisfaction and even subversiveness through problematizing those same conventions, subtly changing the landscape in which women could write. Much of the early work done by critics such as Sandra Gilbert and Susan Gubar and Elaine Showalter focuses on women who used writing as a strategy of empowerment and accomplishment within the limited confines of what was considered "proper."[12]

In a similar way, women writers of detective fiction could not help but be influenced by the expectations and preconceptions of their time period, including the ways these expectations made their appearance in the detective fiction genre. Women's roles are usually secondary in many of the early detective stories written by men, stories which place emphasis on logic and ratiocination or on action-oriented brutality and murder taking place in a city's streets, all of which were considered "masculine" features. As such, these stories portray a world far removed from the sheltered and sheltering image of the home that had been perpetuated as woman's sphere. The detective fiction genre, as it had developed through Edgar Allan Poe and Sherlock Holmes, had little use for women in the starring role.

At the same time, however, women writers could attempt to expand in their fiction these controlling images of women. For example, women often *did* play more active roles in sensation fiction, a genre largely considered woman-centered and which I posit influenced women's detective fiction, in part because it placed women in unusual roles. As inheritors of this tradition, women writers of detective fiction recognized the possibilities available for subverting or expanding earlier images of women. They converted the powerful but often flawed women in sensation fiction into feminine and professional female detectives able to succeed narratively, bringing the story to its expected conclusion and maintaining power within the text. By writing women into positions of authority, women detective fiction writers increased the pressure upon the continually contested sites of the representation of women.

Beliefs about women's nature, as they had been formulated by Victorian society and had been written into its philosophy, appear explicitly and implicitly throughout detective fiction. Women's supposedly innate natural curiosity, gossipy nature, and attention to detail, for example, are used not only to explain the female detective's success at solving crime but also to assure her a place in the genre. The character of the female detective is integral to the ways women writers both capitalized on and transformed traditional images of women. In the process, these women writers were able to carve out a niche for themselves in the detective fiction genre.

There was no area too small to be affected by the Great War, including the detective fiction genre. After the war, people were determined to enjoy themselves, but their entertainment had to reflect the lessons learnt from that experience. As LeRoy Panek explains: "the War undermined many institutions on which the English and their popular fiction ran: honor, heroism, individual effort, trust in authority and the absolutely fixed class system" (*Watteau's Shepherds* 11). The Edwardian crime thriller novel, filled with international escapades and characters who acted "as if Victorian imperial standards were still valid" no longer seemed appropriate after World War I (12). The puzzle format of British detective fiction, with its detached anti-sentimental air and problematic structure, appealed to postwar Britain because it was "exciting without being heroic. The new detective novel fit the bill" (11). The characterization of the fictional male detective changed for similar reasons, as Alison Light in *Forever England* so cogently argues. Because of the war, he went from the "confident, British middle-class hero in the old mould" to one "garrulous and full of badinage and banalities" (73). She argues that the post-war world "had made the notion of the conquering detective unpalatable to some, and it needed to give way to a more modest, sometimes agonised sense of English manliness" (72). Hence, detectives like Sayers' Lord Peter Wimsey, Berkley's Roger Sherringham, and Allinghams' Albert Campion appeared: self-deprecating, foppish, even emasculated.[13]

Changes in the characterization of women detectives before and after the War also occurred, in response at least partly to what was afterwards considered respectable female employment and actions. It was during the war that the first women police appeared; there were no women working in an "official" constabulary capacity before this time. Any pre-war depiction of the female detective was clearly fanciful, and writers had free rein to create anything they wanted since there were no historical and few literary precedents.[14] What women writers created at this time can be taken as a good indication of what they wanted to see, even though they perhaps recognized it as impossible at that moment in history.

Most of the pre-war fictional female detectives were young, attractive, single, middle-class women thrown on hard times. They were also professionals: they made their living through detecting, while at the same time making that profession acceptable for women by showing one could remain feminine and work largely within one's accustomed sphere. They solved crimes using their immense knowledge of the domestic sphere and social world, in which they had been forced to become experts.

After the war, however, the fictional profiles of female detectives changed, partly in response to the outside world. Though women entered the police force during the war, they were expected to quit when the war was over and return to more "appropriate" women's duties.[15] Their refusal to do so quietly went all the way to Parliament and left a sour taste in the public's mouth.[16] The perception of a policing woman became negative, and the fact that there were now real women police seems to have killed the young professional detective in fiction. From the 1920s through the 1940s the female detective in fiction is a much less threatening person to society. She is elderly, often amateur, or if she works at all, works in another profession and accidentally falls into detection. Two of the most popular fictional female detectives from this time—Miss Marple and Miss Silver—fit this general pattern and are indicative of the tendency to reduce the female detective's potential threat.

The detective fiction writers in this study, however, do seem interested in expanding women's limited professional and educational opportunities. Their decision to characterize female detectives in the ways they did seems to bear out this possibility: having the choice, they created women who came from the same economic class and who faced difficulties in the job market that women from their class often faced. Critics Reynolds and Humble in *Victorian Heroines* argue that women writers used certain narrative strategies to express their desire for independence and that these strategies "helped to accustom the reading public to changes in the feminine ideal" (6–7). Similarly, fictional representations of strong female detectives could, I argue, potentially foster greater acceptance of women's entry into the public sphere. While not subversive like many late nineteenth-century New Women writers trying to upset middle-class gender ideologies, women detective fiction writers seem desirous of expanding what those ideologies could contain.

Thus, when women writers created female detectives who solved crimes where men failed, who reconciled despairing lovers upon solving the crime, who perhaps performed "unfeminine" duties but remained feminine and retained middle-class signifiers which separated them from working-class women, they were not just fantasizing or "cashing in" on a craze, though I don't dismiss these as contributing factors. Female detectives certainly were fantasy characters, living a life that their creators' society could not and did not let women lead. But creating fictional female detectives was also a way of entering into the Woman Question debate about women's roles in their society. By creating professional fictional female detectives, they both indulged in fantasy and helped delineate the terms of a larger battle going on in their society.

Women detective fiction writers' emphasis on traditional "womanly" qualities provided one way of making the idea of professional women more acceptable. The one great fear of British society, especially after the War, was that women would take away jobs that belonged to men. Making detectives deliberately feminine and allowing them success in situations for which they, as opposed to men, were specifically fitted, such as crime in the domestic sphere, helped to mitigate this fear. Women writers who created female detectives were not necessarily (or always) arguing that they could replace male detectives, but they did offer scenarios for how women could succeed in a "man's world."

Defining Women's Professional Authority in Detective Fiction

Theories about female literary tradition offer one model for examining the topic of professional authority, in that they address the literary forebears of women's writing and question what these authors might be trying to explore or accomplish through their fictional creations. Some of the most influential literary "parents" in the case of detective fiction by women are the women writers of sensation fiction.[17] Sensation fiction writers such as Mrs. Henry Wood and Mary Elizabeth Braddon expanded the roles for women protagonists by making them "murderesses, bigamists, swindlers, prostitutes, and detectives" (Reynolds and Humble 99). By placing women in a variety of roles other than the Victorian "Angel in the House," sensation fiction is in part "responsible for initiating significant changes in the representation of women in later fiction" (99). Sensation fiction contributes to the formation and success of female detective fiction in two main ways: on a thematic level, the sensation fiction writers "made crime and violence domestic" (Showalter, *Literature* 158) and showed that such topics were not outside a woman's realm; additionally, because women writers of sensation fiction like Braddon saw the creation and production of their writing as professional work, as business, they expanded the realm of possibilities in which women could work and thus helped pave the way for a more professional attitude towards writing. During this time, women's writing came to be recognized as more than merely a "lady's" pastime; it could be as well a moneymaking venture, bringing with it the possibility of economic freedom.

The work done by critics examining the woman's "novel of self-development" or the *Bildungsroman* also provides insights into women's professional authority. Studies like Abel, Hirsch and Langland's *The Voyage In*, Fraiman's *Unbecoming Women*, and Brown's *Poison at the Source* examine the very different results that are produced when the typically male-centered *Bildungsroman* (or *Kunstlerroman*) is appropriated by women writers, who create female instead of male protagonists to play out the characteristic features of such fiction.[18] Brown, for instance, points out the reasons that women's experience of their culture affect their fiction: "the social pressures and expectations are different, the options are different and the ways in which women react to experience are different" (*Poison* 203). Thus, she continues, the format and outcome of a woman's *Bildungsroman* must necessarily be different as well. They tend to "understate personal achievement," for example, in order to deflect potentially negative reactions to their accomplishments, the discussion of which defied the cultural stereotype of the "naturally" demure female (8).

Critical attention has been given to other avenues of achieving authority in women's writing. Mary Jean Corbett writes about women's authority in the Victorian spiritual autobiography and the way it afforded women the opportunity to justify their entrance into the public sphere while remaining within their own private sphere. Women spiritual autobiographers found a way to represent female experience through combining their "religious and domestic authority "in order to "sanction female authorship" (19). Vineta Colby in *Yesterday's Woman* believes "'female domination'" would be an apt subtitle for her book on domestic realism, since women had such a tremendous sway over the genre, even so far as influencing "men novelists to refine their subjects, soften their language, and write about bourgeois family life" (4). These women too helped shape a particular genre through capitalizing on their authority in the domestic sphere, extending it to help establish their authority as writers in the public sphere as well.

In addition to Mary Jean Corbett's work, several other critical studies have appeared in recent years concerning the ways women established authority in their writing. Margaret Dickie studies the ways women modernist poets created authority; Theresa Nicolay looks at strategies that the American writers Anne Bradstreet, Mercy Warren, and Margaret Fuller Ossoli used to forge authority in their works.[19] Nicolay provides a set of concrete questions concerning how these women came to be seen as "cultural authorities, that is, as serious commentators on social, political, moral, and, of course, literary concerns" (1). Among the questions she poses are:

> is their work intellectually and imaginatively sophisticated? Do these women address the most crucial social and political concerns of the day? Moreover, who read their writing? Did their authority extend to both male and female audiences? And if so, of what classes? Finally, what were the interests and concerns of those audiences? [1].

In an audience-centered analysis, Nicolay examines the narrative strategies these writers employed to establish themselves as authorities within their own particular groups—the Puritans or the Transcendentalists, for example—and how that success was parlayed into more widespread fame.

Similarly, I am interested in looking at the ways in which women writers tried to construct for themselves the authority to write in the detective fiction genre with confidence, and their struggles, as products of their society, to do so. The profession of writer, as well as its attendant occupations (editor, copywriter, publisher), was still male-dominated in the early twentieth century. Writing in the detective fiction genre was no exception, though perhaps women writers felt more comfortable taking it up because it was "popular fiction," which had been linked with women since the sensation literature of the 1860s.[20] Nonetheless, women writers had to develop ways of making this fiction their own. Lyn Pykett's discussion of women's 1860s sensationalist fiction and 1890s New Woman fiction coincides in many places with my own study, including her appraisal of the difficulties faced by women in male-dominated fields. Women's writing, she says,

> is marked by the writers' specific experiences as women, and by the ways in which their biological femaleness is structured and mediated by sociocultural concepts of femininity. To this extent these women writers will be seen to rein-scribe their culture's stories about femininity. However, they also participated in a rewriting of this script of the feminine, as in various ways and to varying degrees, they self-consciously explored or implicitly exposed the contradictions of prevailing versions of femininity [5].

Women writers of detective fiction rewrote the "script of the feminine" when they expanded the roles of women within their fiction, creating popular and positive female detectives who successfully solved crimes, often those male detectives could not. My work examines the narrative strategies women writers in the detective fiction genre used to enact this revision, strategies which in turn helped to construct their own professional authority as writers. By professional authority, I mean both the achievement of financial success and critical respect in their field. Women writers established this professional authority by finding ways of expressing their ability and fitness to write in the detective fiction genre and adapting it as a vehicle for women's writing.

The character of the female detective was important to this process for many reasons. On a basic level, she served as a professional "double" of sorts, a character moving into a largely male-dominated profession. While I don't mean to imply that there is no difference between the "real life" profession of detective fiction writer and the fictional creation of a female detective, their situations mirrored each other in that both worked to establish a presence in the public sphere and sought recognition as professional women. When women writers wrote in the detective fiction genre, they brought to the genre their own experiences as women, an understanding of their culture that was profoundly different than that of most male writers, whose authority to speak on any subject was rarely questioned. Thus, though the formula for much detective fiction from this time period is the same, women writers maneuvered differently within that formula to make it their own.

In addition, through their female detectives, women writers could point insistently to the value of certain issues important to women. Using domestic expertise to solve crime, for instance, not only gave credibility to female detectives' methods, but it also allowed women writers to highlight in their fiction a set of activities which were seen by their society as strictly woman-centered and thus largely unimportant, in both real life and in most fiction. In detective fiction, however, such activities and pieces of knowledge are vital aspects of professional success. We can see another example of this strategy in the ways that women detective fiction writers often highlighted both the problems and joys of unmarried women. Creating successful detectives and businesswomen out of the despised figure of the spinster cast new light on single women's lives and challenged the stereotype of them as unfulfilled and pathetic. In detective fiction, single women are independent, daring, and intelligent.

Finally, the female detective character provided women writers with a way of more fully examining their lives as professional public women and their struggles for acceptance as members of a male-dominated society. As authors, and specifically as authors in a popular money-making genre, women writers of this fiction were inherently questioning the cultural restrictions which limited the ways and reasons women should make money in their society. When they created professionally and publicly successful female detectives—even more so when they created female detectives who were also writers—they engaged in a very self-conscious exploration of their society's "contradictions of prevailing versions of femininity," to use Pykett's phrase.

Because of the cultural constraints placed upon women based solely on their sex, women's access to professional authority was more limited and more difficult to negotiate than it was for their male counterparts. Women writers who catered to tastes of the populace and did so to make money upset notions about women's proper place, their proper feelings, and their proper roles as members of an ordered society. Yet in directly engaging with these issues, many women detective fiction writers established their careers and proved themselves to be well-adapted to write in the genre.

Later writers, particularly Agatha Christie and Dorothy L. Sayers, were able to draw upon the work achieved by earlier women detective fiction writers and take it further, engaging in self-conscious explorations not only of their society but of the detective fiction genre as well. Through creating female detectives who are also writers of detective fiction, Christie and Sayers were able to comment on the genre itself, self-consciously playing with its formulas, parodying its conventions, and analyzing its structure, nature, and codes. Through writing detective metafiction, "fiction that includes within itself commentary on its own narrative conventions" (Greene, *Changing* 1), they established themselves as innovators within the genre and were able to change the path that detective fiction would take.

The ensuing success of writers like Christie and Sayers further established the presence of women writers in the genre. In other words, creating a female detective—even if it was done because the female detective's popularity would help sell books—worked as a means for women writers to capitalize on the popularity of the detective fiction genre and solidify women's place in it. The character of the female detective, therefore, was an integral part of the ways women detective fiction writers both constructed and explored their professional authority in the detective fiction genre.

Thus, my study addresses authority in women's writing, using female detectives as the object through which to discuss the question. While the topic can be informed by work done by critics in other fields, examining authority in women's detective fiction is more interesting and exciting than it is in genres like spiritual autobiography or domestic realism because detective fiction deliberately steps outside the boundaries of what were considered acceptable subjects for female writing. Women writers in this genre, though they drew upon many traditional gender stereotypes, were at the same time expanding those stereotypes when writing about professional women in a male-oriented sphere. They may have faced difficulty justifying their entrance into the detective fiction genre, yet at the same time, they had more to gain in challenging society's viewpoints concerning appropriate roles for women. Their characterization of female detectives, as intelligent and logical yet often stereotypically feminine, as groundbreaking yet conservative, highlights their challenge to societal norms and at the same time their inability to break from them completely.

In addition, developing a definition of professional authority in women's detective fiction must take into account the fact that it was foremost a market-driven popular genre, and authors shaped their texts based in part on the perceived interests of a reading public in order to sell books. Thus the questions Nicolay poses, for example, while largely appropriate, are not directly transferable: certainly the work of female detective fiction writers was read by a diverse audience, and the very idea of a female detective inherently addressed social concerns about women's limited employment opportunities.[21] On the other hand, detective fiction as a genre could not be considered universally "intellectually and imaginatively sophisticated," nor was the question of women's roles considered the most crucial political concern by their society in light of more obvious occurrences like World War I or the Great Depression.

Women's roles did change during this time period. The effort made by women writers to explore the limited roles faced by women in their culture coincided with a larger societal questioning of the nature of women's "calling," which, especially during and after the War, was undergoing rapid change, as women struggled to find ideological bases upon which to rest authority in the professional world. Women needed, or at least believed they needed, a variety of arguments to make a place for themselves, adapting accepted ideas about women's moral superiority and traditional femininity into new forms of professional authority.[22]

Clare Stewart's discussion of Victorian women writers of ghost stories advances an argument similar to my own. Recognizing that this popular medium provided women writers with a venue through which to articulate the tensions surrounding women in the marketplace, Stewart argues that the ways women wrote within the male-dominated ghost story genre reflects their desire to see fewer strictures around what could be considered women's appropriate sphere, both within their fiction and in everyday life. She writes: "the work of women writing ghost stories in many ways exhibits similar concerns about women's lives, and allows them, in common, to depict strong, capable, determined and independent notions of womanhood normally denied them" (112). Traditionally-minded women writers who manipulated and restructured the ghost story in order to voice beliefs "which frequently challenge contemporary patriarchal ideology" (112) is analogous to the work of women writers of detective fiction, who often seem to uphold traditional female roles but whose fiction inherently argues for an expansion of what those roles could contain.

The female detective provided women writers with ways of consolidating arguments about women's fitness to write in the detective fiction genre, keeping the ideals of middle-class femininity intact while expanding the sphere of women's influence in the genre. They characterized female detectives as lady-like and decidedly middle-class women who solved crimes based on their knowledge of the household and through using "natural" female intuition. Women writers created detectives out of the spinster, a figure in their society seen as burdensome or pitiable. In doing so, their fiction expanded the perceived boundaries of women's goals and means of fulfillment, both personally and professionally, and showed awareness of the difficulties facing women, especially spinsters, in the professional sphere.

At the same time that women writers of this fiction sought to imbue it with feminine traits and female detectives, they were in their own lives crossing over the boundary of acceptable female actions and the division between public and private spheres, as they made money from writing in this genre. Women writers of detective fiction, in treating their writing as their profession and in writing for a market, were questioning the restrictions which limited the ways and reasons women should make money in their society, forcing their contemporaries to take them into account, whether in a negative or positive way.

Here again, the image of the feminine but daring female detective was helpful in articulating women writers' struggle for authority. Their female detectives went forth into the public world, dealt with the problem of professional authority in a male sphere, and used writing as part of their job. They were often portrayed as writers as well as detectives, and were financially and personally successful at their chosen profession, all the while retaining womanly qualities. For women writers, this not only offered a model of professional authority but also presented them with an opportunity to discuss in their fiction specific problems faced by women writing in a popular genre. Through participating in the detective fiction genre, a well-received fictional format; through being published and making money, women writers were able to contribute to society's debates about the roles of women and engage in those issues which helped them construct and explore their own professional authority.

In focusing on how women writers used female detectives to help explore underlying social, sexual, and professional tensions in late Victorian through post–War England, I re-examine the important and ever-shifting problem of women's prescribed roles in society. This study begins with a historical examination of women's employment during the late nineteenth and early twentieth centuries to provide a framework for discussing fictional female detectives. In subsequent chapters, it focuses on individual authors and the narrative strategies they used in their detective fiction. The opening chapter looks at various jobs women actually held during this time period, focusing in particular on those portrayed by women authors in their detective fiction: governess, typist, newspaper correspondent, psychoanalyst, and nurse. Importantly, women in police work (largely in an unofficial capacity) function as the closest real life counterpart to the fictional female detective. Rooted in these historical connections, the chapter lays the groundwork for discussing gender ideology and women's roles in the workplace both historically and as they are portrayed in women's detective fiction.

The second chapter looks at the ways women writers capitalized on one of the most pervasive ideals of Victorian womanhood—the domestic Angel in the House—in order to forge a space for a specifically female brand of detection. These women writers, including C.L. Pirkis, L.T. Meade, and Baroness Orczy, wrote stories in which female detectives could use their knowledge of the domestic sphere and their "natural" female intuition to gather clues and solve crimes, often ones that their fictional male counterparts could not. Female detectives read clues extending from domestic disturbances, social situations and human nature to help discover motives and to solve crimes. In these ways, female detectives who were raised to be middle-class managers of the domestic world show that their skills can transfer to the male-oriented world of work for pay. Through these characters, women writers examine and complicate traditional middle-class ideologies of womanhood in an attempt to expand those boundaries, as their characters translate their "separate sphere" into a means of enhancing their authority in an unconventional profession.

By the 1930s, women detective fiction writers were not only accepted by the public and the literary world, but were in fact among the defining figures in Britain's Golden Age of detective fiction. In the female detective world, the Golden Age became the era of elderly spinster detectives, which I posit was both an unexpected outcome of World War I and another inventive way in which women writers expanded society's traditional views of women. Chapter Three looks at the ways women writers used the character of the spinster, women usually considered superfluous and lamentable in both real life and fiction, as productive members of society uniquely fitted for crime-solving. This includes both the "young" thirty-year-old spinster, especially in the detective fiction of the near-forgotten Marie Connor Leighton, as well as the more familiar elderly character, the detectives created during the 1920s and 1930s by Agatha Christie, Dorothy L. Sayers, Patricia Wentworth, and Gladys Mitchell. The fiction of these later writers was shaped by both societal changes and by permutations in the genre itself; as a whole, the detectives created during the 1920s and 1930s are unmarried professionals, working in some way (if not by detecting) for a living. This chapter adds another example to the ways that women writers, in exploring topical concerns important to them as women, established parameters for negotiating and establishing their professional authority.

As writers, these women were themselves performing work that straddled concepts of appropriate behavior. It was largely acceptable by the 1890s for women to become professional writers, but their relationship to the world of popular fiction remained ambiguous and fraught with difficulty. Chapter Four examines the ways that women writers like Georgette Heyer and Agatha Christie used female detectives to investigate problems women faced as writers of popular fiction, focusing on the particularly effective strategy of creating female detectives who were also writers. These women writers parody the genre through their female writer-detectives, engaging in a type of literary playfulness not seen earlier in the century, and they create detectives who are also writers of detective fiction, offering themselves yet another avenue through which to discuss the roles of professional women in society. Their creation also exhibits the measure of authority which later writers achieved in the detective fiction genre: Agatha Christie, for one, shows a mastery of traditional detective fiction plots and conventions in the very act of changing them. Thus this chapter introduces further and more specialized ways women writers constructed and explored issues of their authority in this genre, while they continued to create narratives with cultural resonance for women.

The final chapter focuses on Dorothy L. Sayers and her detective/writer Harriet Vane as the most complete example of the ways women writers who created female detectives could explore issues of professional authority in their detective fiction. Her achievement can be seen in both her command

and manipulation of the genre's conventions and in her ability to use her work as a way to comment on social issues that mattered to her. Sayers created female characters that use intuition and knowledge of the domestic sphere to solve crime, and she created a spinster-detective to help highlight the injustice of society's treatment of women. She also created a female detective/writer who helped her introduce desired changes to the detective fiction genre, allowing her to transform her fiction and reach her artistic goals. In order to create the intelligent and well-rounded Vane, Sayers needed to dispense with standard conventions of the detective story genre and make it a more complete, less-formulaic tale. She did this most completely in *Gaudy Night* in two ways: by intelligently discussing one of the important social problems in the 1930s—the problems faced by women juggling higher education and the workplace with love and marriage—and re-introducing growth of character and thematic structure. Consistently throughout the Vane novels Sayers discusses problems that occur during the act of writing, the problems women face as professional writers, and the difficulty of maintaining one's professional independence. The ways in which Sayers, through Vane, examines literary and professional issues makes her a paramount example of the potential productivity that can occur when women writers create female detectives.

While establishing women's professional authority in detective fiction was not necessarily a rigid step-by-step process, it is true that later writers I discuss in this study were able to build upon the work of earlier writers. For instance, nearly all of these women writers have their female detectives recognize and use certain "domestic" clues to solve crime, and many use the character of the spinster as their detective. Because writers earlier in the century made these aspects of women's detective fiction acceptable and successful, writers from the 1920s and 1930s could take such elements of crime fiction for granted and move onto other, more pointed ways of using their fiction to explore questions of authority, such as creating detectives who were also writers of detective fiction. And only later writers could use the burgeoning popularity of the genre itself as an additional means of establishing authority, capitalizing on a trend and expanding their presence into a genre-changing force.

Taken as a whole, then, my study examines the critical importance of early female detectives, both in their own right and as part of the larger genre of detective fiction. Many critics and editors have dismissed these early detectives as conventional and trite, ignoring the genre's rich variety. Yet fictional female detectives appear as both paid professionals and gifted amateurs; single, married, widowed; older spinsters and young adventurers; detecting for pleasure and to clear their own or a loved one's name. By using the logic and intelligence necessary to any detective, along with their own specialized knowledge, female detectives negotiated within societal strictures a specifically female authority and professional identity. In choosing to create female detectives who were both varied and unusual, women writers confronted some of their own literary anxieties and effectively expanded conventional roles for women. The women writers who created these detectives ultimately were able to explore the ways in which women could negotiate and command authority within a male-dominated culture, creating new routes to women's authority in the detective fiction genre.

ONE

Professions for Women

It may be added that, although women police are
employed occasionally on detective work, there are no
women in the C. I. D.: *Lady Molly of Scotland Yard* has never
had a counterpart in real life.
—J.F. Moylan, *Scotland Yard and
the Metropolitan Police* (1929)

How did a fictional character gain such a hold over the people's imagination that an official history of Scotland Yard, in its small section on women in the police force, felt compelled to mention her? Why, if there were no women in the Criminal Investigation Department, was the character of "female detective" so popular in the fiction of this time? What jobs did women in the police force actually perform, if they were barred from detective work? And how were they perceived by their fellow officers and the public? I believe the answers to these questions and others about women and their entrance into the workforce can help shed light on the way women writers portrayed the character of the female detective in their fiction and the character's fate in Britain during the late nineteenth and early twentieth centuries.

The single greatest factor that brought about changes in women's employment was World War I, as women during this time entered into many types of work that before the war would not have been accepted as appropriate by their society. When the war ended, however, society stalled in permanently accepting women into such previously male-only professions, and even women who had ably performed men's work during the war were asked either to return to their former jobs (already sanctioned by British society as appropriate female work) or to quit altogether. For example, though the work of women police was gratefully accepted during the war, the women who served had great difficulty after the war convincing the public (and the standing male police force) that they were still needed. Except for a tiny group of women appointed by the Home Office, women police remained (or were reduced to) objects of public benefactors, dependent on charitable funds for their existence, with no professional status or career opportunities, as this chapter will relate.[1]

A similar phenomenon is seen in the fate of the female detective created by women writers, the closest fictional counterpart to a policewoman. While still a popular character, she usually holds amateur status following the war and does not work as a paid professional detective. Most female detectives appearing in the late 1920s and after are either elderly or hold other occupations and get involved in detecting accidentally or both. In these scenarios, fictional detectives raise fewer questions as to women's proper roles in the established police force or in the work force; they present fewer overt challenges to expectations of what roles women should fill in society.

Michele Slung, in her introduction to one of the first collections of stories starring fictional female detectives, *Crime on Her Mind* (1975),[2] offers one possibility for this seemingly backward step in the evolution of the female detective, from young professional to elderly amateur. "It might be," she writes, that:

> despite the gradual erosion of traditional roles, society's ideas concerning women could not metamorphose at the same rate as could that creature of the imagination, the fictional detective, and the unspoken tastes and preferences of the reading public were for the retention of illusion in heavy doses when it came to their heroines. [...] It almost seems as if the question of dealing with a new kind of woman detective was shoved aside for the duration [of the 1920s], until the internal changes in the genre and the external ones of the public world could catch up with each other [xxiii; xxv].

Slung's tentative language—"it might be"; "it almost seems"—speaks to her hesitation as to the possible motive for detective fiction writers' "overcompensation" (xxiii) in response to potential pressures from their society. However, Slung does not assign any specific historical reasons for her view and thus seems to arrive at too quick a conclusion.

This chapter supplies historical details about women in the work force in England during the late 19th and early 20th centuries, providing some background for Slung's supposition. It looks at the jobs women were performing at this time and how the underlying ideology of their society surrounding women and work may have informed the fictional representations of a specific group of working women—detectives. It focuses primarily on women in the police force, as the closest counterpart to the fictional character of the woman detective, but it also touches briefly on other professions that in some way appear in detective fiction, either as jobs previously held by female detectives (and which they are invariably glad to have escaped) or jobs which they hold simultaneously with detective work, sometimes as a cover for their detective work and sometimes as their actual profession (if they appear in fiction as amateur detectives).

Women did not enter the police force until the War; any depiction of women police detectives (like Lady Molly) before this time sprung solely out of the authors' imaginations. Yet looking at the jobs women did do, especially those which, like in detective fiction, place women in a traditionally masculine field, will hopefully present a clearer picture of the society that accepted and admired fictional female detectives and of the ways they were portrayed by women writers.

Though "working"-class women held industrial and domestic jobs all through the 19th century, acceptable paid jobs for middle-class women beyond teaching, governessing, nursing, or selling "fancywork" were few. It is suggestive, therefore, that primarily middle-class writers of detective fiction created middle or upper-class detectives. Women writers, when choosing unusual jobs like detective for their heroines, were undoubtedly aware of the difficulties faced by women in the job market. Beatrice Heron-Maxwell's Molly Delamere, for example, in *Adventures of a Lady Pearl-Broker* (1899), takes on the unique job of pearl-broker, in the course of which she solves pearl-related crimes. Despite the high element of danger from thieves and con-men, she is grateful for the job, and when her boss expresses concern for her safety, she dismisses his fears, saying she prefers danger to the hardships she would most likely incur working in a more traditional job:

> "Nonsense, Mr. Leighton," I said, "you are over-cautious and over-sensitive. You are giving me, at my earnest desire, the opportunity to earn a comfortable living in a congenial way. If you take it from me, then I must become a governess, or a companion, or a typist, or something equally arduous, and for an income that will only just clothe me" [109].

As a recent widow, she understands how few opportunities she has to maintain a decent living: "poor widows are looked upon in society so often as adventuresses. People seem to think it a disgrace that one's husband should not leave one enough to live on" (5–6). Indeed, though it was well-known how extremely poor widows or spinsters could be, society offered them very few ways to support themselves. Mrs. Delamere, declaring that "it is worth some risk to have an assured income" (5), shows an awareness

"traditional notions of 'womanly' behavior as they created 'domestic' or 'female' spaces for themselves in the public domain" (Ardis 16). They also felt that if women were better educated and trained in fields related to those already socially acceptable and already expected of them, like visiting the sick and the poor, they could perform these duties better. Lee Holcombe, in her history of middle-class workers, writes that feminists "wanted to see such amateur ladies bountiful [who visited the sick and poor] replaced by well-educated, competent women with a sound knowledge of social problems and with the ability to take a meaningful and constructive part in such concerns as the administration of workhouses, of schools and of hospitals" (9).

Women writers who created fictional female detectives often argued along these lines. Because women, according to commonly-held notions, were "naturally" inquisitive, detail-oriented, and familiar with human nature, female detectives could use these skills, rather than brute force or rough questioning, to ferret out the solutions to crimes. In this way, fictional female detectives used their own specialized skills and knowledge to gather evidence, solve crimes, and gain authority as detectives. Women writers who created female detectives frequently capitalized upon these arguments about the "natural" gifts of women and put their detectives in settings and situations—usually involving the household or other specialized women's milieus—where they could succeed better than men because of these traits.

Women who entered the male-dominated police force during World War I, the closest counterpart to the fictional female detective, also used this strategy. As a whole, they maintained that their entrance into the force was needed because they could fill specific roles for which women were better suited, those having to do with other women and with children. By using the argument that they were better suited for crime prevention in youth because of their already comprehensive dealings with children, they carved a niche for themselves in a completely male institution, going so far as to "feminize" at least this specific branch of it.

Published in 1924, the autobiography of Mary E. Hamilton, New York City's first official policewoman, offers insight into the reasons women felt they were qualified to do police work. Her philosophy is imbued with the domestic ideology with which she and the rest of her generation were raised: "In many ways the position of a woman in a police department is not unlike that of a mother in a home. Just as a mother smoothes out the rough places, looks after the children, and gives a timely word of warning, advice or encouragement, so the policewoman fulfills her duty" (4). In taking on police work, she writes, "women have not forsaken the home ideals, but invariably work out their programs and develop their activities in accordance with the traditions of the home" (4). She argues that while women can perform many roles within the police department, they are better suited to and qualified for those which relate in some way to their womanly duties, and that "to this may be attributed much of the success of women in their work today" (4).[4] This statement echoes the common belief of women who began working at the turn of the century—that while women's place does not *literally* have to be the home, women who leave the home have the responsibility of taking those qualities which were part of the domestic sphere into the public sphere, where they can also do good.

It is impossible to say what Hamilton's personal beliefs were on this issue of why women made good police officers, whether she truly believed these arguments or whether she advanced them primarily to smooth the way into male-dominated professions like police work. What is more important is that she deliberately employed a rhetorical strategy prevalent in women's writing—claiming that women possessed "natural" abilities in order to justify their entrance into a field—and chose to write her account in a way which confirmed aspects of the traditional domestic ideology surrounding women.

In their fight for more employment opportunities, middle-class mid-Victorian feminists also used arguments which did not uphold the typical ideology of separate spheres for women and men. As Holcombe delineates, to those who argued that women could not handle the strain of hard work, they pointed out that many women (at least of the working class) already did manual labor—in the fields and factories and the workshops—and that it was actually the lack of employment which made women weak and fragile. To those who said that women had inferior intelligence, feminists argued that they merely had inferior education. To those who argued that women would take men's jobs away, they offered arguments based on economics, positing that all of society, men as well as women, would benefit by women's increased employment. The amount of work was not a "fixed quantity," and new occupations were continually being made available to educated workers (Holcombe 10). With a better educated and better trained workforce, England would maintain economic supremacy.

But the argument which held the most sway was the irrefutable fact that there were simply more women than men in their society, over one million more by 1900, and nearly a million and a half according to the census taken in 1911 (Holcombe 11). Since not all women could get married and fulfill their "natural" calling, activists argued, they ought to have a means of supporting themselves to prevent them from being destitute and burdens to their society. The disproportion of women to men was greater in the middle-classes than in the working classes, which posed a more serious problem since it was middle-class women who had so few socially acceptable jobs available to them.[5] It would make more sense to educate and train these women so that they could contribute to the nation's welfare rather than be a drain on it.

Though this population dilemma existed in other periods of England's history (Melman, for one, points out that women outnumbered men in Britain since 1802),[6] the Victorians seized upon this and other aspects of the "Woman Question" in their attempt to formulate a clear response to their rapidly changing industrial society. The problem of "superfluous women" held the nation's attention and was debated everywhere from Parliament to the pages of newspapers, periodicals, and novels. What jobs should they be allowed to pursue? What should England do with them? The solutions ranged from proposals to send them to the colonies where men outnumbered women to the establishment of schools for women to learn office work.[7] Women thus began to train as typists, secretaries, and stenographers.

Furthermore, the expanding British economy led to more jobs in general, jobs into which women had already made some inroads. Increases in medical technology opened up more positions as nurses; the Education Reform Act of 1870 opened up more opportunities in the teaching profession, particularly as elementary school teachers.[8] The teaching field expanded to include university lecturers and secondary school teachers as well; no more were unmarried middle-class women doomed to become governesses. Finally, women worked in many "male only" jobs during World War I, and while most gave up their jobs when the War was over, their able performance of this work expanded their society's beliefs about women's abilities.

In 1919, a further step was taken in opening up professional positions for women. The Sex Disqualification (Removal) Act made it illegal to bar women from certain professions, most noticeably as members of Parliament, because of their sex or marital status. The Act also opened up the possibility of women serving as magistrates and on juries and in working in the legal profession. Though many supporters of women's equality saw the SDRA as a weak compromise for a more far-reaching emancipation bill, the Act did legally establish the right of women to pursue jobs from which they previously had been barred.[9]

One last point ought to be made concerning the changing status of women. In 1918, the power to vote was granted to women over thirty, and in 1928, it was extended to all women over twenty-one. Enfranchisement was gained partly because of the unremitting pressure women's rights advocates put onto members of Parliament and partly because of the increased work women performed during the War. Whether consciously or not, women who worked at men's jobs advanced the case for women's civil rights by showing, as Arthur Marwick states, "the absurdities of the many preconceptions about what they [women] were capable of" (158). Thus when the antiquated voting rules for men, which had been based on residency, were changed after the War, supporters of the vote for women argued effectively that during this re-structuring, women should be taken into account and granted what many felt was their long-overdue right to contribute to their nation's politics.[10]

Employment and Education

Higher education was also made available to larger numbers of women to provide them with necessary skills to hold these new positions. Establishing women's colleges and opening the doors of previously male-only colleges was seen as vital in increasing women's occupational opportunities. Says Levine, "Feminists consistently yoked education and employment together as necessarily linked aims"; education was seen as "a prerequisite for professional status" (*Lives* 126).

Teaching as an independent profession, as opposed to being a governess dependent on someone else's good graces, became solidified during the late 19th and early 20th centuries, and several universities began offering teaching certificates which practically guaranteed their holders a better wage. Though college education opened many doors in the working world for women, most college graduates taught at some point, and many attended college for that very reason. Indeed, it was the most common career path for women after graduation.[11]

Women could attend several colleges by the 1890s, but they were not considered equal in any way by the male students and dons at the universities. Carol Dyhouse, in *No Distinction of Sex? Women in British Universities 1870–1939*, explains that women's confused status depended in part on definitions. "Women attending universities" was a murky subject depending on how one defined "attending." Women could in some instances go to lectures but could not be fully admitted to the university; women could be considered fully admitted but were still not be allowed to take degrees; women could take degrees, as long as it wasn't in the field of medicine.[12]

The one item that *was* held universally true was that, in the structure of university life, women were not on the same footing as men. The inequities extended to the courses they were allowed to take, the deplorable classrooms and living conditions as compared to men's colleges (a picture Sayers paints in her Oxford-based novel *Gaudy Night*), and their inability to receive degrees, despite having taken the same course of study and passing the same standard of examinations. Oxford did not confer degrees upon women, making them full members of the university, until 1920; Cambridge did not do so until 1948. Durham University did not think it "'convenient that the scholarships now open to men should be taken away from them or thrown open equally to women students'" (in Dyhouse 29); therefore, a separate benefactor's society was set up to offer scholarships to women. Edith Morley writes in *Women Workers in Seven Professions* (1914) about the near-impossible task of women getting appointed to faculty posts at universities:

> At Oxford and Cambridge a woman is, at this stage and always, definitely at a disadvantage by reason of her sex. [...] At almost all the new Universities men and women are nominally alike eligible for every teaching post. In practice, women are rarely if ever selected for the higher positions. [...] indeed it is certain that a woman must be exceptionally qualified and far more distinguished than her male competitors to stand a chance of a professorial appointment even in the most liberal of co-education universities [...] [15–16].

There was also the derogatory implication that true "ladies" would never wish such an inappropriate thing as a university education. Writer Mabel Tylecote says about this split that approximately half of the women at the Women's Department in Manchester were only taking a single course here and there: "'The 'ladies' were not registered students, but possessed cards admitting them to certain lectures. The registered students were termed 'women'" (in Dyhouse 24). Elaine Showalter points out that in a common medical argument of the time, to be too brainy was to jeopardize one's fitness to bear children: the New Woman "was dangerous to society because her obsession with developing her brain starved the uterus; even if she should wish to marry, she would be unable to reproduce" (*Anarchy* 40). The implication, and indeed the common perception, was that women who wished to be educated on the same footing as men were unnatural; Mother Nature herself would punish these women by denying them child-bearing abilities.

Even so, women went to college, and this fact affected all women, whether they wished themselves to attend or not. As Constance Maynard reminisced, though only "'one girl in a hundred has any sort of university career, the other ninety-nine are unconsciously affected by it, and their standard of life and its work altered'" (in Mitchell 49). The idea of "college" quickly began to spread, and beginning in the 1880's girls' magazines and publications began printing stories about college life and the freedom that girls who went to college possessed; these themes quickly made their way into the popular fiction of the day.[13] As they did so, college for women seemed less strange; as job opportunities for women increased, college for women became a necessity.

In these ways—through the expanding economy, more job opportunities, and better education—came the vital (though perhaps subtle) shift in society's beliefs about women's abilities. Holcombe sums up this transition most succinctly when she writes: "in the mid-nineteenth century ladies who had to work for their living were a surplus and depressed minority, who were pitied and who pitied themselves. By 1914 middle-class working women, a respected and self-respecting group, were an essential part of the country's labour force" (20).

Women in the Professions

Regardless of the profession, women were not usually well-paid for their work. It was seen almost always as a stop-gap measure, based on the assumption that women would quit work after marriage and allow their husbands to be the sole breadwinner. Indeed, most girls did not want to work after marriage, believing that marriage meant they didn't have to. Even the success of women in certain jobs did not increase their pay but instead led to the belief that only women should perform them; in this way jobs became "feminized," complete with all the attendant low status associated with "women's work." Men began to refuse certain jobs like typists at lower levels on the business ladder; women themselves began to expect lower pay, and the job's worth in society's eyes decreased. After all, went the circular logic, if women are doing it, it must not be that important since they aren't serious about work.[14]

Paying women low wages was thus both a justification as well as an incentive to ensure that women would stop working after marriage, and married women who did want to work faced strong cultural proscriptions against it. Teresa Davy's interviews with shorthand typists reveal one woman who did try to work after marriage and was told she was taking away bread from someone else's mouth—a single girl's. She took off her wedding ring and called herself "Miss Adams" in order to find work (in Davidoff and Westover 142). Joan Perkin, in her study of Victorian women, states that "by 1913 nearly all the organized forces in society were against the married woman worker, whatever her circumstances" (198).

Thus, despite better education and more job opportunities, women were still greatly limited by what society thought they could and should do. Though women got better educational opportunities, what women could do with their education—the role of women in the public workplace—was still a controversy. Furthermore, women who did choose careers were often expected to remain unmarried and dedicate themselves solely to their profession, focusing the "natural nurturing instincts" society assumed all women possessed onto those in their care. With this choice before them, most women worked before marriage and then quit. There was no middle ground.[15]

to be better educated and come from a slightly higher economic class in order to compete with men who were less educated or from a lower class. Scott's study done for the Fabian Women's Group in 1917 found that "women of good education, sometimes in possession of degrees, find themselves in competition with men of an inferior social class. [...] the average woman clerk is invariably a person of better education and manners than the male clerk at the same salary" (in Morley 296).

Conditions for typists and clerks left much to be desired. By 1917, a glut of typists flooded the market, and many were badly trained and poorly educated, making conditions for all typists poor. Often there was no room for advancement, making their jobs after several years boring and undesirable. When asked why they weren't promoted like men in the office, the employer would give the typical line about marriage: "while the office boy, if promoted and given increasing pay, may be expected to stay with the firm for a lifetime, there is not the same certainty of continuity of service from women clerks, who may at any time leave to get married" (Scott in Morley 297).

This is exactly the point of view Dorothy Sayers relates in her 1929 novel, *Strong Poison*. An exasperated Mr. Pond, head clerk in a law firm, explains to Peter Wimsey the difficulties women cause in the working world:

> "Here's our young lady clerk—I don't say she wasn't a good worker—but a whim comes over her and away she goes to get married [...]. Now, with a young man, marriage steadies him, and makes him stick closer to his job, but with a young woman, it's the other way about. It's right that she should get married, but it's inconvenient [...]" [74–75].

Sayers finds Mr. Pond's point of view slightly ridiculous and old-fashioned, made clear in further conversations between him and Miss Murchison, the woman he eventually hires. But Sayers' appraisal of her society's stereotypes is certainly correct. Scott, in her thorough study, cites only one case of a woman "who entered a firm as a young girl, continued with the firm after marriage, and is now, as a widow, working for the same employers. There is no reason why such cases should be exceptional" (in Morley 297). Scott believes that women leave after marriage mainly because it isn't made worth their while to stay; low pay, poor conditions, and, more importantly, overpowering ideological beliefs about the roles of women prevail in the end.

Newspaper Journalists

Of the jobs that appear in detective fiction (excluding the job of detective), that of writer is most common. Since the relationship between women writers and their female detective creations forms the basis of this study, the role of writing in detective fiction will be discussed in full detail in later chapters. This subset of women writers, those working as journalists, faced greater difficulties finding work and being accepted than women novelists because this work demanded much greater visibility outside the home and hence uncomfortably extended the ways in which women could (or should) write for money.

Like with most jobs for women, circumstances and perceptions concerning women's entrance into this profession changed over time. For example, when Christie's Anne Beddingfeld in a 1924 novel hits upon the idea of becoming a newspaper correspondent to finance and disguise her detective work, only one character in the novel questions its seemliness. But earlier in the century, newspaper work for women was discouraged. An informal survey run by the *Ladies Home Journal* asked 50 female and 50 male editors if they would approve of their daughter going to work in a newspaper office. All but three of the women who responded (42 of the 50) said they would not like it and would not approve. All of the men who responded (30 of the 50) "were unanimous and emphatic in their opinion that the newspaper office was not a fit place for a girl" (*The Writer* 30).

On the other hand, E.A. Bennett's British publication, *Journalism for Women: A Practical Guide* (1898), initially sounds much more positive. Bennett offers market-oriented advice about the importance of being business-like, so as to raise oneself above non-technical women journalists. He encourages women to go every day to public reading rooms and study all publications (not just those that interest them) because one must learn "intimately the complicated topography of all the daily papers—on what days certain features appear; what length of article is affected by each paper; and the subtle variations of tone which, apart from grosser differences, distinguish one organ from another" (50–51).

Bennett is harsh towards women who try to enter the field without understanding the maxim that "business is business" in journalism. However, though he thinks that women journalists are as a class "unreliable," he blames their often-deplorable technical skills on a lack of early training, not on biological sex: "the female sex is prone to be inaccurate and careless of apparently trivial detail, because that is the general tendency of mankind. In men destined for a business or a profession, the proclivity is harshly discouraged at an early stage. In women, who usually are not destined for anything whatever, it enjoys a merry life" (17).

But in this guide, working in an actual newspaper office is barely touched upon, as Bennett does not consider it practical. The only "proper way of entering upon journalism" is to work as an "outside contributor," working at home and sending in articles or even mere paragraphs to various papers (24). Thus the journalism field is another example of the employment philosophy which deemed it acceptable for women to work in certain aspects of a field which could be construed as more appropriately "feminine." Writing certain types of novels might be acceptable, for instance, but working for a newspaper, which took women out of the domain of the home, was looked down upon. Bennett's advice about becoming an outside correspondent bears out this point; while women could be published in a paper and make money for themselves, it was best and most appropriate if such money-making not be done in a public way.[24]

Within the limited scope of his advice—most of his book is written on the assumption that women will work solely as outside contributors—Bennett's work is unusual in its practicality and assumption that working is a natural and obtainable goal for women. It is also invaluable as an example of the ways women who wished to make money adapted to prohibitive cultural prescriptions against employment in the public sphere.

British Psychoanalysts

Of the jobs discussed in this chapter, this was certainly the most uncommon for women in the early 20th century, but it deserves mention because one major figure in this study, Gladys Mitchell, created a woman psychoanalyst to serve as an amateur detective in her fiction. Though uncommon as a profession, it was not unrealistic that such a character appeared in fiction; women had been involved in psychoanalysis since its inception in Britain and had a large impact on the ways Freud's theories were disseminated.

Women's entrance into the field of psychology (the precursor of psychoanalysis) had its beginnings in the cultural belief that women possessed certain bases of knowledge which were uniquely theirs, giving them an advantage over men. In this case, it was knowledge and understanding of children; women had larger roles in children's lives and were thought to better "naturally" understand children's ways. With this accepted ideological construct supporting them, women were able to make inroads into the field before it was even an established science. Mary Carpenter, as early as the 1850s, worked to establish a link between juvenile delinquency and psychology. According to L.S. Hearnshaw, a historian in the field of British psychology, Carpenter's two books, *Reformatory School* (1851) and *Juvenile Delinquency* (1853), had much to do with the passage of reform legislation in 1854.[25]

The work done by women in child psychology also shaped the ways that Freud's psychoanalytic theories were circulated in Britain in the early twentieth century. Several women analysts practicing in England had been trained by men in Freud's inner circle, and others were active in the translation of his theories.[26] Perhaps the most well-known woman in early British psychoanalysis, Melanie Klein, became famous for her disagreements with Anna Freud on the specific issue of child development. Her ideas were so influential in Britain that the Kleinian variant of psychoanalysis is often labeled the "British School" of psychoanalysis (Hearnshaw 240). Appignanesi and Forrester too call work with children "a characteristic factor of psychoanalysis in Britain," highlighting the contribution women of this time made to the development of the field (353).

Mitchell's fictional Mrs. Bradley is thus believable as a woman psychoanalyst when she appears in 1929. However, Mitchell makes it clear that though Mrs. Bradley's profession is plausible, it is unusual. None of the supporting cast of characters in Mitchell's novels know how to classify Mrs. Bradley or her profession. Several characters in *Speedy Death* align her work with witchcraft, and in *Mystery of a Butcher-Shop*, the profession is seen as a fad, discussed along with subjects like crash diets and crystal gazing. One character, explaining Mrs. Bradley's presence in their village at the time of a murder, exhibits this uncertainty as to her "calling":

> "I don't know what they [psychoanalysts] do, quite. I believe it's something mad but brainy. The thing was all the rage two or three years ago, and the mater [...] collects these new movements. Well, she tried to collect Mrs. Bradley, who appears to be rather a brass hat at the business, but the old dame wasn't having any" [*Butcher-Shop* 74].

Mrs. Bradley is an amateur criminologist in the first several novels in which she appears, but her success in this line eventually leads to her appointment as Psychiatric Consultant to the Home Office, where she combines her psychoanalytic and crime-solving skills to serve in an official capacity. Such an appointment might have possible in more than just the world of fiction—in 1927 Beatrice Edgell of Bedford College was made the first woman Professor in Psychology in Great Britain. She was later appointed the first woman president of the British Psychological Society, pointing to the possibility of women's advancement in this field.

World War I and Women's Employment

Like most branches of work done by women, war work—nursing, military attachments, and police work—was also framed around the rubric of the home in order to make it ideologically convenient. And, like fictional women detectives, who purposely played upon and used stereotypically feminine traits to succeed, women coming from the middle and upper classes who wanted to perform war work justified themselves in society's eyes by arguing that they could fill certain positions—those requiring a woman's touch—better than men.

That being said, it is true that the largest employers of women during the war were the munitions factories. Nearly one million women worked in a job that was both difficult and dangerous, in a place decidedly *un*-feminine. The general factory workers were usually from the working-classes; most middle-class women were employed as "quasi-professional" supervisors, inspectors, welfare workers, or women police or patrols (Woollacott, *On Her* 2). But middle-class women worked on the factory floor too, as a story in Gilbert Stone's collection of women's war experiences makes clear.[27] Naomi Loughnan puts out an impassioned plea to her middle-class sisters to "come in their hundreds and use their fine gifts of culture and education for their country and for humanity," to take up work in the even more dangerous filling factories (in Stone 41). Far behind her seem the days of "dogs and novels, tennis rackets and golf" (38) as she works "shoulder to shoulder with the children of the slums" (37).

But even though this "woman's work" could not be directly cast in terms of the home, it was cast in terms of sacrifice, another socially acceptable reason for women to work. The main motive for women's work during war time was patriotism; though they were working "unwomanly" jobs, they did it for the men on the front lines, recasting what might be construed as rebellion in times of peace as noble sacrifice instead. Most women working for the war effort—whether as nurses, munitions workers, or potato planters—cited patriotism as the main reason for signing up, the feeling that they weren't doing enough. For Ellie Rendell, a young nursing recruit with the Scottish Women's Hospital and member of the suffragette movement, viewing war propaganda movies was the impetus for her spur-of-the-moment decision to become nurse. She writes to her mother:

> You will probably think me quite mad when I tell you that I have decided to go to Russia for 6 months with the Scottish Women's Hospitals people.
>
> We went to see the war pictures at the Scala on Monday night and as a result of that I felt it to be my duty to offer my services [...] [in Figes 226].

However, as Elizabeth Crosthwait's article, "The Girl Behind the Man Behind the Gun," makes clear, patriotism coincided with a unique chance for independence and difference for women. Crosthwait describes the space "created by the war's disruption of normal life for women to have some independence":

> They could live away from home, and although women had to accept official discipline and work hard, at least they had escaped family constraints. And despite hardships and problems, this independence was exhilarating: "For two years we worked long hours seven days a week, we were cold, dirty and badly

fed. Did we care? Not a bit! We were young, we kept on falling in and out of love, and we have got our fingers into the war pie" [171–172].

The exoticism of going to the Front or to France thus fueled these women to do something for the war effort; dogs and novels, as Loughnan points out, seemed as remote and meaningless as munitions did before the war. I do not mean to discount patriotism as women's primary motive for action, but in the course of being patriotic women were able to change the course of their lives and expand the scope of their abilities. Most women welcomed that opportunity.[28]

World War I was the single greatest factor changing women's employment patterns. But allowing women into some areas of war work required much decision-making. For the first two years of the war, the Armed Forces declared that women were not wanted in anything but nursing. By 1916, when the country became desperate for men to serve as soldiers, the government began to think differently (D. Mitchell 222). All sorts of organizations were formed for women in wartime, in addition to their work in munitions and other factories: women police; women auxiliary forces to the army (the WAACs), navy (WRNS), and air force (WRAFs); the Women's Land Army; and the Women's Legion Motor Transport Section.

The propaganda surrounding these jobs, in addition to their patriotic mien, usually focused on the work these women could do specifically as women, thus employing the same justifications feminists had used in the past to give women a foot in the working-world door. Women police at home could bring a stabilizing influence on young people. Those joining the paramilitary organizations could bring "a woman's touch" to the troops and their camps overseas: a home-like atmosphere, improved hygienic conditions, cleaner camps and better food. The Volunteer Aid Detachments (VADs) and other nursing units could attend to the sick, since nursing had always been a woman's domain (and since the work of Nightingale and others had made it respectable for middle- and upper-class women). These tasks did not greatly disturb commonly-held notions of respectability and would serve as good training to make young middle-class women successful wives and mothers.

There were exceptions, of course; there was nothing in the training that women in munitions factories received that could be considered training for future household management. And Crosthwait's article about women who served in the paramilitary attachment to the army, the WAACs, enumerates some of the difficulties women had when they broke into one of the last bastions of pure masculinity, the military.[29] At the base of society's dilemma concerning women in the military was the belief in women's paradoxical nature: on the one hand, women were domestic angels, dedicated to making a lovely and moral home, even if it was away from home, so therefore it would be good to have them serve; on the other hand, women were sexual temptresses whose immorality could only be fueled by such close proximity to men. Serving in the army would coarsen women, and any women wanting to be part of such a male institution must be "sexually suspect" to begin with; it was assumed they would not be able to control themselves around the forces (Crosthwait 178). This, as we will see, is the same reason women police were hired in Britain, as patrols to control not the men but the young girls invariably suffering from "khaki fever."

However, because of class issues, women serving in the WAACs may have experienced more difficulties overcoming negative public opinion and perceptions of immorality than their counterparts in the WRAF and the WRNS. Though staffed by educated women of a higher social class, the WAACs were primarily comprised of working class women, whereas the WRAFs and the WRNS "'catered for the nicer girls'" (S. Rowbotham 75).[30] On the whole, however, regardless of their members' class or education, women's military attachments proved highly beneficial at replacing men in non-combat situations, thus freeing the men to fight. Building on the success of the WAACs in early 1917 (in which 57,000 women served), the country created the WRNS that same year (in which 3,000 women served) and the WRAF in 1918 (which admitted 32,000 women).[31]

Paramilitary groups like these gave women the opportunity to serve with other women in what had been an exclusively male institution, to prove themselves capable of hard work, and to serve their country in a way unlike anything before. They knew that their work would end with the war, and, like most women who served in what was clearly a war-time capacity, they gave up their work when they were expected to and became wives and mothers, or returned to being wives and mothers if their husbands and sons hadn't been killed. Their jobs simply no longer existed, and they usually accepted this with equanimity. Nevertheless, work during war time more than any other single force expanded the opportunities available for women in the workplace and altered the public's perception of what they could do.

Nursing

Nursing for the most part presented no such problems to society's standards or beliefs about what work women should do during wartime. It had become a common respectable job for "ladies," and it was even assumed that women would take up some kind of nursing work when the war began. Agatha Christie, in her *Autobiography*, writes that every young girl went to first aid classes in 1913, though with no real comprehension of how soon they would need their skills. When war did break out, Christie just seemed to know where to go: "I hurried to my attachment in the V.A.D.s to see what was going on" (267). By 1914, women had so completely proven them-selves in this field—and it coincided so well with what society saw as fitting duties of women—that "few thought of military nursing as a man's job" (Summers 269). Indeed, though the Volunteer Aid Detachments were designed to employ both men and women, it was very difficult to get men to apply, and the Red Cross reported that those who did were largely apa-thetic (Summers 253).[32]

The VADs were started in 1909 at the request of the War Office to fill in gaps in territorial medical services. Women's detachments were to set up rest stations, to take care of soldiers too weak to travel, and to help when necessary with nursing in nearby hospitals. In general, they were looked down upon by members of the regular nursing profession because they were so poorly trained—they actually set back the professions' hopes for creating uniform standards and a sense of professionalism. However, the conception behind the creation of VADs was always that they would be "amateur." Recruiting appeals were made to the genteel (volunteer work had always been expected of them), and male organizers were quick to choose women who were in no way connected with suffragette movements to run the group. By the end of the war, nearly 50,000 women were members of the VAD (Summers 237).

Though connected to the military, detachments of VADs were not con-sidered military posts by the War Office or by the nurses and volunteers serv-ing. Ellie Rendell speaks to her mother in a disparaging tone about the women in her unit who had served already in "semi military organisations" and writes that "the military spirit has crept in," to the annoyance of the sisters running the hospital:

> some of our leaders have been bitten with the military craze & they love salut-ing, giving orders etc without having quite grappled with the essentials.
>   They rather like making us salute them for example without ever dreaming of returning the salute [in Figes 227].

Yet at its inception, the VADs were trained to see themselves as adjuncts to "military" movements. For example, one exercise asked them to suppose that "a battle had taken place on the Northumbrian coast [...] and soon after a heavy roll of casualties was reported" (in Summers 258). How would they respond? Some detachments took these exercises very seriously and were therefore taught how to dress a wound in the field without bandages, how to build a stretcher, how to cook over an open fire. They spent weeks in tents as well as in hospitals. When male organizers learned how aptly and avidly women were performing these unfeminine duties, including heavy stretcher training, they quickly interceded and revised the language of the organizations' documents. But the damage was done; these elements of thinking on one's feet, improvisation, and leadership training made work in the VAD exciting for women who had no previous display for their intelligence.[33]

When war broke out, any attempt to quell the more adventurous units of the VADs was quickly banished for more pressing concerns. Casualties started arriving, and the volunteer-oriented, middle- or upper-class women who thought VAD work would be fun but were not particularly willing to get their hands dirty were shocked by what they saw and were being asked to do. Christie writes that many middle-aged women especially had the idea that nursing involved primarily "a good deal of pillow smoothing, and gently murmuring soothing words" (229). When tasks like cleaning bedpans, delousing soldiers, and bandaging suppurating wounds presented themselves, these "idealists gave up their tasks with alacrity" (229). VAD nurses quickly realized that their basic first aid training did not prepare them in the least, and they almost immediately got tough or they dropped out.

Therefore, while nursing in the VAD was a respectable and common women's role, it offered, like most positions in wartime, a chance for women to extend their boundaries. Most women who joined the VADs, as Summers points out, were those "whose home backgrounds denied them access to political activities and professional competence and who, but for their VAD work, might not have ventured beyond tennis parties and fundraising bazaars" (290). Agatha Christie is a classic example of this sheltered type. Even women like Vera Brittain, who as a Somerville student was already functioning in an unusual role, could not resist war work and became a VAD in order to "join up in a London hospital and thus be on the spot when Roland [her fiancé] came home wounded or on leave" (Youth 146). Regardless of recruits' social background or original reason for joining, serving in the VADs gave women experience and responsibilities that many found difficult to relinquish when the war was over.

Policewomen

Serving on the police force was another way for women to expand their opportunities, contribute to the war effort, and change public opinion about women's abilities. While several other countries already had policewomen in some capacity before the war, with duties therefore not defined by it, in Britain the war became the catalyst for the appointment of women police.[34] Though various women's organizations had been lobbying for admittance into the force for some time, it was only the need for women to serve as patrols in newly established army towns that pushed the issue through. But though women police from this time are the closest counterpart to the fictional female detective, their status was a far cry from that of their independent-minded fictional contemporaries, both in duties they were allowed to perform and in how they were perceived by society.

Women were attached to London's police force in minor ways before their official recognition in 1918. Two women were hired in 1883 to supervise women convicts (this was later cut to one), and in 1905 a woman was hired to help interview women and children (Owings 2). This latter job was subsequently changed to the title "police matron" and became a different branch from women police.

Two separate groups were fundamental in establishing women police at the beginning of the war: the Women Police Volunteers, later called the Women Police Service (WPS) and the National Union of Women Workers of Great Britain and Ireland (NUWW). Both of these groups primarily were concerned with patrol work, in towns with troops suddenly stationed nearby, in parks, railway stations and later in munitions factories. Mary Allen, one of the first Commandants of the WPS, gives an excellent first-hand account of the movement from its inception, and writes that in the beginning, their mere presence was the only weapon they had. They often had no powers of arrest (especially at first) and simply walked back and forth in front of people whom they suspected of committing indecent or illegal acts, trying to "move them along." They were not primarily concerned with professional prostitutes, who were already basically lost, but with girls and women who "were so attracted to men in military uniform that they behaved in immodest and even dangerous ways" (Woollacott, "Khaki" 325).

This outbreak of "khaki fever," as it was soon dubbed, swept through towns where base camps were newly created. Though both "idle boys and girls of all classes" (Allen 18) succumbed to the disease, it was the reputations of respectable girls which caused the uproar and whom police patrols tried to protect. These girls were not necessarily criminals, and the police would not usually get involved with preventive work of this sort. Women patrols, seeing the need, basically created a job for themselves in London and in military towns.

Protection of women from harm was the foremost idea of women police from the outset; Owings writes that the thread running through the policewoman's past was the realization that women would be the best force to protect "little girls" from "men of degenerate sex tendencies" (6). But as Angela Woollacott and others point out, in actual fact this gradually became turned around: though they saw themselves as protecting women, they were seen by the military and their male counterparts as protecting the soldiers from women.[35] The women and girls were the ones who needed policing, and whether they liked it or not, women police often had to go into women's homes to enforce the law.[36]

Women police began solely as volunteers, having been brought in by private organizations wishing to see their presence in their town. This piece-meal placement of women patrols meant that there was no real regulation of women police, no requirements except those self-established by the WPS or NUWW, and no authoritative duty description or pay scale. Each town's Chief Constable could do as he pleased with women recruits.[37] In some cases, the women were sworn in, given powers of arrest, wore the same badges and got the same pay as male constables. In others they were treated only as volunteers supported by the local organizations that had originally brought them in. Their forcefulness in these situations was severely ham-pered by their inability to make arrests, and their "distinctly anomalous" position was concealed as much as possible from the public (Allen 49).

Though their actions were self-described as preventative, women work-ing as police, especially from the WPS, were anxious to distinguish them-selves from social or rescue work or other more traditional areas of women's work. They wanted to be defined as police and to get paid (as opposed to mere "volunteering" like earlier patrols) for doing work they saw as neces-sary for police to do. In November 1915, after seeing how well they per-formed their "arduous and unenviable duties," the two women stationed at Grantham were sworn in as members of the police force. They were paid out of police funds, and worked under the orders of the Chief Constable (Allen 38).[38]

According to Allen, the existing male police force usually accepted the women recruits after a few weeks; even when the Constable initially objected, he was "promptly reconciled" to the policewomen after reading the women's diaries, in which they recorded their activities over the past week. The men on the force too, were "inclined to be both friendly and help-ful; and the Inspectors themselves, as soon as they realised that their female colleagues were prepared to salute them with becoming gravity, and to treat them in every way with due respect, were equally inclined to cordial rela-tions" (48).

The towns where they were stationed also appreciated the work of the women patrols, both in protecting women from falling into lives of prosti-tution, and, in the eyes of the military, protecting their soldiers from women. General Hammersly of the Grantham camp, on hearing that the two police-women stationed there were going to be removed, wrote a letter to the Chief Constable asking that they not be taken away:

> The services of the two ladies in question have proved of great value. They have removed sources of trouble to the troops in a manner that the military police could not attempt. Moreover, I have no doubt whatever that the work of these ladies, in an official capacity, is a great safeguard to the moral welfare of young girls in the town [in Allen 37].

Notice the order of importance in which the General lists their work!

Allen also provides a few newspaper accounts showing the public's support of women police. The *Grantham Journal* late in 1915 wrote: "'the presence of women police is a distinct advantage to the town'" (38); and the London *Evening News* provided the following accolade:

> Everybody admits that the policewoman has done splendidly. She has "moved on" with the utmost success; she has turned disorder into calm [...] all by the power of the eye. She draws no staff, she administers no push, in many cases she does not even speak. She just looks, and he who is looked at melts thoughtfully away [...] [qtd. in Allen 55].

Even the conservative *Times* came out in favor of providing women police with full powers in 1917 to help deal with the rampant prostitution in London (Lock, *Policewoman* 58).

Undoubtedly, some measure of the policewomen's success stemmed from the odd mixture of sex with class: the public was "confounded by the privileged class stature of the early recruits. It was not just that those in the streets were women, they were ladies" (Levine 64). This posed difficulties in determining their potential staying power, as "it is impossible to measure how far their early success derived from class deference rather than their legal authority, a puzzle which the women themselves recognized" (Levine 63). Allen, for instance, was aware of the courtesy they were given as "ladies," and says she found that in addition to being able to control women better than male constables, they could also control soldiers better: "It is a most curious fact, confirmed by a thousand instances, that the rougher elements among mankind are more easily controlled by women than by men, far more easily than the so-called 'upper-classes'" (22). A private of a lower class would turn into a "shamefaced and penitent boy" at a policewoman's reproofs (Allen 22), as "'the natural authority of their [the policewomen's] class'"often made working-class men and women likelier to comply with the women's instructions (Levine 64). An officer of an equal class to the women, on the other hand, was more likely to "turn furiously upon the policewoman who ventured to interfere with his pleasures, and to 'damn her impudence!'" (Allen 22). However, though they sometimes encountered hostility from men in socio-economic classes equal to their own, none of the women reported any worse treatment than verbal abuse, and this usually came from drunken working-class women.

While it was obvious that wartime groups like women's paramilitary attachments or the VAD would not last beyond the war, the future of women police was not so clear. The WPS believed that they had conclusively proved their worth, beyond patrol work of army towns, in their service for women and children and in the establishment of prevention as police work. Dorothy Peto, a NUWW member, wrote in 1916 in *The Englishwoman* that "the steadily increasing demand for such workers is, in itself, an assurance that no suitable woman need fear that she will find any difficulty in obtaining a post" (27). Priscilla Moulder, writing in the feminist magazine *Life and Labour*, believed optimistically that policewomen "have demonstrated their ability so successfully that it is now a foregone conclusion that they have come to stay" (121).

But in Allen's eyes at least, the women police "experiment" which the new Police Commissioner decided to form in 1918 was deliberately designed to fail. Not only did Sir Nevil Macready opt *not* to use the fully trained and experienced force of the WPS put at his disposal, he did not even want the type of women so carefully screened by them: "his actual words, with regard to educated women, were 'that they would pin-prick the men,' and he did not want any friction" (Allen 128). The new women police were in no way to be higher (in class, education, pay) than the male constables. Regardless, at the end of 1918, the Police Commissioner sanctioned the Metropolitan Police Women Patrols as members of the force. This first officially recognized body of women police was to be comprised of one Superintendent, one Assistant Superintendent, 10 Sergeants, and 100 Women Patrols. In February 1919, the first 24 were sent out on duty.[39]

These women police were from the start limited by what the male police structure saw them as being able to do. If one took away the title of Metropolitan Police, there was little left behind: these women had no powers of arrest, "were not to be sworn in, they had a meagre status in comparison with many provincial policewomen already in the field, and their duties were correspondingly curtailed" (Allen 130). Furthermore, they were not even allowed to be called "women police," as Macready objected to the term, but had to settle for "patrols" (Lock 90). Given this restrictive atmosphere surrounding their abilities, combined with the end of the war, women police came to be seen as unnecessary; even those cities which had once found them useful began to think of them as a luxury. In December 1919, Dorothy Peto wrote to amend her once-positive stance into a urgent plea for Parliament to quickly decide the policewoman's uncertain future so as not to throw away the opportunity to lay "the foundations of valuable and permanent work for Society" (*Englishwoman* 176). Though a Committee set up in 1920 to look into a permanent women police force said "there is not only scope, but urgent need for the employment of policewomen," the issue was scuttled. By 1922, the country had done a complete turn-around, and that year's expenditure report suggested doing away with women police altogether, saying "'their powers are very limited and their utility from a police point of view is, on the evidence submitted to us, negligible'" (Owings 31). The

Commissioner of the Metropolitan Police Force began executing an order from the Home Secretary which rescinded the women police.

It was only after numerous Parliamentary debates and protests from women's groups of all natures that the complete abolition of women police did not occur. Yet of the 110 positions originally created for women in the London Metropolitan Police, only twenty were retained, to be raised incrementally to fifty.

Levine comes to the conclusion that "within the boundaries established by gender, policewomen enjoyed significant successes" (76), especially in initiating and defining preventative work as part of the proper role of police. However, though the public was pleased with women police during the war, supporters had difficulty sustaining professional interest and public opinion in favor of their continuance beyond wartime, whether because of the depleted post-war economy, the general depression which hit England earlier than the United States, or simply because of the continuing belief that women should not perform men's work. This sentiment was especially strong in the light of soldiers returning home from the war; under these circumstances, it was thought that, like women in other "men's" jobs, they should relinquish any oddity in employment, since it was only "part of the abnormal times, it was reasoned, that women should be doing these grotesque things" (Allen 14).

WOMEN POLICE AND FICTIONAL DETECTIVES

The rise and fall of policewomen in society's eyes is particularly interesting in light of the trend that appears in fiction concerning female detectives. Women police during the War seem to have much in common with their fictional counterparts in the early part of the century. First, women initially recruited for police work were often unmarried—either single or widowed—and were older, between thirty and forty.[40] Secondly, they were well-educated and, according to Levine, "not women who typically would have engaged in paid work" (46). To illustrate, of the 1080 women the WPS says it trained between 1914 and 1919, 40 percent of them did not need to work—they were upper-class women who had private means of support. Another 50 percent came from fields of work already entered by the middle-classes and made respectable: 130 women were nurses, 75 were teachers and another 167 called themselves "certificated" (both of which suggest above-average education), and 59 women came from business (Allen 157). Only 10 percent of the nearly 1100 women came from working-class backgrounds, mostly domestic service, and Levine calls their move from subservience to positions of authority a "striking" fact (47). Finally, policewomen, as can be seen from their level of education, were recruited largely from the middle- and upper-classes, creating a very different profile than male constables, who were usually considered lower middle-class or working class. Interestingly, women writers of detective fiction pre-figured this trend when creating their very refined, well-educated, even aristocratic women detectives.

The pre-war fictional detectives are young professionals, confident, successful, unmarried, and, though most are working to make money, are by no means working-class. Rather, they have chosen detection as a line of work suitable for their intelligence, combining their brains with specialized "feminine" skills to succeed on the job. Five of the eight professional detectives in this study appear before the war; between 1912 and 1919 only Lucille Dare, created by Marie Connor Leighton, fits this description.

For the most part, after the war amateur (rather than professional) detectives appear in fiction, both male and female.[41] The two professional fictional detectives who do appear in the late 1920s are elderly spinsters, completely unlike the young brash detectives of earlier years and who thus cannot be considered threatening to established ways. But the women in this study who appear in fiction published after the war work as detectives on a mostly amateur basis, or, even more commonly, only as a sideline to other jobs or professions—typist, psychoanalyst, writer. The correlation is clear: the professional policewomen had fallen out of favor with the public; and similarly, in fiction, "a few backward steps were taken, perhaps in reaction to the shifting societal patterns" (Slung xxiii). The fictional female detective during and after the 1920's, like the initial 1914 policewoman, is largely amateur; if a professional detective appears, she is elderly and therefore non-threatening.

"SHADOW" DETECTIVES?

However, I have found in several histories of this time various oblique references to women working as detectives before they were "officially" hired by police. It is possible that these rather unknown women may actually be the fictional female detective's true counterpart. In two separate first-hand narratives, references are made to detective work done by women. Says Mary Allen: "Scotland Yard has for years made use of women in detective work; but the idea that the 'weaker sex' should actually be considered at all on a basis of equal standing with men in the police force was regarded, in 1914, as positively revolutionary" (21). Mary Hamilton seems to have the same situation in mind when she writes: "long before any one thought about employing policewomen, women detectives were engaged in the work of ferreting out crime by applying their intuition, versatility, and natural feminine guile to cases whose solution demanded these qualities rather than the methods of the male sleuth" (Hamilton 77). I have found no details on either of these reports of the apparently common use of women in detective work; I have no idea what work these women actually did. Official histories of Scotland Yard are silent.[42]

Hamilton reads Scotland Yard's comments about women police as admitting the need for women as detectives, regardless of what they are officially named, because the Yard "pointed out that in several important murder cases it was they [women] who secured information which proved the most important clues" (79). She continues:

> Sir Nevile [sic] Macready, until lately head of the metropolitan police in London, declared that all types of women detectives were needed; those who could put on evening clothes and mix with people at social events, as well as women who could don the make up of a woman of doubtful morals and frequent the underworld on an equal footing with the men and women hiding there from the law [79–80].

Though Lock's version of the above comments is simply about Macready choosing women to be police in general, Hamilton substitutes the word "detective," since in her eyes the use of disguise is an aspect of detective work. These references made by actual policewomen shed a different light on the potential role women may have played in an unofficial capacity before they were hired as policewomen.

To be sure, women were not "officially" attached to the police until the War years, and here there is a concrete reference. Lancashire during this time employed 19 women officers with the title of detective. The Chief Constable there (since each Chief Constable could choose how to employ women police) personally selected out of his clerical staff those women he felt would make good detectives, and trained them in theoretical aspects of crime-solving before sending them out on assignments. Owings reported that they are "attached to the Detective Division, rank as inspectors, sergeants and policewomen, and have the same conditions of service and pay as men officers of similar rank" (45). These women were employed as "detectives," and, in a sharp contrast to most women police, did no preventative or patrol work at all, making it a point "'to keep perfectly clear from any sort of welfare work.' The women police handle any kind of work as it is reported (A-941) whether murder, housebreaking, burglary, or other charges" (46). Though they were not put in charge of cases, this suggests at the very least that women police in boroughs had much more freedom and room for advancement than in London.[43]

Moylan's statement presented at the beginning of this chapter bears repeating in light of these comments: "although women police are employed occasionally on detective work, there are no women in the CID" (223). The definitions of "employed" and "detective work" in actual practice sound increasingly vague, and it is unclear what these women's connection to the department actually was. Might the general public have known about these women's unofficial detective work? Could these detectives have been the

model for the popular fictional woman detective? If so, why have no histories of women's detective fiction mentioned them? These seemingly off-hand
remarks about the years women were used in detective work may hold more
of a key than their writers appreciate. Even if no solid facts ever come to
light, these references make it clear that the position of female detective is
more complicated than even the most detailed account of the policewoman's
past can adequately explain.

The goal of this chapter has been to highlight women's place in the
working world, to better understand historical aspects of the society in which
women writers were living and which may have contributed to the characterizations of their female detective creations. Though women's roles changed
drastically during this time period, most notably because of the Great War,
an unremitting ideology which by and large did not approve of women working outside the home retained its influence. This was despite the fact that
women *were* working outside the home, and in male-dominated professions.
Rather than recasting culturally-laden middle-class assumptions in a different
light, it was easier to make certain justifications: that these things were just
temporary; or just in certain cases; or just for single women until they got
married; or, if they worked to support a male relative, then only because
their love for their brother or nephew demanded this great sacrifice of them.

Acceptable women's jobs, such as a governess, nurse, or typist, were
often arduous and low-paying, and fictional detectives refer scornfully to
these jobs, acknowledging that one reason they took up detective work was
to escape the drudgery and low status associated with typical women's work.
Women detective fiction writers, predominately middle-class and thus aware
of the limited possibilities open to women in their social position, drew
upon this knowledge when creating female characters to fill the role of detective in their fiction. In doing so, they seem to express dissatisfaction with
the domestic ideology that saw inherent limitations in their ability to work
outside the domestic sphere. Their characterization of female detectives as
feminine and lady-like shows a desire to expand the boundaries which could
contain such women.

TWO

Female Knowledge; Of Domesticity and Intuition

[...] everything that a lady could require in dressing lay ready to hand. The dressing gown lying on the back of a chair had footstool and slippers beside it. A chair stood in front of the toilet table, and on a small Japanese table to the right of the chair were placed hair-pin box, comb and brush, and hand mirror.
—C.L. Pirkis, "Drawn Daggers" (1894)

Feminine realism and, by extension, domestic realism in general were thus defined in terms of woman's nature and woman's social role. Given the prevailing views of woman, and also the actualities of women's lives, it is not surprising that feminine realism was repeatedly defined as a lack. [...] Women writers were deemed capable of submitting everyday events to minute scrutiny, but lacked the power of "generalization" and "reasoning."
—Lyn Pykett, The "Improper" Feminine (1992)

The above quotations—one a description written by a woman and the other a commentary on the act of "description" by women writers—highlight the common perception of women's experiences and women's writing, as well as the way their supposedly inherent female characteristics were construed by late Victorian society. It was thought that women's literary powers extended from and mimicked their natural gifts. In the same way, women's narrow sphere in life was reflected in their fiction: they wrote works that were detailed but insignificant, clear and sharp but lacking intelligent cohesiveness.

Yet woman writers who created female detectives presented a challenge to that constructed "lack" in women's writing and experiences. Rather than seeing women's supposed detail-oriented nature as a flaw, women writers (and also female detectives) often turned this conventional "womanly" trait into a tool for success in the world of detection, a world which relied on the more "male-oriented" powers of generalization, reasoning, and deduction for its success. This chapter looks more closely at this powerful narrative strategy: women writers use traits which extended from what society thought of as women's naturally detail-oriented lives—knowledge of the domestic sphere and of "natural" female intuition—as key crime-solving tools. Instead of seeing traditionally female traits as handicaps, women writers provide their female detectives with these tools emanating from their status as middle-class women to successfully solve crimes. By validating women's areas of knowledge as valuable and worth writing about, women writers helped establish authority in the detective fiction genre.

As a whole, women writers of detective fiction wrote pieces in which class distinctions were upheld and which displayed their carefully cultivated domestic and middle-class values. Their fictional female detectives, despite their foray into the professional male-oriented world, emerge with their femininity and middle-class values intact, thus reflecting this socially conservative ideal. Indeed, their crime-solving ventures often have the effect of returning society to the status quo and upholding traditional values.

At the same time, however, these female detectives—who often receive money for their work, a decidedly unfeminine act—are placed in a socially equivocal position, one which reflects society's ambivalence about professional women. One of the ways women writers of detective fiction explored the ambiguous position of working middle-class women was through creating female detectives who were able to turn their specialized "female" spheres of knowledge into tools which would help them in a male profession. In addition to the stereotypically "male" traits of logic and analysis needed to solve crime, female detectives added tools that were specifically associated with women's sphere. Though they usually did not leave their prescribed societal roles as middle-class women, they attempted to put those roles to new professional purposes through using what society considered traditionally "female" knowledge, knowledge gleaned from doing or supervising housework and caring for children.

The methods fictional female detectives employed, though stemming from issues common to the woman's world, were considered very unorthodox by the detecting world. Many of these cases are solved by women who are able to do so precisely *because* they are women. They can read the crime scene in ways that their male counterparts cannot, ways which provide them with vital clues. Success in solving crime made these methods, and therefore the female detectives who used them, credible.

Thus, by invoking the traditional domestic ideal in conjunction with these successful and unusual characters, women writers were able to challenge and expand that ideal. Female detectives who acted like the ladies they were brought up to be simultaneously changed the definition of what a "lady" could do. The existence of aristocratic female detectives makes this point even more convincingly; for the aristocracy to enter a profession was to almost immediately legitimize it. Women writers employed "femininity" in a strategic way, showing that even within limiting cultural boundaries women could do more.

Women writers who created female detectives, therefore, helped create new images for women and played an active part in the expansion of women's roles. As Craig and Cadogan point out, despite the tacked-on marriages and sentimental endings of many of these works, "the general idea behind the use of a female detective is bound to appear progressive, irrespective of how it is worked out" (12). By participating in this expansion of women's roles— exploring in their fiction a topic which affected the roles of women in society—women writers challenged the cultural boundaries limiting women's roles and worked to establish new parameters for their own professional authority in this burgeoning new genre.

Creating situations in which female detectives could succeed in this new genre was not difficult for women writers, in part because these situations were closely related to the ones created in the earlier schools of sensation fiction and domestic realism. These subgenres were considered "women-centered" for two reasons. First, their protagonists were usually women, often placed in unusual but traditionally "feminine" marriage narratives.[1] Second, the narrative success of these genres relied upon skills which society felt occurred more "naturally" in women writers. For example, using large amounts of realistic detail was a rhetorical strategy considered particularly feminine. As Robert Buchanan wrote in 1862:

> The lady-novelists are the most truthful of all aesthetic photographers. Narrow as their range necessarily is, they have been encouraged to describe thoughts and emotions with which men are of necessity unfamiliar [...]. Disciplined in a school of sorrow, closely observant of detail, and painfully dependent on the caprice of the male sex, they essay to paint in works of art the every-day emotions of commonplace or imaginative women, and the domestic experience of sensible daughters, wives, and mothers [134–135].

Echoed in the above description of realism in women's works are the two factors discussed in this chapter: knowledge of the domestic sphere and human nature. According to Buchanan, whose opinion is indicative of what was considered appropriate for middle-class women, these characteristics are necessarily present in women's fiction because domestic and emotional details are what women know best. For similar reasons, women writers could argue that they were well-suited to writing detective fiction: its success as narrative depends in part on its attempt at realism, the fact that the plots do not overstep the boundaries of what could happen. Increasingly, the crime story's setting was the home, a place with which women were intimately familiar.

This chapter then, looks at the ways in which women writers used traditionally feminine traits to establish both their own authority in the detective fiction genre and the authority of their characters. Though during this time the character of "female detective" itself was considered unconventional, the detectives themselves often acted in fairly conventional ways to achieve success. Furthermore, the tools they were given to succeed required that they have access to knowledge inscribed as "feminine" by society: specialized knowledge of the domestic sphere and an intimate knowledge of human nature, bound up in assumptions about women's "natural" intuition.

Knowledge of the Domestic Sphere

In creating realistic and detailed settings for their detectives, one of the areas women writers drew upon was their immense knowledge of the home. As the "cult of domesticity" became one of the most entrenched philosophies among the middle classes, the women writers in this study, all of whom were middle or upper-middle class, drew upon the assumptions of this philosophy concerning what was expected of middle-class women and provided their detectives with knowledge of practices surrounding the home.[2]

Among the duties of a middle-class Victorian wife falling within the sphere of the house were the establishment and maintenance of certain social signifiers seen as necessary for sustaining clear class boundaries: from the "increasingly complex rules of etiquette and dress, to the growing formalization of Society and the Season, to the proliferation of household-help manuals, to the institution of household prayer and the custom of house-to-house visiting, to cookery and eating behavior" (Langland 9). The implications of this list stretch far beyond what we think of today as "household" knowledge, and the vast responsibility involved in acquiring all this knowledge was no small feat. The house, both symbolically and literally, held tremendous sway over the imaginations of the Victorian middle-classes; says Dickerson: "the house had never so powerfully, explicitly, and strictly defined society as it would in nineteenth-century Britain" (xiii). Middle-class women's position in the house was also strictly defined, and girls were brought up knowing the important practices of their middle-class standing and what they signified.

But women's strategic role within the house, that which so "powerfully, explicitly, and strictly defined society" (and a role especially important to the middle classes), has often been undervalued. With the rise of the middle class came the desire for its members to formalize and regularize their actions and behaviors so as to distinguish themselves from those below, the lower middle classes or the working classes. In this defining of one's place, middle-class women had considerable power, both as the paradigmatic Angel in the House, creating a safe haven for working husbands, and as managers of the household and servants. Jessica Gerard's essay about the work performed by the "chatelaine" bears this out: these women "were not frail and idle, but self-assured, energetic and willing to do their duty [...]. Far from being idle parasites, they performed real work demanding significant skills, time and effort [...]" (in Dickerson 200). Reynolds and Humble point out that "the feminine ideal was empowering as well as enfeebling" (8); and Elizabeth Langland, in *Nobody's Angels*, forcefully argues for a re-reading of the common perception of idle and powerless wives, to see them in addition as "key players in consolidating power" (9). Though they acted within their accustomed spheres, or rather because they did, they wielded power and effected change while upholding not only domestic ideology, but ideologies regarding gender and class relations as well:

> Frequently interpreted only as victims of patriarchal oppression, bourgeois women were both oppressed as women and oppressors as middle-class managers. And they helped facilitate change not as agents fighting against oppression to generate new opportunities, but as subjects positioned unevenly within those power operations [Langland 18].

In other words, women did not necessarily have to rebel against standard social practices in order to negotiate their power or bring about changes to their sphere. Mary Poovey points out, for example, that women in the 1840s and 1850s who went about changing divorce laws in ways society perceived as "womanly"—quietly, steadily, deferentially—were vastly more successful with Parliament than Caroline Norton, whose behaviors and writings put her constantly in the public eye and scandalized society.[3] I don't mean to minimize the vital work of people like Norton and other early women's-rights activists, who helped usher in the immense changes to women's spheres occurring later. But it is equally false to retain a picture of Victorian middle-class womanhood that does not take into account the powerful opportunities women could seize within their own spheres, especially as creators and regulators of cultural ideology.[4] Women writers of detective fiction—again, middle-class and usually socially and politically conservative—pass onto their detectives both their domestic knowledge and the power emanating from it, giving them specialized skills to use to their advantage. Fictional female detectives often work within prescribed roles, but it is the knowledge originating from those roles that allows them to solve a crime, often in cases where male detectives fail. They act in ways acceptable to society while expanding what is considered acceptable.

Earl Bargainnier points out that many of the crimes involving female detectives occur in the house itself, where women are "*necessarily* present and involved in the happenings" (*10 Women* 1). But to see this merely as a "plot device," used to justify female detectives' presence on the scene of the crime, belittles the strategic narrative choice of women writers who place their detectives in a position of authority and expertise. Crimes are solved by female detectives who have specialized insight because they possess knowledge of the normal functioning of the household: the schedule and habits of servants, the intimacies of those living in the house, and the proper organization of items within the house itself. More importantly perhaps is what the absence of these signifiers of ordered life—which are always apparent at the scene of the crime—say to these women. Based on their knowledge of domestic practices, they are able to find clues that male detectives cannot.

C.L. Pirkis' Loveday Brooke (1894), the first professional female detective created by a woman, displays this alertness to housekeeping and domestic details that are often slightly askew and therefore a clue to the crime. She is at the same time an utter professional: she is highly educated and respected by her boss; she often places herself in danger for the job; she does not quit the detective profession to get married, making her somewhat of an anomaly among female detectives. Loveday Brooke is Pirkis' only detective, appearing first in a series of short stories for *Ludgate Monthly* and later collected into book form, *The Adventures of Loveday Brooke*. It is also Pirkis' last work; after this book she quit writing to concentrate on animal rights issues with her husband.

As what Ann Ardis calls "single-issue social reformers," women like Pirkis "presented only local challenges to Victorian social conventions" (15) because they continued to endorse "traditional sex, gender, and class distinctions" (16). They did not seek sweeping changes in the way society was run but worked only to solve particular issues. While they often advocated more job opportunities for women, these jobs usually corresponded to their middle-class status: fields like social work and nursing merely extended out of their earlier roles as domestic caretakers. They remained firmly within society's culturally-prescribed professional boundaries while simultaneously exploring what the expansion of those boundaries could mean.

Like most of the women in this study, Pirkis' young detective fits neatly into this mold; she is a professional using traditional womanly traits to succeed. Loveday works for a "well-known detective agency in Lynch Court, Fleet Street" ("Black Bag" 401). She is very much admired by her boss, Ebenezer Dyer, who "would at times wax eloquent over Miss Brooke's qualifications for the profession she had chosen" (403):

> she is the most sensible and practical woman I ever met. In the first place, she has the faculty—so rare among women—of carrying out orders to the very letter; in the second place, she has a clear shrewd brain, unhampered by any hard-and-fast-theories; thirdly, and the most important item of all, she has so much common sense that it amounts to genius—positively to genius, sir [403].

She is often sent on cases where her sex is a requirement: they need a woman to "hob-nob with the maids" (402), or to play a "lady of impoverished means, who would gladly take the duties" of an amanuensis to a elderly scholar ("Troyte's Hill" 530). One time she is sent, rather than a male detective of the agency, because her boss believes that "'the idea seems gaining ground in many quarters that in cases of mere suspicion, women detectives are more satisfactory than men, for they are less likely to attract attention'" ("Redhill" 581). Indeed, as Klein has pointed out, Loveday's plainness and her status as a spinster make her particularly invisible: "she is doubly unnoticed; as both a detective and a woman she can expect to be overlooked by a society which has clear but restricted ideas of her value" (*Woman Detective* 68). Though her sex matters to the cases on which she is sent, Pirkis does not in any way play upon Brooke's sexuality, preferring to focus on other aspects of her character. The one description of her comes in the first story, beginning with "she is best described in a series of negations": "She was not tall, she was not short; she was not dark, she was not fair; she was neither handsome nor ugly. Her features were altogether nondescript [...]. Her dress was invariably black, and was almost Quaker-like in its neat primness" (402).

And, like most female characters who engage in detective work, she is penniless and friendless and takes up detecting because she does not like other more "suitable" women's work, even though this "cut[s] her off sharply from her former associates and her position in society" (402). She is also very well educated, though her education leaves her without what society considers "marketable accomplishments" (402).

Society has educated her about the domestic sphere, however, and she uses that particular knowledge to solve crimes. In "Drawn Daggers," a young heiress, Miss Monroe, convinces a fellow-passenger on their return ship to England to switch places with her so that she can marry her lover without the knowledge of her father or her guardian, with whom she is going to stay.

Since the Monroes have been in Hong Kong for twenty years, Miss Monroe's guardian, Mr. Hawke, would not recognize her, and once Miss Monroe and her lover married, the "impostor" Miss Monroe could return to home in Ireland. Loveday Brooke, who is called into the case for something apparently unconnected, surmises that Miss Monroe is not who she says she is upon seeing her bedroom: "The one point, however, that chiefly attracted Loveday's attention was the extreme neatness that prevailed throughout the apartment—a neatness, however, that was carried out with so strict an eye to comfort and convenience that it seemed to proclaim the hand of a first-class maid" (137). Loveday's interest is piqued when she discovers that Miss Monroe requires no help; much to her maid's disgust, she does everything herself, "'even to placing the chair in front of the looking glass.' 'And to opening the lid of the hair-pin box, so that she may have the pins ready to her hand,' added Loveday" (137).

These seemingly trivial details mean nothing to other observers, especially to Mr. Hawke, who cannot believe that Loveday has unraveled the whole conspiracy in one afternoon based on the neatness of a bedroom. But Loveday confirms that this fact allowed her to piece together the possibilities:

> The orderliness of that room was something remarkable. Now, there is the orderliness of a lady in the arrangement of her room, and the orderliness of a maid, and the two things, believe me, are widely different. A lady, who has no maid, and who has the gift of orderliness, will put things away when done with [...]. I don't think, however, it would for a moment occur to her to put things so as to be conveniently ready for her to use the next time she dresses in that room. This would be what a maid, accustomed to arrange a room for her mistress's use, would do mechanically. Now the neatness I found in the supposed Miss Monroe's room was the neatness of a maid—not of a lady, and I was assured by Mrs. Hawke's maid that it was a neatness accomplished by her own hands [141].

This convinces her that the occupant of the room is *not* the heiress Miss Monroe, who must have always had a maid perform these tasks. Here, Pirkis deliberately organizes the solution of the crime around a class distinction, discernible only through rigidly ordered household details. Loveday solves the crime because, as a middle-class female detective, she notices when certain domestic signifiers of upper- and middle-class respectability are missing. So clearly delineated are the distinctions between classes that a case of switched identities can be cleared up based on those details alone.

Pirkis perhaps implies the need for such distinctions, as Loveday's detection has the effect of re-establishing class boundaries and hierarchies. Though her detective has a job and can discern details which signify working-class practices, Pirkis makes it clear that Loveday herself is not working-class.

She maintains all the qualities of a lady, showing that women can work even in a male-dominated profession and retain both their feminine sensibilities and their social positions.

Assumptions about women and their domestic roles were not limited to the Victorian Era but appear throughout the time period covered in this study. For example, finding a vital clue based on domestic practices is also present in Gladys Mitchell's 1929 novel *Speedy Death*. Like Pirkis, Mitchell created only one detective throughout her extensive writing career, Mrs. Lestrange Bradley, a middle-aged psychoanalyst. Since she is about 55 years old in this first novel (born in the 1880's),[5] Mitchell implies that Mrs. Bradley is fully versed in late Victorian and Edwardian social practices and assumptions about prescribed women's roles, including the domestic practices that would have been taught her. Though Mrs. Bradley, as a professional psychoanalyst, has gone beyond the usual role for women, the training she would have received as a young woman—her domestic knowledge—serves her just as well as her psychoanalytic training in the sleuthing field.

One of the first clues to the murder of Everhard Mountjoy involves a missing bathroom stool, upon which the murderer must have alighted from the window sill in order to step down quietly. Both Mrs. Lestrange Bradley and Mr. Carstairs, a friend of the Bing household where both are staying, have figured this out; the stool is "missing" because it must contain some sort of shoe print. Carstairs is greatly disappointed, therefore, when he relates to Mrs. Bradley that the trail was a false one—the stool wasn't really missing at all: "Through some oversight, the maids appear to have put the two stools in the upper floor bathroom and none in the lower one" (51). Mrs. Bradley sees the improbability of this situation immediately:

> I can assure you, out of my housekeeping and servant-managing experience, that no maid ever moves bathroom stools. They won't even dust them unless you insist [...]. And tell me why it should ever occur to a maid to carry a bathroom stool up on to the next landing. And again, although I grant you girls are fools, even housemaids have eyes in their heads, and bathrooms are not extraordinarily large or particularly overstocked with furniture. They must have noticed that they were putting a second stool up there, mustn't they? [52].

Indeed, the murderer had cleaned off the stool and returned it later, hoping the story about the maids' incompetence would be believed. Carstairs never questioned the story, having no experience with household affairs; but Mrs. Bradley, knowing both household activities and human nature, laments the loss of the clue. It is so shocking to Carstairs that she could figure this out—it is so far out of the realm of his experience—that he accuses her of having knowledge no person should have: "'Are you a witch?' demanded Carstairs. 'No. Merely a fairly observant human being,'" Mrs. Bradley replies (52). Through this exchange Mitchell can reiterate that such amazing discoveries are simply part of the normal sphere of knowledge for a middle-class woman, demanding only the "human" power of observation to see the clue through to its logical conclusion.

Class in Women's Detective Fiction

One way women writers used female detectives, therefore, was to expand acceptable roles for women by showing how knowledge thought of as traditionally feminine could contribute to a predominantly male profession, while allowing women to retain their femininity and respectability. In turn, women writers of this fiction used the respectability of their detectives as a means to make the genre itself, as well as their contribution to it, more respectable.

By the end of the nineteenth century, the novel had already been divided into two distinct camps: mass-produced "popular" fiction versus its "high-culture" counterpart.[6] Detective stories, popular as they were, were subject to the same criticisms that surrounded most "mass" publications. Sub-genres such as sensation fiction and detective fiction were consigned to the lower level of literary production for a variety of reasons: they often appeared serially in periodicals first; if they did appear in novel form, they came out in cheaply produced editions (hence the term "penny-dreadful"); and sensation fiction, at least, was designed to appeal to the emotions, aligning it with the "feminine." Sensation fiction and detective fiction also were both associated with working- and lower-class readership, though the middle-classes too read them voraciously. In the sensation genre, books by Ellen Wood and Mary Elizabeth Braddon were best-sellers; Braddon's *Lady Audley's Secret*, for example, went through nine editions in three months.[7] Though men like Charles Reade and Wilkie Collins were famous writers of popular sensation fiction, it was considered primarily a "feminine phenomena" by the critics (Pykett 32). And while detective fiction was not seen as a woman's genre, it was, like sensation fiction, certainly thought of as a secondary, popular literature.

Since women writers of popular fiction often wrote to make a living and to support their families, they had a vested interest in making their writing succeed. This is especially true of Victorian era women, as financial necessity was one of the few socially acceptable justifications for picking up the pen, and it is true of many women writers of detective fiction, including well-known ones like Christie, Sayers, Meade, and Orczy. The debate surrounding the "inferiority" of popular fiction was well-known in late Victorian society. Discussion of it appeared in all types of literary publications, since even critics who didn't read it felt the need to comment upon it (Cvetkovich 16). Knowing women's long-standing relationship to popular fiction and its poor critical reputation, it is possible that women writers choosing to work in the new detective fiction genre tried to make it not only successful but respectable too. One way of doing this was to create female detectives who embodied middle-class values, who were well-versed in domestic knowledge and in class-conscious behavior. In effect, they were not only arguing for the respectability of their heroines, but for the respectability of the genre in which they were writing. Indeed, creating respectable heroines was a prime means of doing that.

Perhaps for this reason—the middle-class writers' desire to imbue writing in the genre with more respectability—women writers also created aristocratic female detectives, able to solve crimes while retaining all the signifying practices of wealth and femininity. Creating upper-class detectives may have helped transform the negative associations society had, not only about women entering the professional marketplace, but also about the "popular" genres of fiction commonly associated with women and in which women often wrote to make a living.

I am not arguing that these women writers were trying to turn the genre itself into "high" art; they knew it was popular and perhaps consciously used the fact that it was very publishable to their advantage. Indeed, many might have chosen to write in the genre *because* it was popular.[8] I do think, however, that the fact that all of these detectives are middle- and upper-class is more than mere fad or coincidence, and more than an expression of a desire to see expanded working opportunities for women. The respectability of women writing in these popular genres was also an important issue at stake; creating such detectives can also be seen as an expression of their desire to make the genre respectable not only for middle-class readership but for middle-class writers.

Within the genre of British detective fiction as a whole, aristocratic detectives were plentiful, seen as necessary in solving the crimes of their own class. In general, policemen are portrayed as unable to infiltrate the upper ranks themselves, so when crimes involving the upper classes are committed they need adjunct helpers. T.J. Binyon, in *Murder Will Out: The Detective in Fiction*, explains the existence of aristocratic detectives:

> While the police were quite capable of dealing with the brutal, common, and sordid crimes committed among the general populace, they were not only intellectually, but also socially, incapable of comprehending the nuances of the more subtle, refined, delicately plotted murders met with among the upper classes. [...] when confronted with a landowner, nobleman, or tycoon, they found themselves out of their social depth [...] [79].

These staples in British detective fiction—aristocratic sleuth and clumsy bobby—say something about the society which produced the genre, one largely committed to retaining class boundaries through both educational disparities and an array of class signifiers. The perception that working-class policemen would not be able to solve the more witty and "delicately plotted" crimes of the upper classes were perpetrated through this fiction, underscoring how important class distinctions were. Binyon's observation makes it clear that women writers were not alone in holding certain assumptions about class and the need for maintaining class boundaries.

American authors too, though seemingly not as class-conscious as the British, invoke class when the wealthy are involved in crime. Anna Katherine Green's Inspector Gryce of the New York police, trying to explain to Mr. Raymond why he needs his help, feels this distinction between classes keenly:

> "Have you any idea of the disadvantages under which a detective labours? For instance now, you imagine that I can insinuate myself into all sorts of society perhaps, but you are mistaken. Strange as it may appear, I have never by any possibility of means succeeded with one class of persons at all, I cannot pass myself off for a gentleman" [*The Leavenworth Case* 130].

Since he cannot "pass himself off for a gentleman," Inspector Gryce needs Mr. Raymond, a successful lawyer to the wealthy Leavenworth family and therefore on more equal terms, to get information for him. His lower-class standing shuts him out. Similarly, Anna Katherine Green's Violet Strange, "a girl of gifts and extraordinarily well placed for the purpose," can solve the crimes of upper-class young women with the proper amount of respect due that class, criminality notwithstanding. But the minute her connection to the sleuthing business comes out, says her boss, "her value to us will be impaired" (in Slung 154). She cannot be known as a police associate and still be fully accepted by those in her class.

In addition to Anna Katherine Green, Elizabeth York Miller and Baroness Emmuska Orczy created detectives who were also "ladies," and for this reason, their detectives, Madame Saroff and Lady Molly, respectively, are invaluable to solving cases involving the upper classes. They know the intricacies of how "the Season" is run and the habits and dress of the upper-classes, especially upper-class women. They solve crimes that the police with whom they work cannot. For example, Valeska, Madame Saroff, has many high society connections and a knowledge of women's social situations which allow her to see clues in "The Matter of the Savoy Thefts" from a different angle than Mr. Harris, the male working-class detective hired to solve the case. It is made clear many times in this story that a policeman could not possibly understand crime amongst the upper classes. The criminal is also of a lower class and trying to pass as upper-class, a cover that Valeska, like Loveday Brooke, is able to see through when solving the case.

Most of these authors attempted to account in some way for the reason their main characters chose detection for their careers. Elizabeth York Miller was no exception. Valeska, who appears in two stories in *London Magazine* (1908/9),[9] is an American whose Russian husband has just "singed" her, forcing her to return to London, poor and alone. Valeska's friend Sir Alec Campbell, knowing she has no money and needs to make a living, assumes that she will enter one of the few acceptable lady-like professions and open a bonnet-shop. But Valeska feels there is more to life: "I wonder if you can't inhale, as I do, the subtle breath of an hundred intrigues? It's everywhere. I have but to close my eyes—so, and it comes prickling up to me [...]. *And you talk of bonnets!* [...] *I am going to be a detective!* I am going to earn my miserable living prying out mysteries" (291).

In "The Matter of the Savoy Thefts," Miller creates a venue for her female detective that allows her to address one of the larger issues faced by women of her day, the very real need for professions for women, regardless of class. In keeping with many of the women writers creating these characters, Miller cogently raises the question of socially acceptable work. The issue raised in this chapter—the value of women's specialized knowledge— is also highlighted, as Miller has her detective give weight to certain clues and discount others based on that knowledge. This story therefore provides a very thorough example of the way that women writers use issues important to women to articulate a response to their culture, in the process establishing women's fitness to write in the detective fiction genre and thus their professional authority.

Women's knowledge of class signifiers, combined with upper-class society's desire to maintain strict class boundaries, plays a major role in this case. For instance, Valeska's main advantage over Mr. Harris in this case is her knowledge and understanding of the crowd at the Savoy Hotel. Crime here— amidst "the sea of white shoulders, the soft hues of exquisite fabrics, the jewels, the flowers, the rare wines" (291)—is clearly out of place, and Mr. Harris and the hotel manager are out of their league in trying to discover the thief. But Valeska is at home as a patron. Her "disguise" is as a regular customer: no one suspects she is there for any other reason except to be seen, and seen as Valeska, Madame Saroff, not as a private detective. No one else working the case has this advantage; two male detectives on the scene have to pretend they are waiters, and Mr. Harris doesn't come at all.

Miller further highlights class as an important issue through the identity of the criminal, also a member of the working-class, and, as a further condemnation, a foreigner. A former "Slav" courier of Lady Kathleen O'Shaugnessy, who has (rather improbably) disguised himself as a woman, is taking revenge for his spurned love by framing Lady Kathleen in the series of thefts, stealing something from another lady whenever at least the three of them—the courier, Lady Kathleen, and the victim—are in close proximity. Suspicion begins to settle on Lady Kathleen, a poor woman known to have gambling debts, but since she is part of the upper-class "Set," people are unwilling to give evidence against her. Says one party, after being asked who the other lady in the cloakroom was when a lorngette chain was found missing: "The lady's name does not mattah. Come, Milly. It's the chain you want, not to make trouble" (295). And since Mr. Harris is clearly *not* a member of this small social circle, he is not told the information he needs to solve the crime. The police are clearly intruders: even having to say "the odious term 'officer'" makes that patron's "soul shrivel" (294). Lady Kathleen pronounces Mr. Harris' name "with such infinite scorn that the little detective fairly withered away under it" (302).

Mr. Harris finds Valeska an invaluable ally in this situation. Much to her dismay, the fact that she must work incognito so her wealthy friends "do not know [she is] in a position to pry upon them" (299) works to her advantage with Mr. Harris: "I am sorry to say that [...] my society connections have done more to impress Mr. Harris with my value to him than anything really clever I may ever have accomplished" (299). Because he has none of those connections himself, he sees how valuable they are.

But even the working-class Mr. Harris can recognize certain pieces of evidence, and in this case the evidence seems clear: the first clue is a note in Lady Kathleen's writing, "the large conventional hand affected by fashionable ladies in their correspondence" (295) which accompanied a few worthless items that had been returned to the Savoy. Secondly, the stolen items have been retrieved from a pawn shop, originally brought there by a veiled lady who dropped a visiting card out of her muff, clearly identifying her as Lady Kathleen. But the most damning piece of evidence against her is not these obvious pieces of physical evidence, but her strange actions in the mornings. Mr. Harris reads the following from a notebook:

> "Spends part of each day away from home. Leaves house in Grosvenor Square, dressed shabbily; takes a 'bus and disappears upon some mysterious errand in the city. Has been traced to an office building on—- Street. Lets herself into a room on the fourth floor with her own key. [...] Does not reappear again for some hours. [...] Is visited frequently by a strange-looking man, shabbily dressed and somewhat unkempt. He is seen carrying flat parcels, which sometimes he leaves with her, and sometimes takes away with him.
>
> "The lady on these surreptitious excursions is always veiled, and seems anxious to avoid scrutiny" [299].

Even Valeska is overcome by this news and "dropped down helplessly into an armchair" when she hears it. Lady Kathleen's suspicious actions prove she is hiding something. Who would voluntarily go to an office building in the mornings, rather than make a more appropriate round of social calls? After Mr. Harris confronts Lady Kathleen with the thefts in front of her fiancé, with these damning suppositions given as evidence, her fiancé wants only "'one thing'" explained him. "'Only one. Then I will be satisfied. What does he mean when he says you spend much of your time in that dingy office-building? Why is it that you are always 'busy' in the mornings?'" (300). The accusations of theft, of breaking the law, the inevitable disgrace of it— these are all secondary. What Lady Kathleen does in the morning is the true mystery. And so she confesses that in order to pay off her bridge debts and for her upcoming wedding, she has become a writer: "'That little office is my workshop. I—I couldn't work at home. There were too many interruptions. I write silly stories, and a man comes for them and takes them to the publisher, and brings me the proofs to correct'" (302).

With this introduction of writing as a way to make money, Miller poses yet again the question of suitable work for women into her fiction. Four different professions have been mentioned in this story: Sir Alec has suggested the bonnet-shop as the obvious and acceptable choice for a "single" woman; when Valeska demurs, he guesses that she will go on the stage; Valeska then shocks him by her intention of becoming an incognito detective; and Lady Kathleen, in what is portrayed as the most shocking move of all, has become a popular writer to support herself.

Miller gives the reader this news in a matter-of-fact way, at the very end of the story, with no authorial stance except to say that there is a "flicker of a smile about the corners of her mouth" (302) as Lady Kathleen explains. But surely Miller means to say something about it. In a society that has such limited views of women's capacities, the fact that one must write and that one must often write in solitude are mis-read as criminal acts in this story. Furthermore, Lady Kathleen, because she is a "lady," has to hide her money-making fiction because she is committing a social indiscretion, a fact which is portrayed as the worst crime of all. One suspects that if Lady Kathleen were writing something more "worthy" than "silly stories" directed toward mass readership, her need to hide would be less acute.

It is unclear how close a parallel Miller means to set up between herself and Lady Kathleen. Detective fiction stories like "The Matter of the Savoy Thefts," written for a monthly magazine, might very well have been deemed "silly" by those in Miller's social sphere. It is clear, however, that Miller self-consciously plays on the notion of the criminality of women writers, perhaps to emphasize in a more forceful way the need to establish women's professional authority. Lady Kathleen's suspicious behavior in the mornings, when she writes, is just as disruptive as the crime, if not more so, because it prevents her from behaving in a socially traditional way. As a writer herself, Miller sees the injustice of a society having such restrictive views about what is important in women's lives. To emphasize the importance of this theme, Miller deliberately has this penultimate discovery of "writing for profit" overshadow the revelation of the thief's identity. Though Valeska unmasks him over the next few paragraphs, vindicating Lady Kathleen of at least physical theft, the mystery already seems over.

Just as important as these questions of class and profession are the questions of women's roles and the place of women's knowledge in society. Even within the limited framework of what a woman can do to make money, Miller highlights the immense activity of women within what society considered their proper sphere, with an emphasis on their relationships and areas of knowledge.

A "woman's network" runs clearly throughout this story. First, though Valeska scoffs at the idea of opening a bonnet shop, her relationship to this vital part of women's lives gives her an inside lead to the Savoy thefts. When she is in Mr. Harris' office asking for employment, he receives a call which she realizes she understands: "Like a flash of lightning I recalled a whispered conversation I had overheard between two ladies at my dressmaker's the other day. One always does listen to whispered conversations, doesn't one?" (292). Based on what she tells him she knows, he hires her on the spot. And rather than telling Mr. Harris how she got her information, she lets him think she got it in "some mysterious way" though "[t]here is nothing specially clever in eavesdropping" (292). To Valeska, overhearing a conversation at the dressmakers is commonplace, though it is a realm men cannot enter.

Secondly, her social connections in Vienna, where these thefts seem to have originated, allow her access to information no one else has: "Maud French, the American Ambassador's daughter, was one of my dearest girlhood friends, and if there was anything of importance to be discovered in Vienna, I am by way of discovering it" (297). From her friend she learns the background of these thefts and is able to fill in large gaps in Mr. Harris' theory.

Finally, her way of looking at clues in general comes from a deeper understanding of the motives and actions of a woman, which Miller stresses that Mr. Harris could not possibly understand. Most importantly, though she says she is technically "as certain as Mr. Harris of Lady Kathleen's guilt" (300), she opts to follow a different trail based on what her specialized knowledge tells her is true. She does not believe it was Lady Kathleen at the pawn shop, and therefore suspects Lady Kathleen is being framed, partly because she believes the note was forged and partly because of "one other thing: *Never before have I known a woman of fashion to carry her visiting cards loose in her muff. They are too easily soiled. It's an effort to keep them presentable in one's cardcase even*" (300).

So she follows her own instincts and discovers that at the time Lady Kathleen was supposedly pawning items, both the landlady and the liftman at the dingy office where she goes in the mornings verify her presence there. Mr. Harris, fully believing that it was Lady Kathleen at the pawn shop, never bothered to check this. Valeska knows for certain now that Lady Kathleen is being framed, and that Sunday night, the mystery is solved.

"The Matter of the Savoy Thefts" is a classic early example of an author exploring problems of acceptance and authority through a character also struggling with those problems. The situations of both the female detective and the struggling writer emphasize flaws in society's ideology concerning the roles of women. Though in this case the detective is not herself the writer (as will be the case in later chapters), she works just as effectively as an onlooker and sympathizer to this sub-plot, able to detect and expose the woman writer's difficulties and clear her from the suspicion of crime. This remarkable short story, however, has never received critical attention, despite its expert delineation of the often conflicting routes that women, whether as detectives or writers, must navigate in order to affirm a place in their society in the manner they wish.

Baroness Orczy's Lady Molly is another "lady" detective, more unusual in that she is an actual member of the police force. Even more unusual is the fact that this does not work against her socially, for she is able to maintain her "position in Society [...] whilst exercising a profession which usually does not make for high social standing" (260). Her antecedents, that she is the daughter of the Earl of Flintshire, are kept a secret, as is the reason she joined the force, to clear her husband's name from a false accusation of murder. The tales are narrated by Mary Granard, Lady Molly's former lady's-maid and now erstwhile partner in crime-solving, who treats her ladyship with all the deference due her position.

Baroness Orczy displays quite openly her concern with class attitudes and her desire to maintain the privileges and respectability associated with the upper-classes. Though the Orczy family lost much of their wealth before they moved to London due to a peasant revolt on her father's Austro-Hungarian estate, they were nonetheless aristocracy, and London society treated them as such. Baroness Orczy moved only in the highest circles, studying art and exhibiting at the Royal Academy, playing piano before Franz Liszt, dining with the Churchills. After her marriage, she and her husband, a painter, struggled financially for a few years, but after the success of her novel *The Scarlet Pimpernel* in 1905, their fortune was made.

This ideological investment in the aristocratic way of life is reflected in much of her work, including *Lady Molly of Scotland Yard*. Says Klein: "Baroness Orczy's stories embody an aristocratic superiority that brings the lower orders to justice but often allows the upper classes to hush up their crimes" (*Great Women* 259). Many of Orczy's upper-class perpetrators conveniently commit suicide when their crimes are discovered, so as to not have to go through the humiliation of public trial. And Lady Molly's privileges and status are made perfectly clear, especially through the tone of the volume: the men on the force, including the chief, all call her "my lady," and Mary says, "she could do anything she liked with the men, and I, of course, was her slave" (48). But Mary is not merely obsequious; Lady Molly deserves her status on the police force. Over five years, she has worked her way up from a small post to become the head of Scotland Yard's "Female Department," through "analysing and studying, exercising her powers of intuition and of deduction, until at the present moment she is considered, by chiefs and men alike, the greatest authority among them on criminal investigation" (275).[10]

Her intuitive and deductive powers, as well as her specialized knowledge of the upper-classes and women, help her solve "The Woman in the Big Hat," in which a man is murdered in a tea shop with a poisoned cup of chocolate. The title alone suggests the chief clue and the need for a woman who understands feminine sartorial details to solve the crime. The inspector in charge is relieved to find Lady Molly already on the scene: "The chief suggested sending for you [...]. There's a woman is this case, and we shall rely on you a good deal" (232). Unfortunately, a huge hat hid the female murderer's face, and, say the waitresses, unless one looked directly at her, one could not see above the chin. Therefore, none of the waitresses think they could recognize the woman again, although they are quite sure they would recognize the hat.

Lady Molly correctly figures out that the murdered man's wife, Lady Irene, is guilty, rather than the tall beautiful woman whom Lady Irene is trying to frame and whom Scotland Yard arrests, though they do not have enough evidence for trial. Lady Molly tricks Lady Irene's maid into commenting on a huge hat that she put back together "with the scraps [she] found in the dusthole" (255)—a hat Lady Irene wore only once and then cast off. When she hears this damning evidence, realizing that Lady Molly has put it all together, Lady Irene kills herself.

The men at Scotland Yard are stunned by the solution; however, to Lady Molly, who "had been right from beginning to end" (258), the clue was obvious and the solution simple:

> "The big hat," replied my dear lady with a smile. "Had the mysterious woman at Mathis' been tall, the waitresses would not, one and all, have been struck by the abnormal size of the hat. The wearer must have been *petite*, hence the reason that under a wide brim only the chin would be visible. I at once sought for a *small* woman. Our fellows did not think of that, because they are men" [259].

Millinery, therefore, has a greater importance to society than the mere making of hats. A thorough understanding of this and other women's milieus can lead, Orczy emphasizes, to effective police work. Both this story and "The Matter of the Savoy Thefts" point out the intricate and important relationships women have to each other through such female networks, giving them a greater understanding of each other, access to potential clues, and different eyes through which to see crime. The policeman who told Lady Molly that "there's a woman is this case, and we shall rely on you a good deal," obviously understood something of this situation. When the police cannot find clues, they must call in someone who can.

Baroness Orczy achieves the same goals in this book as many other women detective fiction writers, including a re-emphasis of class structures and a re-evaluation of those things perceived by society as insignificant because they belong to the women's sphere. Nearly all of the fictional female detectives of this time period "are able to interpret some clues because of their special social training as ladies—an expensive hat, the scent of perfume, fragments of will and letters [...]" (Blake 31). Because these women's domestic training and specialized knowledge of the home give them particular insight into crime scenes, they succeed many times where, their authors emphasize, male detectives cannot.

Additionally, Orczy's use of an upper-class detective argues for a re-evaluation of the respectability of women's detective fiction as a genre, in that Lady Molly's aristocratic background (and Miller's Valeska as well), works to counteract the negative associations of women writing for a "mass" readership. These detectives' ability to remain feminine and respectable while performing their jobs suggests a renewed hope that women writing in the popular detective fiction genre may perform and make a living from their literary "jobs" with similar expertise, maintaining their own femininity and respectability.

Knowledge of Human Nature

Along with specialized knowledge of the domestic sphere, female detectives are portrayed as having knowledge of human nature and natural "intuition" which they use to solve crimes. Both male and female authors associate this resource with women and imply that it was largely unavailable to male detectives. However, women authors seem to focus more on this skill as a valuable tool of female detection.[11] Women writers allowed their detectives to use intuition, often associated with a knowledge of human nature, to help solve crimes. They thereby make a traditionally "womanly" trait both valuable and marketable.

Terminology in this case tends to be confusing. Was natural female intuition really seen as "natural," or was this trait seen as socially acquired, cultivated by society's desire to explain what women should be like? Was women's often-hailed "knowledge of human nature" really a form of knowledge, something learned? Or were women thought to be born with the ability to intuit? Authors' interchangeable use of these terms adds to the confusion.[12] Indeed, society itself was confused about this so-called "natural" trait. Herbert Spencer attempts to sort out this confusion by locating female intuition in evolutionary history in his influential *Study of Sociology*, when he states that in humanity's primitive days, "the weaker sex naturally *acquired* certain mental traits" (emphasis mine), including the ability to "interpret the natural language of feeling. Hence, from the perpetual exercise of this power, and the survival of those having most of it, we may infer its establishment as a feminine faculty" (qtd. in Vrettos 19).

What I want to establish here is simply that society's belief in the origins of this trait were laden with contradiction and were being increasingly questioned (hence Spencer's desire to ground it scientifically). Regardless of these female authors' attitudes towards women's intuition—whether they thought of it as a learned behavior or as a natural attribute—women writers often emphasize this advantage in their female detectives. We can see a parallel here in the way women's rights advocates justified women's entrance into certain fields of work that they were "naturally" better suited to perform. Indeed, for women writers to call intuition a form of knowledge was to give it social value. Baroness Orczy, for example, refers to Lady Molly's "knowledge of human nature" and "knowledge of psychology" interchangeably throughout her book, and the narrator of the tales calls Lady Molly "the most wonderful psychologist of her time" (24). Adding the new term "psychology" to explain women's abilities reframes them as scientific and professional rather than merely feminine. But as Chapter One showed, psychology had been a discipline to which women could contribute; one of the most prominent and long-lived amateur detectives, first appearing in 1929—Gladys Mitchell's Mrs. Bradley—is a professional psychoanalyst.

Women writers applied a similar tactic to justify their entrance into the writing field; they argued that they were naturally equipped for this particular profession. Elaine Showalter, in *A Literature of Their Own*, writes of the need to reconcile women with novel-writing success in the 1840's:

> The least difficult, least demanding response to the superior woman novelist was to see the novel as an instrument that transformed feminine weaknesses into narrative strengths. Women were obsessed by sentiment and romance; well, these were the staples of fiction. Women had a natural taste for the trivial; they were sharp-eyed observers of the social scene; they enjoyed getting involved in other people's affairs. All these alleged female traits, it was supposed, would find a happy outlet in the novel [*Literature* 82].

These same assumptions, I argue, may be applied to women writers of detective fiction, and to female detectives, well into the twentieth century. If women writers achieve success by applying their "natural" talents to fiction writing, it follows that they give their creations the same skills, the same tools they "naturally" possess, in order to succeed. Female detectives succeeded in part because "detecting" came easily to women: they were seen as nosy, detail-oriented, and naturally inquisitive. They could go to places socially that men could not and gather information. They could use their intuitive insights to peer into the hearts of their fellow creatures and see hidden truths.

A *Quarterly Review* article from 1894 echoes this belief, that women "excel in fiction" in part because they are already "trained" in studying human nature:

> They observe minute traits of conduct; they spy unconsciously upon the men their masters, and learn the signals which betoken storm and sunshine [...]. When a woman sits down to write a story, she is exercising the same kind of faculties that enable her to overcome mere strength by delicacy of interpretation and natural tact; she has but to throw her feelings upon paper, to describe the scenes which she habitually notes in her thoughts, and [...] she will produce the outline of readable fiction [Barry 305].

Thus Barry reiterates Spencer's "scientific" interpretation of women's ability to decipher others' actions. He also takes it a step further in showing how that natural talent can be transferred to their ability to write; indeed, women apparently need only to be able to physically put pen to paper in order to become an author, so adept are their observation skills.

Women writers of this time period often reiterated these beliefs about what women could and should write, which included proper roles for women in their fiction. Many prominent women, believing that heroines of fiction should be appropriate role models for young girls, took great offense to the sensation fiction of the 1860's and the New Woman fiction of the 1890's because the heroines were so "unnatural." Margaret Oliphant, one of the most prominent critics during the 1860's as well as a writer herself, was disgusted that Mary Elizabeth Braddon chose to denigrate the "wholesomeness and cleanliness" (257) of the English novel by creating such passionate and immoral women as heroines of her fiction:

> Women driven wild with love for the man who leads them on to desperation [...]; women who pray their lovers to carry them off from husband and homes they hate; [...] who give and receive burning kisses and frantic embraces, and live in a voluptuous dream [...]. Now it is no knight of romance riding down the forest glades, ready for the defence and succour of all the oppressed, for whom the dreaming maiden waits. She waits now for flesh and muscles, for strong arms that seize her, and warm breath that thrills her through [...] [259].

That it is a woman who has created such a character is the worst part of it all: if a man wrote such things "its openness would be less repulsive" (259), but that this "new and disgusting picture of what professes to be the female heart" was written by a woman "is not in any way to be laughed at" (260).

The New Woman novels of the 1890's discussed more fully and frankly the subject of women's sexuality, again to the dismay of many readers. But they offend even further, as the New Woman became associated with a variety of society's ills: they were linked to not only the major political issues of divorce and voting laws, but to social attitudes and habits like smoking, riding bicycles freely in public, and daring to wear pants while doing so. Mrs. Elizabeth Lynn Linton berates these "Wild Women," whom she labels "social insurgents," for welcoming lower class habits and ways of life. They are, she says,

> bound by none of the conventions which once regulated society. In them we see the odd social phenomenon of the voluntary descent of the higher to the lower forms of ways and works. "Unladylike" is a term that has ceased to be significant [...]. Women who, a few years ago, would not have shaken hands with a dressmaker, still less have sat down to table with her, now open shops and set up in business on their own account—not because they are poor, which would be an honorable and sufficing reason enough, but because they are restless, dissatisfied, insurgent [...] [599].

Linton's opinions reflect the general sense of unease surrounding the mixture of the classes that was still widely prevalent at this time period. Appropriate reading material for women in many cases demanded the inclusion of a highly codified class structure and the portrayal of "ladylike" women, sexually virtuous and mindful of the conduct befitting their class.[13]

The early women's detective novels too seem to emphasize that being what society considered lady-like was still important, indeed crucial for the respectability of the genre, the female detective, and her author. Despite their socially-suspect profession, and the possibility that they might have to sit down with a dress-maker, female detectives did not stray far from what would be considered acceptable middle-class behavior. At the same time, showing that they could perform the act of detecting and still remain "womanly" worked to expand the definition of what a woman could do. Within these novels, women writers emphasized natural feelings, abilities and traits to give their female detectives credibility and authority.

I want to reiterate that providing their female detectives with intuition was a deliberate rhetorical strategy on the part of women writers. Many, of course, may have believed that "feminine" intuition was an inherent trait, and so the creation of a detective without that trait was unthinkable; others may have deliberately used the trope only to subvert it later on, or to show how insignificant a part it played in the lives of professional women, detecting or otherwise. But regardless of their attitudes, the outcome was largely the same: intuition was transformed into a *tool* used by women to achieve professional success. Using it in their fiction gave women writers a means to emphasize the femininity of their heroines, as well as transforming femininity into a condition of authority.

In Orczy's "The Woman in the Big Hat," for example, Mary tells us that, if only they had been eating at the same tea shop, her "dear lady is quite sure—and needless to say that I share her belief in herself—that she would have anticipated the murderer's intentions, and thus prevented one of the most cruel and callous of crimes" (230). The implication is that Lady Molly, simply by seeing a woman with murderous intentions, would have been able to see through seemingly normal actions or mannerisms and determine what the woman was about to do.

Indeed, according to Mary, all of the successes achieved by Scotland Yard's "Female Department" can be attributed to a knowledge of human nature:

> We of the Female Department are dreadfully snubbed by the men, though don't tell me that women have not ten times as much intuition as the blundering and sterner sex; my firm belief is that we shouldn't have half so many undetected crimes if some of the so-called mysteries were put to the test of feminine investigation [1].

As Mary makes clear, what is mysterious to men might not be to women because of their specialized psychological knowledge. Mary spends the book detailing cases in which Lady Molly's glorified intuition has solved the crime at hand. In "The Ninescore Mystery," the first murder case to be put into the hands of the Female Department, Molly draws a young mother out of hiding by placing a false paragraph in the newspaper stating that her child was dying. In the emotional battle between hiding out to shield her lover's crime of murdering her sister (who was blackmailing him) versus seeing her baby before it died, seeing the child wins out, as Molly knew it would: "How well she had known human nature in pitting the child against the sweetheart!" (24). Though male inspectors have been working steadily on the case, Molly solves it in two days, based on her understanding of female psychology: "'Oh, Mary, what a wonderful thing is human nature, and how I thank Heaven that gave me a knowledge of it!'" (20). Confronted by Molly, the mother is also tricked into naming the father of her child, after Molly tells her it will go to the workhouse: "'The workhouse! And her father a lord!'" (22). Thus, the mystery is cleared up, as Lady Molly's "strange intuition in the matter" (23) draws the truth out.

This is clearly a crime that a woman can solve; as Mary sums it up:

"don't tell me that a man would have thought of that bogus paragraph, or of the taunt which stung the motherly pride of the village girl to the quick, and thus wrung from her an admission which no amount of male ingenuity would ever have obtained" (25). Here, "male" intelligence is deliberately ranked opposite and inferior to "female" feeling, though it is clear that Lady Molly has used a great deal of intelligence (as well as leg-work, deduction, and other traditionally male crime-solving skills) to help solve the crime. Having placed an aristocratic and sensitive woman in a predominantly male and working-class profession, Orczy strategically emphasizes her distinctly feminine qualities and the professional authority they allow her to achieve.

In "The Fordwych Castle Mystery," "a case which more than any other required feminine tact, intuition, and all those qualities of which my dear lady possessed more than her usual share" (73), Lady Molly and Mary are sent to clear up the mystery about which "the ablest of our fellows at the Yard were at their wits' ends to know what to do" (73). Lady Molly seems instinctively to know before they even arrive on the scene: "'I know exactly where our fellows are wrong, and why they cannot get on'" (90), she says on the train ride up to Fordwych. Roonah, the Indian companion of Joan Duplessis, one of the heirs of a wealthy aunt who owns Fordwych Castle, has been murdered. At the inquest, Joan makes the accusation that her older sister Henriette is illegitimate (their father married their mother while his first wife was still alive) and therefore is not the true heir. Roonah carried papers on her body proving this, and now she is murdered and the papers are gone. Henriette is of course implicated in the crime, though there is no proof.

Again, though men from Scotland Yard have been working months on the case, Lady Molly solves the crime the day after arriving, having suspected all along that the missing papers—and therefore Joan's claim—were false. Lady Molly has Joan's room illegally broken into and searched for the papers, and Joan, confronted with their appearance, jumps over the side of the hotel into the gardens, killing herself. "'I know my own sex pretty well, don't I Mary?'" says Lady Molly afterward. "'I knew that Joan Duplessis had not destroyed—never would destroy—those papers'" (96). Here again, Lady Molly's knowledge of female psychology tells her that women are likely to hold onto damaging papers for sentimental or other reasons. Orczy seems to imply that Lady Molly knows this only by being a woman herself, since this possibility never occurred to the men working the case.

However, Lady Molly is not so willing to ascribe all of her success to female intuition. She knows the laws she must follow and police procedure, and she understands the limits of her profession as a policewoman. In the above case, she must break into Joan's private possessions to find the papers, knowing it is illegal: "'if I was wrong I would probably be dismissed [from] the force for irregularity, as of course, I had no right to do that'" (95–96). She can read the available clues that support her hunch—in this case a well-thumbed Bible and a locked communicating door. And she sometimes loses patience with Mary's lack of acumen: "'Don't repeat all my words, Mary; it is silly and wastes time'" (91); when Molly's actions are questioned, her reply is succinct: "'Mary, you are stupid,' was all the reply I got" (18).

However, by having Mary narrate these tales, Orczy re-establishes certain class assumptions. She implies that since Mary is of a lower class, it is understandable for her to attribute Molly's success solely to natural female intuition, not recognizing the part that logic and intelligence play when solving crimes. She is not as educated as Lady Molly, nor has she seen as much of the world, and therefore she cannot be expected to have skills needed for detection or recognize that intuition is only one such skill among many. Having an assistant unequal in intelligence narrate the exploits of the main detective is a staple of detective fiction, and Orczy is the first to turn this Watson/Holmes relationship into one involving two women.[14] But Mary is unequal not only in intelligence, but in class as well, and class is an issue for Orczy. Though Lady Molly has elevated the status of her relations with Mary to that of a "friendship" and "partnership" (1), the rise is only temporary; after Molly is reunited with her husband and quits the police force, there is no doubt that Mary will return to being Molly's servant. And, implies Orczy, nothing would give Mary greater joy.

Orczy supplies female intuition liberally, making it Lady Molly's overriding trait. Most other writers do not rely on intuition as a tool of female detection as frequently, though they do invoke it. Pirkis' Loveday Brooke displays her feminine feelings and innate understanding of humanity in "The Redhill Sisterhood." Here, a nondenominational group of Sisters is implicated as scouts of sorts for criminals; the houses to which they go begging for scraps of food are later robbed. But Loveday is convinced that these women are not criminals when she sees the "tenderness" with which one of the sisters handles a child: "'there was something absolutely beautiful in the way in which she lifted the little cripple out of the cart, put his tiny thin hand round her neck, and carried him into the house'" (594). She therefore looks elsewhere for the perpetrators and discovers that the Sisters' neighbor has been spying on them and using them as a red herring to commit the robberies.

Michele Slung sees this incident as "the most significant thing about Loveday Brooke," showing that she is "neither sexless nor oblivious to her sex. Her empathy for women in unfortunate situations makes her more than one-dimensional" ("Introduction" xii). Loveday Brooke is portrayed by her author throughout most of the book as rather sexless, with an emphasis on her keen eye and deductive abilities. However, with this incident Pirkis makes Loveday's "femininity" clear as well and shows that despite her profession "she is a woman all the same" (Slung xii). She also has the ability to intuitively understand the actions and feelings of her sex.

In "The Black Bag Left on a Doorstep," Loveday Brooke uses knowledge of human nature to clear a convenient but innocent French maid. Where the police read everything—her lapses into French, her hysteria, her contradictions in speech, her running away—as indicative of blame, Loveday reads these actions rightly as abject fear; when the police are positive that she has run away to meet her accomplices by the only train to Wreford, Loveday says gravely: "'I can see another possible destination for the girl— the stream that runs through the wood we drove past this morning'" (409).

In several novels, intuition plays the role of an impetus for the solution or a reason for investigating a person. For example, Dorothy L. Sayers' Miss Climpson in *Strong Poison* cannot convict Harriet Vane of murder in the face of overwhelming physical evidence because she believed that "the prisoner's demeanour was part of the evidence" and she should be allowed to take that into account (37). Since this results in a hung jury, Peter Wimsey and Miss Climpson can then spend the book clearing Harriet of the charge. Patricia Wentworth's Hilary Carew in *The Case Is Closed* tries to goad her partner into action by exclaiming her belief about the identity of the murderer, "Henry, it's a hunch!" (130), and even though "Henry frowned upon the hunch" she moves forward with her belief and uses logic and reasoning to prove it correct.

Even though the role of intuition is smaller in these cases, their authors do employ it, solidifying certain assumptions about the ways women can solve crimes. It is not seen as a downfall to have this trait, but as a valuable tool, one which gives female detectives insight to crimes and a greater understanding of their fellow humans, especially women. The authors of this fiction further imply that it is a mistake for society to overlook this valuable tool. By having their detectives use feminine intuition and domestic knowledge to solve crimes, they imply that both they and their fictional detectives can remain feminine and respectable, as well as successful and self-assured professionals.

During Britain's Golden Age of detective fiction, women writers' use of intuition as a detecting tool underwent a marked decline, as writers sought to find less gender-specific and less limited ways for their detectives to solve cases. We can note, for instance, in the two above examples (both in novels from the 1930s), the different names under which intuition is brought into the story. Christie, through her alter-ego Mrs. Oliver, both makes fun of it and validates it, but not without touches of humor. "'My instincts never lie,'" Mrs. Oliver says in *Cards on the Table*, declaring that Dr. Roberts must be guilty (25). But she changes her mind and becomes convinced she is wrong when new facts come to light on three separate occasions before Poirot proves her original guess correct, whereupon she says "happily, if not quite truthfully: 'I always *said* he did it!'" (220). Mitchell's Mrs. Bradley and Sayers' Harriet Vane scorn any suggestion that natural female intuition has a place in their logic, preferring more professionally-based reasons for their understanding: Mrs. Bradley relies on her training as a psychoanalyst to read people's motives, and Harriet Vane uses her "artistic sense" to point out flaws in a poorly thought-out solution. But even in these cases, despite the protagonists' wishes to disassociate themselves from this trait, intuition is seen by other characters in the novels as natural and inherent, a reminder of its importance to the social construction of "womanhood" in both real life and in the pages of fiction.

Women writers, when seeking to establish professional authority for their female detectives, thus relied primarily upon socially accepted traits as a means of incorporating women into male-dominated spheres, regardless of their own beliefs about those traits. At the end of the nineteenth and beginning of the twentieth centuries, emphasizing women's "natural" abilities was a common and productive way of reaching this goal of entering male-dominated spheres. As society's beliefs about the proper roles for women expanded, it seemed less necessary to rely on arguments about women's natural talents, and women writers eventually sought new ways to emphasize how women could achieve success in the world of detection.

Women's knowledge of domesticity and their "natural" female intuition were invaluable methods of making female detection credible and were two of the most commonly-used techniques used by women writers in their detective fiction. Women writers drew upon their means of authority in the domestic sphere and transferred it to the public sphere, building upon society's existing beliefs about womanhood to build professional authority for their detectives. By creating feminine and upper-class detectives, women writers also found a way to preserve women's respectability despite their entrance into the professional world, including their own respectability as professional writers of popular fiction. In establishing women's fitness to solve crime, women writers were able to establish their own fitness to write in the crime fiction genre.

THREE

The Spinster as Professional Woman

"Dear old tabbies are the only possible right kind of
female detective and Miss M is lovely."
—Dorothy L. Sayers in a letter
to Agatha Christie, after
Murder at the Vicarage (1930)[1]

Sayers, in her introduction to *The Omnibus of Crime* (1929), had made
clear her unhappiness with what appeared to her a profusion of young, inexperienced girl detectives who inadvertently solved crimes. She believed that
"the really brilliant woman detective has yet to be created" (16). In an effort
to portray a more logical and successful woman detective herself, she had
three years earlier followed the same advice she gave to Christie, creating
Miss Katherine Climpson in *Unnatural Death* (1927) to work as Lord Peter
Wimsey's adjunct crime-solver. Sayers' note to Christie upon the appearance of Miss Marple, however, is more than an affirmation of her own belief
about the role of women in crime fiction. It is also a testament to the changing beliefs about women's abilities and their roles in society. This chapter
looks at the ways women writers used the character of the spinster, a "tabby,"
as a crime-solver, contributing to a re-examination of the largely negative
view of older unmarried women.

The perception of the Victorian old maid had changed only slightly by
the beginning of the twentieth century, both in real life and in the pages of
fiction, despite the inroads in education and employment for women.
Though the "New Woman" and the "Odd Woman" of the 1890s made

valiant and often successful attempts at starting careers in the business world, they were unable to overturn their society's fundamental beliefs about unmarried women. Spinsters were to be pitied, as they had no families of their own and were therefore lacking the one item society saw as natural for women's fulfillment.

However, as they appear in the pages of detective fiction, spinster detectives are successful, daring, and unusual, the exact opposite of what society had deemed "old maids" to be. Women writers who employed the spinster in their detective fiction used the stereotype to challenge and complicate the gender constructs of their society. Recuperating the spinster-character is thus another powerful way women writers used detective fiction as an avenue through which to discuss issues of importance to women. Women writers' use of this character was a forceful narrative strategy through which they could establish authority, as they subverted traditional stereotypes surrounding spinsterhood and questioned the limited roles of women in the workforce, highlighting instead the importance of unmarried women.

There are abundant critical studies examining the role of unmarried women in society of this time, seeking to recast them in a more positive light. In *Woman and the Demon*, for example, Nina Auerbach explores the ways in which Victorian women who were located in some way outside the family structure could be considered dangerous by society. This includes the spinster, for though the spinster was defined by the negative—what she did not have—her freedom was nonetheless something enticing. In the forward to Laura Doan's *Old Maids to Radical Spinsters* Auerbach writes: "the Victorian old maid, after all, was forced into deprivation so that her life would not be attractive enough to tempt young women and threaten the family" (xi). Doan echoes this sentiment in her introduction, saying of the spinster: "society has deliberately deemed her pathetic to mask its fear of the unmarried woman" (1).

Books like Martha Vicinus' *Independent Women* and Sheila Jeffreys' *The Spinster and Her Enemies* discuss various types of women-centered institutions in an attempt to highlight the positive activities of single women during the Victorian and later eras. Spinster women were not altogether idle, despite this impression from fiction that has come down to us and despite the pervasive cultural if not legal prohibition against women working outside the home. Their lives centered around socially acceptable activities—religious sisterhoods, nursing, and the Governesses Benevolent Institution—as well as the more visible and discordant suffrage activities at the beginning of this century, discussed in depth by Jeffreys.

Yet as these studies make clear, as do all studies on single middle- and upper-class women during this time period, unmarried women were habitually considered by their society as either unfulfilled (at best) or burdens to others (at worst). In light of this, the work of female detective fiction writers in portraying single middle-class (and middle-aged) women as productive and active members of society cannot be overemphasized. In this chapter then, I am particularly interested in the way women detective fiction writers re-work the cultural stereotype of the spinster, transforming her life in fiction from one of worthlessness to one of fulfillment and independence.

Like their "real life" counterparts in the bourgeois world of women's work, most fictional female detectives remain single. Only Agatha Christie's Tuppence Beresford continues detective work after her marriage, and she is provided with those opportunities through her husband's career in the Secret Service. However, the fact that most middle-class women who worked were single, as well as its reverse—that most middle-class women who married did not work—does not prevent most feminist critical studies of early female detective fiction from coming away disappointed, viewing female detectives' careers as mere aberrations in the life of a woman. Because female detectives often marry and return to domesticity at the end of the story, this criticism runs, these detectives negate any radicalness they displayed in their lives as single women. Kathleen Gregory Klein echoes Sayers' beliefs when she comments that "women might be successful amateur detectives so long as they employed the more stereotypically feminine talents of gossip and intuition, but they were barred from detective careers" (*Woman Detective* 3). This statement, however, unfairly dismisses the efficacy of these crime-solving tools, the importance of which I showed in Chapter Two, and seems to deliberately overlook the fact that many of these women were professional detectives.

Critical discussion of authorial intention is also largely negative. Klein, for instance, argues that fictional female detectives are deliberately sabotaged by their authors, doomed to fail, because of the inherent incompatibility of the two scripts, "woman" and "detective," with the latter implying masculine traits like logic, action, violence. In completing these tales, "authors decided that their character was either not a proper detective or not a proper woman" (4). Craig and Cadogan introduce their collection about female detectives with the similar observation that "the apparent feminism of many of the early stories featuring women sleuths is at odds with the sentimental endings which popular authors often felt obliged to append to their works" (11–12). Fay Blake, though she calls women detectives (as opposed to lady sleuths) of this period "truly subversive females," believes they were only created to startle readers and "become interesting characters *despite* their authors' intentions because of their accomplishments in an all-male profession" (39; emphasis mine).

Yet such statements seem a direct contradiction to what actually occurs in women's detective fiction stories: obviously there were professional female detectives in fiction, seeing as how Klein herself examines just that category in *The Woman Detective*. And they did succeed if and when they used the more "masculine" traits of logic and reason in conjunction with those traits demarcated "feminine." To posit, therefore, that women detectives are either failures as women (because they do not marry but have careers as detectives) or as detectives (because they marry and end their careers as detectives) represents not only circular logic but a rejection of the ways women writers were coming to terms with the important debate about women and work in their society.

In this study, I accept as a starting point that the opportunities of middle- and upper-class women who worked—both in real life and as they were represented in popular fiction—were limited by society's expectations, and that women writers, knowing this, chose to work within existing formulas when creating their stories. At the same time, I argue that women writers of detective fiction sought to expand these limited options for women, and by writing about women facing difficulties in the working world, they did more than merely uphold the status quo. They reworked those scripts, developed them, and if nothing else, at least in their fiction wrote women into unusual positions of power.

The "Young" Spinster

An understanding of the spinster in these detective fiction stories must take into account the fact that the age at which a woman could be considered an "old maid" was much younger than it is today. While today's definition of the spinster as an elderly women certainly held true in the 1890s, it was also true that women who had not married by the age of thirty were called spinsters as well; by then they were truly considered unmarriageable. Many detectives in this study fit into this age group: Loveday Brooke, Florence Cusack, Joan Mar, Lucile Dare. None of these characters marry at the end of their tales. Their status as professionals—and their choice to be so—nearly always signifies that they will not marry. This chapter is therefore comprised of two major sections. The first section examines young female characters who are portrayed as desiring work and whose status as professionals can be taken as an indicator of their spinsterhood. The second section addresses fictional representations of spinsters beyond marriageable age.[2] Women writers, in creating such a wide range of characters, more fully enter into the debate on women's roles in their culture and explore the professional opportunities for women in their fiction.

While all unmarried women posed a potential threat to established social norms, young spinsters were an additional source of anxiety because they harbored the possibility of unsanctioned social and sexual activity. Vicinus, in *Independent Women*, argues that during the Victorian period in England women were divided into one of three symbolic representations: an "ideal wife/mother or a celibate spinster or a promiscuous prostitute" (5). Spinsters, in order to distance themselves as much as possible from the other single woman in the triad, the whore, often embraced the doctrines of piety and celibacy, presenting to society a virginal demeanor and lifestyle. In theory, at least, they sublimated their sexual energy into performing self-sacrificing acts for others.

And yet, this asexual status was one "thrust" upon them, to use Vicinus' term, though again it was a label and lifestyle spinsters often chose. The truth is that the spinsters' status as "Other" gave them freedoms other women could not have, including the potential of being sexually active beyond the boundaries of respectability. The changing definition of "spinster" is enlightening; for instance, Jeffreys notes that by the 1920s, the definition had changed from simply "unmarried women" to mean "women who had not done sexual intercourse with men" (qtd. in Doan 4), a fact which blurred the lines between the definitions of lesbian and spinster, while celibacy itself, on the other hand, came to be seen as unnatural and abnormal.

Whether spinsters actually indulged in sexually "deviant" behavior, with men or with other women, was not as important as the symbolic implications of spinsterhood; it was just as much their potential threat, what unmarried women represented in their freeing status as "Other," as it was their actual threat. A more common manifestation of spinsters' "non-respectable" behavior took the form of working: women with ambition and education could try to find meaningful work, especially by the late 1800s and early 1900s, work which they actually enjoyed rather than simply took up to escape poverty. Vicinus writes that "many single women looked forward with relief to turning thirty, when they could put aside any pretense of being marriageable and concentrate upon their own interests" (40). This is indeed the manifestation most common in detective fiction; for the most part, female detectives as portrayed by women writers maintain the spinsters' designated "asexual" status, bringing uneasiness into their social surroundings not because of their licentiousness but because they engage in paid work.[3]

Hints of sexuality in these stories were usually present in the much-subdued and conventional form of the romance. Despite the dislike that Sayers and other inter-war writers expressed for a love-interest in the detective story, many stories starring female detectives do have an element of romance in them.[4] One reason for this might be its importance in the traditional "female" plot, in which the path to love and marriage forms the major part of the narrative. Although these women writers were exploring elements of professionalism in their fiction and were writing in the "masculine" genre of detective fiction, they may have felt that it was expected and even necessary to include love as part of the story line.

But the extent to which this element is included varies. Sometimes the detective herself was involved in a romance. In *Lady Molly of Scotland Yard*, for example, Lady Molly becomes a detective to free her husband, whom she secretly married at her own request the day before he was arrested, and to clear his name. After a touching love scene when this is accomplished, she gives up her job. In Beatrice Heron-Maxwell's *The Adventures of a Lady Pearl-Broker*, Molly Delamere is a widow who takes up pearl-brokering to support herself and through it gets involved in criminal schemes and conspiracies; she gets remarried at the end of the final story and gives up her job.

However, in some stories the detectives engage in no romance at all. Tales like those starring C.L. Pirkis' Loveday Brooke or L.T. Meade's Florence Cusack are short stories about crimes and the female detectives who solve crime, leaving little time to develop extraneous plots. Though these two detectives do not themselves engage in love affairs, their crime-solving often has the effect of bringing other young couples together. Often they take a case because a friend's happiness in love is at stake.

Such is the case with Florence Cusack, the woman detective created by L.T. Meade and Robert Eustace. All of her cases end with the continuing (or newly-created) happiness of a young couple. In "Mr. Bovey's Unexpected Will," an inheritance in gold is stolen, without which the couple cannot marry (Cusack finds the gold); in "The Arrest of Captain Vandaleur," a husband's gambling habit with a cheating partner is ruining the health of his wife and hastening her towards an untimely death (Cusack exposes the cheating partner, the husband reforms and the wife recovers); in "A Terrible Railway Ride," jewels entrusted to a young man are stolen after he is drugged on a train, thereby ruining his reputation and preventing his impending marriage (Miss Cusack connects this theft with several others, exposes the thieves and saves his reputation and engagement); in "The Outside Ledge," a stock exchange mystery implicates a younger partner about to marry (Miss Cusack exposes his role in the affair and the marriage is prevented, although the young lady does get married to someone much better in the last half of the last sentence); and in "Mrs. Reid's Terror," a woman gambles away her fortune and is about to face exposure to her husband through a blackmailer (Miss Cusack tricks the blackmailer and saves the marriage; the wife reforms).

Kathleen Gregory Klein argues that advancing the marriage plot in such stories reduces he efficacy of detectives like Cusack, that "her successes [as a detective] are presented as subordinate to her traditional female roles and responsibilities" (73). In other words, marriage and a husband remain the primary focus of these women's lives, even if it is not for them. The fact that marriage does not occur for the detective herself signals her failure as a woman, just as her inadequacy as a detective is highlighted because she turns over the capture of criminals to the police or male associates—the female detective can advance the marriage plot, but the "real" detective work of putting criminals in jail remains the privilege of men.

But Klein's insistence on focusing only these authors' inability to reconcile opposing scripts forces her to overlook the ways in which their detectives do achieve measures of individuality and freedom within the scripts presented to them. What stands out most about Cusack, for instance, is her unique status as a turn-of-the-century female detective: she is a single young woman of independent means and does not need to take up detecting for money or to clear a husband's or loved one's name. In fact, Meade and Eustace offer no concrete reason for her entrance into the detective profession. None of the other female detectives of this time period are thus unencumbered. While romance is certainly featured as a sideline in these stories, the focus is rather on the detective herself and her work.

L.T. Meade was a prolific writer. She was such a regular contributor of short stories to the many literary journals of her day that according to Hugh Greene, who edited several early detective fiction collections, "one can hardly open any of the magazines of the period without finding examples of her work" (Rivals 14). Over the span of her long career, she authored over 250 novels; along with Evelyn Everett-Green and Charlotte Yonge, she is one of the best-known writers of "girl's fiction," a literary blossoming that reflected as well as sculpted the cultural landscape of middle-class girlhood at the turn of the century.[5] Most of these novels feature "career" girls of some sort: secretary, a newspaper correspondent, a nurse, a journalist, girls who go to college and make money without shame. She carried on her crusade to transform what girlhood could contain as the founder (and editor for six years) of Atalanta magazine in 1887, a well-written bi-monthly journal that was designed to reach the daughters of the upper- and upper-middle classes.[6]

Though a working woman, Meade was not poor and did not work with the "printer's boy at the door" waiting for copy. She worked because she wanted to, keeping a regular schedule of dictating in the morning before any domestic chores, going to edit the magazine in the afternoon, and in the evening working with the material she had dictated in the morning. In an interview reprinted in The Writer magazine, Meade said that she was quite young when she told her father that she "should greatly like to earn money"; alarmed and dismayed, her father reminded her that there hadn't yet been "'a woman of our family who earned money,'" though he admitted that getting paid for writing books "'would not be quite so disgraceful'" (28). She was just fifteen she began work on what would be her first published book, and at times in her life she wrote several books during the course of a year, not to mention the near-continual magazine publishing.

Meade created several types of mystery stories during these years. Sally Mitchell claims that Meade "apparently invented" the subgenre of the medical mystery with the publication of "Stories from the Diary of a Doctor" in *The Strand*, arguing that her contribution to this Watsonian formula was to include some type of medical or scientific twist that helped solve the crime (11). The Cusack stories are also narrated by a medical man, Dr. Lonsdale.[7] She also wrote at least two series of stories in which the woman is the villain, "The Sorceress of the Strand" and "The Brotherhood of the Seven Kings." The stories starring Cusack ran in *Harmsworth Magazine* from 1899 to 1901.[8]

Readers meet Florence Cusack and Dr. Lonsdale in "Mr. Bovey's Unexpected Will," when Cusack goes to Dr. Lonsdale to get help for her "periodical and very acute nervous attacks" (259). She is, as we learn from Lonsdale's point of view, an enigma to society; he says in the opening paragraph that "I never visited her without the hope that some day I should get to the bottom of the mystery which surrounded her" (259). This mystery-within-a-mystery is why Cusack would choose to work, much less in a profession unpopular and unladylike, when she clearly doesn't have to: she is young, wealthy, lives in a large house at a fashionable address, keeps many servants, and is popular in society. This contradiction piques the interest of her society: "As one glanced at this handsome girl with her slender figure, her eyes of the darkest blue, her raven black hair and clear complexion, it was almost impossible to believe that she was a power in the police courts, and highly respected by every detective in Scotland Yard" (259).

Her nervous attacks are most likely related to her detecting work, as she asks Dr. Lonsdale not to "ask too many questions or look too curious [...]. I know well that my whole condition is abnormal" (259). By stating that her "whole" condition is abnormal, Meade pathologizes Cusack's desire for work, her strange "state" of employment. Her illness can in this case be read as a metaphor for, or symptom of, the larger "condition" of women. No doubt Cusack is sick; but her condition stems not from a physiological ailment as much as the internal struggle between what she wants and society's judgment upon her for wanting it. Her sickness and fatigue are both caused by her job and symbolic of it.

Her motives for taking up detection are unknown; she tells Dr. Lonsdale she is "forced" to do what she does: "I have no choice; I am under a promise, which I must fulfil" (259). However, though the authors felt the need to provide some reason (vague as it may be) for a young woman of independent means to enter a scorned profession and perform duties, as Cusack calls them, "at once herculean and ghastly" (259), they never give an answer for this mystery. Cusack simply exists. A very possible reason for this lack of an ending could simply be the magazine format. These stories were never collected in book form and are not dependent upon each other; nor are the cases connected, although introductions of the doctor, the detective and the reason for their friendship are given only in this first story.[9]

On the other hand, the authors may simply have decided that any further explanation of Cusack's motives would distract from the main plot: a young woman becomes a detective. Knowing that at least some of Meade's other detective short fiction stories "end" (the perpetrator in "Sorceress by the Strand," for instance, does get caught), this omission seems to imply something, either about Meade's inability to find a satisfactory way to put Cusack's career to rest (which usually meant marrying her off) or her reluctance to do so. After all, Meade herself worked for what her society would have considered "no reason," as she did not need the money. In keeping with the pattern of the heroines of her girl's fiction, Meade introduces a working woman in such a seemingly unconsidered way that its occurrence appears perfectly natural; even more so, her narratives importantly show how "a career or an education does not destroy 'femininity'" (S. Mitchell 21). Thus, despite the potentially negative connotations of working, much less as a detective, Meade portrays Cusack as proud of her work and her profession: "'You see before you,'" she says "with emphasis, 'the most acute and, I believe, successful lady detective in the whole of London'" (259).

Indeed, the solutions to the crimes in which Cusack is involved require an acuity and well-roundedness that few early female detectives exhibit. In "Mr Bovey's Unexpected Will," the solution centers on clues based on foundry work, as stolen gold is about to be melted down. Another relies on understanding the sleep-inducing effect of carbon dioxide as it melts from a solid to a gaseous state. Two others involve the recognition of curious scents one is a man's fragrance that is used as a code between gamblers, and the other is valerian, used to lure a cat carrying a message in its collar from one office to another in order to thwart business dealings (the cat is fortunately exonerated of the crime). Whatever promise initially led Cusack to detective work, it is clear that her knowledge and power of association suit her ideally for her career.

Thus, romance only occurs as a sideline in Cusack's stories; nor is it featured in the life of arguably the most well-known of these early detectives, Loveday Brooke.[10] Not once are the detectives themselves ever confronted with having to make a choice between romance and career, and the women writers of these stories do not make the choice between the two worlds women could supposedly inhabit—the domestic sphere or the professional world—a focus of the plot. They remain working spinsters and appear satisfied. But the lack of an ending to Cusack's story undermines Meade's forcefulness in stating the case for working women to perhaps balance a profession with marriage. On the other hand, Marie Connor Leighton's two full-length novels about female detectives explore much more forcefully the clash between romance and work in the lives of their single heroines, Joan Mar and Lucile Dare.

Leighton appears in none of the collections about women writers of detective fiction, and her characters do not appear in collections about women detectives.[11] Nonetheless, *Joan Mar, Detective* (1910) and *Lucile Dare, Detective* (1919) highlight through their titles alone the juxtaposition between being a woman and being a detective. Both of these novels are forceful examples of the difficulties working women faced when trying to balance a professional career with what society saw as their natural "career" as wives and mothers. And in both of these cases, their careers as detectives win out.

From the outset of *Joan Mar*, Leighton draws the reader's attention to the negative feelings generated in most of the other characters by Joan's profession, a trend exhibited in most of these stories which reflects society's widespread unease about professional women generally. Though Joan, as an old family friend, has been invited to stay with Mrs. Varley while the rest of the household go on a cross-Channel trip, Mrs. Varley is unhappy with the situation; she says to her daughter: "'I should say that a woman detective was about the most uncomfortable person any one could have in the house. And if this one is as clever as people say she is—why, she must be worse than the others!'" (17). The day after she arrives Mrs. Varley says she "'hates that Joan Mar already!'" (22), and the thought of her in the house gives her a "'nasty, creepy feeling'" because she suspects "'that objectionable woman detective'" is "'lurking about'" (22) listening to their conversations. Similarly, her daughter Cora and Lord Lester's secretary also express intense discomfort in Joan's presence.

The focus in this story is Joan Mar's ability to see, her trained eye for detail. Since the mystery in the story rests on a case of switched identities between Lady Lorine and her cousin Cora Varley, this trait is vital to solving the case. After Lorine's father dies and Lorine succumbs to brain fever during the Channel crossing, Cora assumes Lorine's identity and allows Lorine to go to jail for a murder she planned. However, immediately upon seeing the resemblance between Cora and Lorine (even before the Channel crossing), Joan Mar recognizes the slight difference not only in each woman's beauty but disposition as well, and her training as a detective takes over: "Her whole aspect had changed [...]. she had suddenly become a woman—and a professional woman, too [...]. Her girlish face, so fascinating in its dark handsomeness, had taken on keenness and determination, and showed her for what the world knew her to be—a great detective" (19). When Lorine asks how it is possible for Joan to know that the cousins are not similar in heart and mind, Joan transmits that information with an "interchange of looks" which "said plainly": "'I know, because I am Joan Mar, and it is my business to see more than others see'" (20).

Among the details Joan notices are those extending from the woman-centered or domestic items discussed in Chapter Two. For example, Joan knows that she has not yet seen the owner of the woman's glove found at the crime scene because she hasn't seen a hand to match. The owner of the glove is shocked when Joan confronts that person and demands an answer to the mystery of the glove's placement: "'I had studied the lines of the glove so closely that directly I saw your hand I knew that the shape of it matched those lines. Why do you look at me so amazedly? There's nothing wonderful in my discovering that this glove is yours. It is my business to be observant'" (176). Leighton implies that Joan's social training as a woman also helps—she uses the style and the material of the glove as clues to who its owner likely is.

Unlike the other authors in this study, however, Leighton draws attention to the danger faced by Joan (and Lucile as well, in Leighton's other story) in the course of her detective work. When Lorine asks if it is true Joan's life has been threatened, she answers: "'They have threatened to kill me—yes! Do you think I care for that? It is not the first time that I have been told that I am doomed, and it will not be the last. If I let myself be made afraid by threats of this kind, I might as well give up my profession at once'" (20). Perhaps to balance out this more masculine side of the detective business, Leighton also emphasizes more than any other writer her heroines' physical beauty. When the book opens Joan is described as a "bright-eyed, glowing-faced, quickly-moving girl" (18). As the book progresses and her detective powers are in force—as she becomes "a professional woman"—her beauty becomes more seductive; she is "tall, dark as night, and vivid-faced, with deep, black, unfathomable eyes" (81). She smokes cigarettes, which "perhaps" gives her "the air of dashing recklessness which she certainly had" (82). She has "vividly red lips," and she smiles "a fascinating smile" (82). Leighton obviously wants the reader to understand that though Joan has chosen a profession, she is certainly more than attractive enough to be desired by a man and could marry if she chose to. She is the one author in this study who provides hints of her heroines' sexuality (both Joan's and Lucile's), which, in addition to their professional status, could also be seen as threatening to established mores of respectability.

However, Leighton makes a deliberate distinction between having a career and being able to get married; it must be one or the other. Joan, for instance, develops a passion for Brian, Lorine's fiancé. But she keeps these feelings to herself, and the omniscient narrator of the novel lets the reader know that while Brian cannot help being attracted to Joan, he does not return her love. The final paragraphs of the novel emphasize the difficulties, to use Klein's terms, of reconciling the two scripts available to women:

> "Beautiful, clever Joan! We owe everything to her," Lorine said enthusiastically. "I wish she would marry someone worthy of her who would make her happy."
>
> But Brain smiled as he shook his head.
>
> "She does not want to marry [...] she does not want the sort of happiness we have. She wants to be free—free to work at the profession and get more and more famous in it, till the whole criminal world shall tremble at the name of Joan Mar, detective" [306].

Despite the obvious irony in having Brian draw this conclusion for the reader, what he says is largely true: Leighton implies that if Joan Mar marries she cannot be free to perform her job as a detective, because her "job" would then be her husband and children. Joan Mar chooses to pursue a career, though Leighton leaves the door open for future romance (she is, after all, only twenty-seven).

Like *Joan Mar* before it, *Lucile Dare, Detective* is a romance as well as a detective novel, complete with beautiful heroines, murder, falsely imprisoned suspects, and scorned loves. However, in *Lucile Dare* the conflict that arises between Lucile's career and her love for a man is presented even more dramatically, as Lucile's desire clouds her judgment on the case and almost causes the wrong man to be hanged. Leighton's emphasis on this conflict clearly makes it the important issue; more vital than the mystery itself is the manner in which Lucile's personal feelings damage her professional actions.

Lucile is from the outset of the novel presented as a woman who has chosen to be a professional, unlike her close friend Madeline, whom she is visiting. Madeline is about to be married, and in her own joy Madeline asks Lucile if she will "always be content with the triumphs your cleverness gives you, and never want to know how sweet it is to love and to be loved" (13). Lucile answers "half laughingly: 'I? Oh, I have not time to think of love! And, for the matter of that, I am cherishing a romantic worship for a man whom I have only seen once, and whose name I do not know'" (13). She met this man on a case when she was living "in disguise in a ducal house, tracing the theft of some royal jewels" (11). But she is confident they will meet again, and of course, as fate (and fiction) would have it, the object of Lucile's romantic worship happens to be Madeline's fiancé, Brian Havelock, whom she meets shortly after arriving at Madeline's house. She can see that Brian loves Madeline, and despite herself, this fact infuriates her, and she relentlessly follows clues which are deliberately placed to frame Brian for the murder of Madeline's father. Because, as a detective, she "had taught herself to conceal and repress all sign of feeling" (41), Brian is unaware "how fierce a storm raged against him in the heart of Lucile Dare—Lucile Dare, the fascinating, panther-like woman who was known to him only as an unusually successful pursuer of criminals, and to whom he believed himself to have been, until yesterday, unknown" (66).

In addition to being "fascinating" and "panther-like," Lucile, like Joan Mar, is beautiful and brilliant, with eyes that are "deep, subtle, wonderful" (39). Leighton deliberately sets the description of Lucile's beauty against the possible hazards of a career, letting the reader know that womanliness need not be marred by work: "The sleuth-hound instinct and vast experience which gave her her marvelous power were not visible upon her face. It was a perfect-featured, lineless face [...]. And yet it was a face of strange, weird charm and irresistible fascination" (17).

In fact, concealing her beauty is "often for her the hardest in her detective changes" (81), though she is an expert at disguise. The novel opens with the story of her "playing the part of a distinguished foreign lady" (13) and tracing jewel thieves. During the course of the novel she also disguises herself as a working woman in order to gain access to Brian's study, where she finds incriminating evidence. Leighton's description of how Lucile hides her beauty during this scene, when she is changing from a young beautiful detective to an older working-class woman, is provided in minute detail, down to the method Lucile uses to change the shape of her eyebrows. Such exactitude on Leighton's part emphasizes the need to be familiar with class signifiers and to be able to cross class boundaries, a significant aspect of the way female detectives are alerted to and solve crime; more importantly, it is another way Leighton draws attention to the potential incompatibility of beauty—the hallmark of femininity—and career, a masculine pursuit. Lastly, Lucile transforms herself into the perfect parlourmaid in order to live in the house of the real murderer and find evidence against him, exhibiting knowledge not only of the stereotypical physical look and mannerisms of a servant but the proper work duties of a parlourmaid as well.

But again, the murder mystery itself essentially takes a back seat to the downfall of Lucile's detective ability, caused by distraction for love of a man. It is only two weeks before Brian's hanging, when she is declaring her love for him in his cell, that she becomes convinced of his innocence, and she is stunned and then angered by her previous inability to see the truth: "'There must be a plot against you,' she said hoarsely, at last—'a deliberately-laid plot. And I—I, Lucile Dare—have been the plotter's unconscious helper and accomplice!'" (160). Characteristically, she throws herself into the case to free Brian as fully as she did to jail him. During this time she has second thoughts about her career as a detective, and her mind wanders over the idea of quitting work and finding someone to marry. But the thought is fleeting:

[...] she put the possibility from her as though it were something base, unholy, dangerous. She, the great detective, must not work for her own private ends. She must work for the triumph of justice and right, and the tingling intoxicating delight of personal success.

Never in all her brilliant life had she been thwarted until now. And that a criminal should have had the cunning to blind her, even for a time, was due solely to the fact that for the first time in her professional career she had been influenced by her heart [...]. Her own splendid beauty had been given her, not that she might win and keep a good man's devotion and faith, but in order that she might use its resistless influence in the detection of evil-doing and in the luring of evil-doers to their own self-betrayal [222].

Lucile chooses to use her beauty to the advancement and fulfillment of her career, not to find love and romance. Melodramatic as this soliloquy is, it nonetheless contains a strong claim for women's independence. The limited options available to women are stated repeatedly in this book, most succinctly when Lucile confronts Brian with her feelings in prison: "'I thought that when we met, Lucile Dare, the detective, would give way to Lucile Dare, the woman, the lover, the beloved. But it was not to be so'" (156). I think it possible, taking into account the number of times and ways Leighton looks at this choice, to read these continual references to women's dilemma as a means of questioning the justice of it for professional women. Madeline's exclamation at the end of the book—that despite Lucile's "'wonderful cleverness'" and her brilliant success, "'she has missed the best joys of living. She has never known what it is to love, and to be loved'" (289)— has a somewhat hollow ring. Although there is no deliberate irony in Madeline's statement, one can't help wondering if Lucile really is missing out, and one certainly admires Lucile's brainwork and active lifestyle more than Madeline's passivity. A good comparison might be to Wilkie Collins' *The Woman in White* and the difference between Marian Halcombe and Laura Fairlie: while the reader understands that Laura is supposed to be society's Ideal Woman, Marian shines much brighter.

One major aspect of the argument put forth in this book is that it was important for women writers to create very feminine and lady-like detectives who could work without losing their stature in society, expanding the opportunities for women to find jobs suitable to both their class and their intelligence. Leighton's novels highlight this need for opportunities when the choice between spinsterhood or marriage arises for professional women. In light of her heroines' physical attractions, their decisions to press on with their careers becomes even more forceful. Leighton portrays women who work and yet remain lady-like in society's eyes, women who are attractive and choose a career. The unquestionable beauty of Joan Mar and Lucile Dare works to debunk two myths of spinsterhood: spinsters, in these texts, are not unattractive women who can't find husbands and therefore have to work

to support themselves; nor are they without "natural" feeling for the opposite sex. The force of their choice to remain working is perhaps mitigated
by the fact that they fall for unavailable men, but it does not diminish the
re-discovered joy they find in being successful detectives or the purposeful-
ness with which they continue. They are portrayed as professionals, women
who remain working at the end of the novel, pursuing their careers.

The Elderly Woman Sleuth

In the long run, however, the more familiar image of the spinster detective, an elderly woman detecting usually in an amateur capacity, seems to
have been much more popular and long-lived. The writing careers of Gladys
Mitchell, Patricia Wentworth, and Agatha Christie span five decades, pro-
pelled in part by the success of their spinster detectives—Dame Beatrice
Bradley, Miss Maud Silver, and Miss Jane Marple, respectively. Slung calls
the development of the spinster sleuth during the Golden Age a backward
step (xxiii). I see it rather as a method in which women writers creatively
and successfully transformed the detective in response to their society's needs
at that particular time. While it is largely true that these women were not
professional detectives, they were professionals in other fields, fields that over
time had become more available to women. And that this increase in
women's visibility and abilities appeared in older women—women without
recognized social worth—seems instead a step forward. The longevity and
popularity of the amateur spinster detective should be read not so much as
a sign of society's unwillingness to accept women into professional ranks,
but additionally, as a positive step forward in fiction for women who were
often rejected or dismissed based on age.

Anna Katherine Green's Amelia Butterworth (1897) is usually considered the "grandmother" of fictional spinster detectives. Slung describes her
as "a spinster whose social politesse and notions of decorum are at odds
with her irrepressible nosiness; in other words, she is the prototype of the
elderly busybody female sleuth" (*Crime* xxii). Green's character recognizes
"nosiness" as a trait which comes in handy when trying to gather information from household occupants, and thus is able to transform the popular
negative portrayal of gossip into a useful trait in crime-solving. Later
writers have continued to use this stereotype to their elderly characters'
advantage.

The spinster detective proved successful for many reasons. One reason
for her popularity and social acceptability, as I have previously discussed,
stems from the negative attitudes towards women police after the war. Imag-
inary female detectives had been replaced by real women's patrols, which

led to angry fights, Parliamentary debates, and the perception that women were no longer needed in policing jobs, especially since so many men returning from the war needed them. Women writers, in reaction to post-war anxieties about female police, may have decided that amateur detectives would be a less threatening and more palatable expression of female independence.

At the same time, three of the four spinster detectives I discuss have careers: Gladys Mitchell's Dame Beatrice Bradley is a practicing psychoanalyst (and a widow, rather than strictly a spinster); Patricia Wentworth's Miss Maud Silver is a professional "enquiry agent,"; Dorothy L. Sayers' Miss Katherine Climpson works for Lord Peter Wimsey uncovering various frauds and helping him solve cases. Only Agatha Christie's Miss Marple is truly an amateur spinster detective, although her gardening and bird-watching and knitting have come to define this sub-genre of detective fiction.[12]

Closely intertwined with working status is age—a factor perhaps even more important in the success of the spinster detective. As an elderly woman whose usefulness is usually overlooked, the spinster detective flourishes for just that reason: she is overlooked by those who underestimate her. Women writers who place female detectives in this position of seeming irrelevance, only to have them succeed in the end, make a powerful statement about women's abilities at all ages.

Miss Katherine Climpson: Sayers' Secret Weapon

Dorothy L. Sayers wrote 12 detective novels, all but one starring Lord Peter Wimsey, perhaps the most well-known aristocratic amateur detective. A founding member of the Detection Club, a detective fiction critic, a serious writer who was interested in returning the detective story to more of a novel of manners, Sayers anchored the interwar Golden Age of detective fiction. Though Sayers stopped writing fiction in 1938 to concentrate on translating Dante's *Divine Comedy* and writing religious plays, her impact on the genre is immense, both through her innovations in the genre and her extensive critical output.

Among the themes she dealt with in her writings was the importance of work as a necessary part of one's existence. Her papers and statements about the subject of work are vast in number, to the point that she herself broaches the possibility of "a sort of obsession" about the right attitude one should take towards one's work ("Why Work?" in *Creed* 46).[13] Sayers, a deeply religious person, believed that work should be thought of as a "creative activity undertaken for the love of the work itself; and that man, made in God's image, should make things, as God makes them, for the sake of doing well a thing that is well worth doing" ("Why Work?" in *Creed* 46). In "Are Women

Human?" she addresses the more specific topic of women and work: "every woman is a human being [...] and a human being must have occupation, if he or she is not to become a nuisance to the world" (in *Unpopular* 134).

One way that Sayers expresses this belief in the need for every person to have suitable work is through her use of the spinster in her detective novels. Here, she transforms a class of women that her society labeled as a "nuisance" into a successful and necessary force in the world of detective fiction. Miss Climpson first appears in *Unnatural Death* (1927), as the head of a sort of investigative bureau which helps uncover petty crimes like fraud and blackmail (*Strong Poison* 50). The bureau, which Wimsey in later novels refers to as his Cattery (self-consciously parodying the stereotype), employs only women from "the class unkindly known as 'superfluous'": spinsters, widows without family, deserted women, retired schoolteachers, out-of-work actresses, women who tried to do acceptable female work like open hat shops but failed (*Poison* 49). In Wimsey's eyes, such women are eminently suited for bringing certain male law-breakers to justice, with their success stemming at least in part from the stereotype their society has created for them: harmless, inoffensive, dependent. Since he can't do all of the detective work himself—and since he is not the person best fit to do it—he hires superfluous women.

Sayers is careful to outline the parameters of hiring practices for the Cattery to make a point about the usefulness of women, even if (or perhaps because) they fail in societally-sanctioned branches of female work. Her main protagonist, though male, feels very strongly about the position of women in society, saying that England's neglect of them is

> a manifestation of the wasteful way in which this country is run. Look at electricity. Look at water power. Look at the tides. Look at the sun. Millions of power units being given off into space every minute. Thousands of old maids, simply bursting with useful energy, forced by our stupid social system into hydros and hotels and communities and hostels and posts as companions, where their magnificent gossip-powers and units of inquisitiveness are allowed to dissipate themselves or even become harmful to the community, while the ratepayers' money is spent on getting work for which these women are providentially fitted, inefficiently carried out by ill-equipped policemen like you. My god! its enough to make a man write to John Bull. And then bright young men write nasty little patronizing books called "Elderly Women" and "On the Edge of the Explosion"—and the drunkards make songs upon 'em, poor things [*Death* 42].

In this, Wimsey mirrors Sayers' own view about the importance of work for all people. Though his attitude seems patronizing, it is clear from the importance of the jobs he gives to Miss Climpson and the extent to which he relies on her that this appearance is misleading; indeed, as an aristocrat who does not need to work, he falls into a category parallel to most of these "superfluous" women. He finds idleness intolerable and takes up detective work in part as a way to feel useful, and he hires others and gives them significant employment to help them feel useful as well.

But Miss Climpson serves a greater purpose in the two novels in which she appears than just running the Cattery. Her outside jobs, such as the case in *Unnatural Death* (and later in *Strong Poison*), require the special "qualities" of a spinster. Wimsey explains to Inspector Charles Parker the rationale for sending a woman to ask questions instead of a policeman, a "man with large flat feet and a note-book": "I send a lady with a long, woolly jumper on knitting-needles and jingly things round her neck. Of course she asks questions—everyone expects it. Nobody is surprised. Nobody is alarmed. And so-called superfluity is agreeably and usefully disposed of" (*Death* 43).

In looks, Miss Climpson epitomizes the neatness and primness which has come to define spinster detectives: she is a "thin, middle-aged woman, with a sharp, sallow face and very vivacious manner. She wore a neat, dark coat and skirt, a high-necked blouse [...] and her iron-grey hair was dressed under a net, in the style fashionable in the reign of the late King Edward" (*Death* 37). Like Miss Marple and other early female detectives, she uses the stereotypes surrounding the "spinster" to her own advantage.

When sent out on the case in *Unnatural Death*, Wimsey only gives her the briefest of outlines as to what type of persona she should take on, asking Miss Climpson to use her "remarkable tact and shrewdness" (39) to fill in the details. This includes sartorial details. She is to pretend that she makes about 800 pounds a year, and Wimsey relies on her "'excellent taste and experience'" to "'suggest the correct accessories and so on for creating that impression'" (41). Miss Climpson later sends an itemized account of her expenses bought in order to create such an impression, apologizing for the cost of her underwear: "but wool is so expensive nowadays and it is necessary that every detail of my equipment should be suitable to my (supposed!) position in life" (44). Her detailed knowledge of social conventions includes the ability to ask the right questions of the right people, based on her experience with and knowledge of human nature. Most of the information pertaining to the people in the case is gathered through Miss Climpson's shrewd and inquisitive detective work, in other words, by gossiping and listening and making the right deductions.

Despite (or rather in addition to) such traditionally "female" spheres of knowledge, Miss Climpson is a professional and takes her job seriously. She produces a "business-like notebook" and takes notes when talking to Lord Peter. Coming from a background of dependency and hand-outs, like many women in her position, she hesitates about taking money from Lord

Peter at the outset of a job. When he gives her fifty pounds to start her off on her assignment, he is careful to point out that

> "This is a pure matter of business, of course," said Wimsey, rather rapidly, "and you will let me have a note of the expenses in your usual business-like way."
>   "Of course." Miss Climpson was dignified. "And I will give you a proper receipt immediately" [Death 41].

An old friend of her father's told her she would have made an excellent lawyer, but, as she tells Inspector Parker, "'when I was young, girls didn't get the education or opportunities they get nowadays'" (Death 40). But Lord Peter is careful to point out the usefulness of the qualities she does have: "'Never mind, Miss Climpson [...] you've got just exactly the qualifications we want, and they're rather rare, so we're in luck'" (Death 40).

Her role in *Strong Poison* is even more essential for two reasons. First, Sayers places Miss Climpson on the jury for the trial of detective fiction writer Harriet Vane, in the dock for having killed her lover with arsenic. Miss Climpson forces a hung jury by refusing to find her guilty, believing that the prisoner's demeanor can and should be taken into account as evidence, and Harriet's demeanor—calm, open—does not support what Miss Climpson knows of guilty human beings. This is her version of what most people would call female intuition. She and Lord Peter, who has fallen in love with Harriet, then spend the rest of the novel trying to find the actual murderer so that Harriet can be set free.

Sayers thus provides a venue for the older, never-married woman to "save" the fallen woman, one of the few acceptable philanthropic venues for Victorian spinsters, for it is clear that Harriet is on trial for being sexually active as much as for murder.[14] Though Miss Climpson is old, she is not old-fashioned, and she refuses to find Harriet guilty for living with a man before marriage. This plot device "makes Miss Climpson and the Cattery responsible for saving Vane's life, thereby suggesting the necessary interdependence of all women" (Kenney 132). It also suggests another vital employment for spinsters.

Secondly, Wimsey relies on Miss Climpson to uncover the plot which framed Harriet; while he hunts for clues in town, she is sent to Windle in Westmorland on a job he trusts nobody else to do: "The trouble is, I can't in the least tell you how to set about it. It all depends on what you find when you get there. [...] I don't know who looks after her [the suspect's aunt], or how you are to get into the house. But you've got to do it, and you've got to find out where her will is kept, and, if possible, see it" (169). Without her intelligence and resourcefulness (she poses as a spiritual medium and "finds" the will), Wimsey literally could not have solved the case.

The spinsters in Sayers' fiction extend well beyond Miss Climpson. In *Unnatural Death* there are two sets of lesbian "spinsters" who form the basis of the mystery; in *Strong Poison* a fellow Cattery member, Miss Murchison, gets a job as a female clerk in a suspect's office where she gathers information, picks locks, opens hidden panels, and is invaluable in bringing him to justice. She should have been a musician, she says, but there was not enough money to become one of the first class. The Vane-Wimsey books following *Strong Poison* are populated with unmarried women of all sorts, against whom Harriet Vane weighs her own independence.

Peters and Krause are generally scathing in their article on the sexism in the novels of Sayers, Christie, and Allingham, arguing that despite any seeming advances, their female detectives ultimately return to traditional secondary roles (in this their article is representative of much early feminist detective fiction criticism). Yet they nonetheless have to acknowledge the skill with which Sayers writes about the problems facing single women, not only Harriet Vane (who will be fully treated in the last chapter) but spinsters as well.

Miss Climpson's joy in the freedom of modern times is seen in a letter she writes to Peter after having arrived without problems in Windle. Sayers twists around the platitude of the "good old days" by giving a first-person account of its difficulties for women:

In the *old* days, an *unmarried* woman arriving *alone* at midnight with a *suitcase* would hardly have been considered *respectable*. [...] whatever old-fashioned people may say about the greater *decorum* and *modesty* of women in Queen Victoria's time, those who can remember the old conditions know how *difficult* and *humiliating* they were! [*Poison* 176]

Sayers chooses to dramatize Miss Climpson primarily through such letters to Lord Peter; she writes several in both novels. They are full of italicizations and capitalizations and odd emphases, but though they are strangely expressive and sometimes extend over pages of text, they cannot be dismissed as mere "twaddle," as Miss Climpson herself refers to her writing at times. While they do report people's actions and serve as plot summaries within the text both for Lord Peter and for the reader, they are much more than synopses: they reveal people's characters, their potential motives, and provide intimate details of the setting which end up contributing to the mystery as a whole. Hence, they work towards solving the mystery. Sayers, in choosing to write in first-person letters, highlights the traditionally female epistolary form of writing, showing that such forms of writing and their "feminine" style—full of detail, self-referential and self-deprecating asides, and gossip about others—have an important place in what might be considered the more "male" world of detection, despite their initial awkward appearance. Without the spinster-sleuth's contributions—here in the form of Miss Climpson's letters—the case cannot be solved.

In her introduction to *Old Maids*, Doan writes that Miss Climpson serves "as a positive role model—rather than as a warning for those exploring the nonmarriage option—because her occupation provides her with a new image of herself as well as the means to independence" (13). Though cast in a supporting role to Sayers' main detective, Sayers never diminishes her in the text and is clear in showing Lord Peter's gratitude to Miss Climpson as well as Miss Climpson's gratitude to Lord Peter. Miss Climpson is provided with an independent income and an occupation which requires knowledge of not only domestic matters but intelligence, logic, and common sense as well.

More importantly, through Miss Climpson Sayers makes a powerful case for one of her most cherished beliefs and one of her society's most discussed topics, the importance of suitable work, especially for women. Kenney writes that the appearance of Miss Katherine Climpson provides "a striking example of the tendency of detective fiction to mirror the concerns and experience of its time, in this case, the changing status of women and their quest for fulfilling work" (131). Creating Miss Climpson also helps Sayers establish her professional authority in the genre, as she depicts ways that women can be successful on their own terms.

Miss Silver: Professional Enquiry Agent

Another professional spinster-sleuth, one much more developed and long-lived, is the elderly "enquiry agent" Miss Maud Silver, created by Patricia Wentworth. Wentworth (Dora Amy Elles) wrote well over seventy novels between 1910 and 1961, but she is most known for the thirty-two novels in which Miss Silver plays the primary role. She began writing in 1910, and *A Marriage Under the Terror*, a historical romance for which she won a prize, gave her her first recognition as a writer.

Wentworth wrote her first mystery novel in 1923, *The Astonishing Adventure of Jane Smith*. As in many of Wentworth's stories, the plucky young heroine of this tale is involved in danger and mystery before the requisite happy ending can be reached. The first novel starring a proper woman detective, Miss Silver, was *Grey Mask* (1928), Wentworth's eighth mystery novel. Wentworth returned to Miss Silver after sixteen more mystery novels in *The Case Is Closed* (1937). Over the next eight years, she completed 16 more novels, three starring an Inspector Lamb, seven with Miss Silver, and six featuring no one in particular. But from 1946 on, until the end of her career in 1961, she wrote only Miss Silver novels—twenty-three more books, comprising the thirty-two total.[15]

I have gone over the details of Wentworth's chronology because I believe it exhibits an interesting path of a writer ultimately drawn to the full-time use of a female detective. Twice in her career Wentworth wrote a Miss Silver novel and then abandoned the character, only to return to and finally stick exclusively to Miss Silver for nearly twenty more years. Wentworth's career is a testament not only to the popularity of female detectives but to the ability of women writers to achieve professional authority in the detective fiction genre through the creation of such characters, using them as a vehicle for articulating through their fiction matters of social significance for women.

Both Steinbrunner and Penzler and Nancy Wynne attribute Wentworth's return to Miss Silver exclusively to the detective's popularity with readers, without taking into account Wentworth's own feelings or taste. According to Steinbrunner and Penzler, "by the early 1940's Miss Silver was so popular that all subsequent Wentworth books featured her as the detective" (*Encyclopedia* 417). Wynne writes that after *The Case Is Closed* (1937) Miss Silver "proved to be so popular with readers that she was a part of more and more Wentworth books" (91). Clearly post-war England was the right time for a spinster detective.

While I don't mean to dismiss readers' influence on a writer, I think that returning to Miss Silver must have served other purposes for Wentworth as a woman writer. Certainly these books sold well and made her a commercial success—they are still being reprinted—and this study posits that one way female detectives helped their women creators establish their professional authority was through making them successful in the marketplace as authors. But to base the reason for returning to a character solely on an outside influence, like readers' tastes, overlooks other functions that female detectives may have served for their authors. Like all of these women writers, through her female detective Wentworth had the opportunity to raise awareness about issues facing the women of her day. Joan Hammerman Robbins' article, "A Redefined Sensibility" focuses on the way Wentworth's novels raise issues of importance to women, concluding that "these novels not only perceptively chronicle the social roles of women at the time, they also provide—particularly in the person of Maud herself—alternatives to the dependency and limited possibilities open to women" (431).

Miss Silver's character goes against the general trend of post–World War I female detectives in that she is a professional. Most others detect purely along amateur lines (though they work in other professions). Making their detectives amateurs was one way women writers of this time reduced the cultural anxiety surrounding the issue of women working in traditionally male careers; making them elderly was another. Miss Silver's unmarried status, her continual knitting, and her soothing grandmotherly ways allow her to successfully disarm not only her clients' nervousness but society's as a whole. An ex-governess, who late in life changes careers to become a professional "enquiry agent," Miss Silver works for no one but herself. She does not advertise but gets her clients by word of mouth, a fact which Wentworth tells readers explicitly and which emphasizes Miss Silver's elite connections. She has an office where she welcomes clients, as well as a waiting room; she does all the sleuthing herself, following up on clues and following people who need to be followed.

Wentworth's description of Miss Silver emphasizes her apparent timidity and femininity, focusing on her smallness and blandness: "She was a little person with no features, no complexion, and a great deal of tidy mouse-colored hair done in a large bun at the back of her head" (*Mask* 74). In *The Case is Closed*, she is described as "out of date. She was very neatly dressed in an unbecoming shade of drab. Her indeterminate features gave no indication of talent or character. Her smooth sallow skin was innocent of powder" (146–147). Even her voice is "without tone" (*Mask* 74).

Like C.L. Pirkis' Loveday Brooke some thirty years earlier, who is "best described as a series of negations," Miss Silver may be more effective because she is "doubly unnoticed," as Klein says of Brooke. Neither as a woman nor as a detective does she seem to stand out. Such blandness certainly may help in detection of criminals; with elderly detectives especially, society's perception of their insubstantiality works in their favor. Elderly women detectives are triply overlooked, as professionals, as women, and as old women.

Miss Silver's sex and age work against her at the outset. New clients, seeing that she is an elderly woman, usually do not believe she is capable of doing the job. In *Grey Mask* she tries to convince Charles Moray:

> "I can't take your case unless you're going to trust me. I can't work for a client who only tells me snippets and odds and ends. 'Trust in me all in all or not in all,' is my motto. Tennyson is out of fashion, but I admire him very much, and that is my motto."
>
> Charles looked at her with the suspicion of a twinkle. What a Victorian little person. He became aware of a half-knitted stocking on her lap, still needles bristling. It seemed very appropriate [75–76].

Miss Silver works like most female detectives, capitalizing on the stereotypical gossiping nature of spinsters and using domestic knowledge to give her insight into crimes. In *Grey Mask* she uses to her advantage the fact that a suspect's landlady was very worried about her tenant, in order to get more information from her: "I have always found worried people very willing to talk" (97). She can tell when people are holding things back from her and admonishes them gently: "'Oh yes,' said Miss Silver. Then she coughed. 'You really tell lies very badly, Mr. Moray'" (159).

However, she doesn't attribute her success in "reading" people to some sort of inherent woman's intuition. Like Joan Mar, whose business it is to "see more than others see," Miss Silver is a professional detective first and grants her means of "knowing" to the reason she is good at her job: "'It is my business to know things,'" she tells Rachel Treherne in *Lonesome Road* (5). Though seemingly bound by convention, if her profession demands she do unpleasant things, she does them. She puts herself in physical danger, goes around the law to get into locked houses, and once hired she is determined to find the truth, regardless of whether her clients want to hear it.

In these first novels Miss Silver is largely outside the action, not even appearing in *The Case Is Closed* until mid-way through the book. But with *Lonesome Road* Miss Silver plays a much more prominent part. The book opens with a client, Rachel Treherne, coming to see her, and Miss Silver is present on the 'scene of the crime' throughout the novel. By this point, Wentworth must have understood some of the advantages of having a series character: one, Miss Silver can effectively be used as a medium for portraying and discussing issues facing women, especially employment and education; and two, certain standard characteristics and details can be covered quickly, leaving more time to spend on other issues.

Against the backdrop of Miss Silver, a older woman who has the courage to stop being a governess and become self-sufficient and self-employed, Wentworth can present a variety of types and classes of women and can more thoroughly engage with social issues of her time. Similarly, Robbins notes that "Patricia Wentworth succeeds in using mystery fiction to portray the social issues dominating the era in which she wrote. Her female characters, and especially Maud Silver, further succeed in raising our consciousness about women's lives" (435).

The Unusual Dame Beatrice Adele Lestrange Bradley

Gladys Mitchell was another woman writer, who, having created an older female detective as a series character, could not give her up. Mitchell, herself a "spinster," was born in 1901. She earned her teaching certificate in 1921 from Goldsmith's College, University of London, and continued as an external student at University College, London, getting a degree in English and European History in 1926. Like many college-educated women, Mitchell found teaching to be remunerative as well as a socially acceptable career and remained in the profession even after she became a successful author, though she "retired" twice, once in 1950 and again in 1961. She wrote continually throughout her lifetime, often publishing more than one book a year. She died in 1983.

Mitchell was as prolific as Christie, publishing nearly 90 novels in her lifetime, including nine children's books and eleven or so other novels under two different male pseudonyms. But she is famous for the 66 mystery novels featuring the outlandish Mrs. (later Dame) Beatrice Adele Lestrange Bradley, psychoanalyst and crime solver. Mrs. Bradley is not a "spinster detective" in the strict definition; however, she does fit other parameters: she is over sixty; she lives alone; she supports herself through her work; and she does not rely on economic help from a male relation. She is also non-threatening to the world of male work, since she is not "truly" a detective and since psychology was a more woman-friendly discipline than many others in this period.

Mitchell had had four manuscripts rejected before she turned to detective fiction, and *Speedy Death* was published in 1929 by Victor Gollancz "despite the fact that it 'had every fault under the sun'" (Pike 250). She also worked on historical novels early in her career, but gave it up because "the rewards were so utterly inadequate considering the amount of research involved" (Pike 253). In other words, though they were well-received by the critics, they didn't sell. She therefore continued with detective fiction and children's novels (most of them mysteries also) for the rest of her career. Though she wrote six novels under a male pseudonym and using a male detective, she preferred to remain with the unique persona she created in Mrs. Bradley, saying "I could never get tired of her!" (in Pike 251).

Mitchell herself attests to the charismatic force of Mrs. Bradley's character in these novels, saying that when she began writing *Speedy Death* she "had no intention" of making Mrs. Bradley her detective; however, writes Mitchell, Mrs. Bradley "simply 'took over' and I became so superstitious about her that I would not dare to have another detective!" (in Pike 251). Mitchell seems to go out of her way to create a woman detective as unattractive and unlikable as possible. Her first description in *Speedy Death* is the fullest:

> Mrs. Bradley was dry without being shriveled, and bird-like without being pretty. She reminded Alastair Bing, who was afraid of her, of the reconstruction of a pterodactyl he had once seen in a German museum. There was the same inhuman malignity in her expression as in that of the defunct bird, and, like it, she had a cynical smirk about her mouth even when her face was in repose. She possessed nasty, dry, claw-like hands, and her arms, yellow and curiously repulsive, suggested the plucked wings of a fowl [8].

Mrs. Bradley's clothes are outrageously colored and out of date; her laugh is often described as a shriek, accompanied by a poke in the ribs, and it often erupts at seemingly inappropriate times, since she is the only one to have figured something out. Because she can usually guess what will happen next, she is often thought of as witch-like, as the characters in *Speedy*

Death point out: "little, old, shriveled, clever, sarcastic sort of dame. Would have been smelt out as a witch in a less tolerant age" (5). Only her voice is beautiful, a fact mentioned by many other characters; only small children and animals like her immediately, seeing beyond her physical appearance and peculiar actions.

Mrs. Bradley's methods of detection are based almost entirely on her psychoanalytic training. She gathers information from people using a "psychiatrist's awareness of the power of suggestion," noting reactions, estimating their significance, and drawing conclusions (Craig and Cadogan 186). Mrs. Bradley points out the difference between her methods and methods of others in the world of detective fiction in *Speedy Death* when a member of the house party asks if she is accusing him of murder: "I accuse no one [...]. I know what I know, and I deduce what I deduce. But accusation—that is not my business. I am a psychologist, not a policewoman. Some are killers, and some are not" (25). Intuition, that female standby of detective fiction which women writers use so often to authorize their characters' crime-solving, is made fun of in this book. When Alastair Bing asks how Mrs. Bradley knew Dorothy would be attacked, Mrs. Bradley plays dumb:

> "Just an intuition," she said airily. "Just an idea that came into my head."
> "Oh, rubbish! Rubbish!" snarled Alastair [124].

When someone tells the inspector on the case that only Mrs. Bradley thinks Eleanor was murdered, the inspector can't resist poking fun at her also: "'It's rather interesting to me, sir, that Mrs. Bradley should say that. What does she base it on? Or is it just one of the lady's opinions, based on nothing but intuition?' said the inspector, grinning sarcastically" (227).

In this, she is unlike other female detectives who normally are provided with an array of tools demarcated "feminine," intuition often taking a leading role.[16] But, as Craig and Cadogan point out, Mrs. Bradley "never gossips with servants or befriends distressed ladies on trains and buses [...]. She is not accorded special narrative treatment on account of her sex; her qualities might be transferred to a male detective without loss of credibility" (181).

She is also not very motherly or grandmotherly like the most popular spinster detectives, Miss Marple or Miss Silver, though she alone among these detectives actually is a mother. Her son, the barrister Ferdinand Lestrange, defends his mother against a charge of murder in *Speedy Death*, but Mitchell makes it clear that this is not a situation where a young hero rushes to a distressed heroine's aid. He has been hired because he is the best: "his voice was good, his appearance distinguished, and he was determined to do himself credit, his mother's fate being merely a secondary consideration in his eyes" (277). Lest the reader think that this statement is merely a strange aside by the omniscient narrator, the opening of the trial is seen from Mrs. Bradley's point of view as well: "Ferdinand Lestrange, her son, the leading counsel for the defence, looked distinguished, she thought. Nobody there knew she was his mother. Ferdinand wouldn't care a hand whether she were convicted or not, except in so far as his professional reputation was concerned, but he would take care not to let that suffer!" (265). Even when she tries to be seen doing something grandmotherly and picks up knitting, she does not do it with any real intention of knitting something. The pieces are always awkward and messy and unfinishable; it is clear that knitting is just Mrs. Bradley's sarcastic performance of what society expects from her (and Mitchell's own spoof upon the stereotype).

Unique though she is, Mrs. Bradley does share traits in common with other female detectives. She can read certain household clues, based on the domestic training which she received as a girl (in the 1880s). The previous chapter of this study presents a good example of this from *Speedy Death*, when Mrs. Bradley tells Mr. Carstairs with certainty that the maids would never have dusted, much less moved, a bathroom stool, and that he has therefore lost a clue. And while she still functions as a "mind reader," this skill comes not from intuition or even from feminine socialization, but because of her professional psychoanalytic training. Like Miss Marple's adage, that "human nature is much the same everywhere" (*Tuesday* 69), Mrs. Bradley knows that people's actions give clues to their mental health. Based on her vast knowledge of personality types, she can usually discover the perpetrator based on a recognized series of disturbances.

Mrs. Bradley's profession as psychoanalyst also provides her with a significant intersection between a customarily feminine form of writing—keeping a journal—and a modern use of writing as part of a job. At the end of most books is a section called "Mrs. Bradley's Notebook," a diary of sorts in which she chronologically notes psychological oddities and suspicions as to the murderer. Her notes about "the case" are written out as they would be in a psychologist's casebook. Mrs. Coutts, for example, the perpetrator in *The Saltmarsh Murders*, is down as "a bad case of sadism plus inverted nymphomania" (179). For the reader, these case notes add a fascinating layer to the supposed detection process. The reader sees how early on in the plot Mrs. Bradley names the perpetrator to herself (she's never wrong) and from there either sits still or works behind the scenes to manipulate the other characters in the novel (especially the murderer). This methodical note-taking shows a woman with both an orderly mind and a sense of humor; it also has the effect of highlighting her professionalism. Even though she is only an "amateur" detective, she is never not doing her job. These notes provide insights into both Mrs. Bradley's thinking process and Mitchell's writing process, supplying the reader with a plausible background for her detective's seeming omniscience.

Though Gladys Mitchell claims she is conservative in politics (and agnostic in religion), she uses Mrs. Bradley's character as a medium for discussing rather taboo subjects, subjects that most writers of this time period wouldn't touch, much less discuss with her even-handedness. Mrs. Bradley is sympathetic to adulterers, isn't bothered by erotic literature, and comments without surprise on transvestism and incest. She is at ease discussing birth control, "the arguments for which she was extraordinarily well-versed" (*Death* 282). In *Mystery of a Butcher's Shop* (1930), a character repeats Mrs. Bradley's belief that the Catechism is immoral because village children are led to believe it exonerates their "betters," including fox-hunting squires who do whatever they want and "'factory owners who pay women about half what they would pay men for doing the exactly the same work'" (150).

Mitchell's character is unusual in another way, re-defining stereotypes of femininity and of the proper role of a detective. In the first novel in which she appears, *Speedy Death*, she murders the murderer, taking the law into her own hands. Eleanor has already killed her fiancé and has tried to kill her future sister-in-law. Mrs. Bradley, knowing she is saving other peoples' lives as well as saving Eleanor from a life in an insane asylum, poisons Eleanor and makes it look like suicide. Mrs. Bradley performs a similar action in *The Saltmarsh Murders*. Knowing that Mrs. Coutts (who has killed two young women) has a weak heart, she shocks her to death by naming her as the murderer, rather than allowing her to hang or, again, to have to enter an asylum.[17]

Craig and Cadogan greatly admire Mrs. Bradley's independent actions, saying that she "has the courage not to insist on convictions" (187), in this case the rigid beliefs of a male-dominated justice system. Mrs. Bradley sympathetically takes care of the women perpetrators in what she feels is a more humane way.

Sargeant comments that broaching such topics "was decidedly adventurous of her creator" (254) and humorously speculates on the staffroom fights into which Mitchell must have gotten after the release of some of her novels (she had no pseudonym for these). But Mitchell confessed that her adventure-taking was limited to within the detective fiction format, playful though she is within that venue. In her essay "Why Do People Read Detective Stories?," she writes that she prefers the conservative nature of detective novels over the randomness of more modern novels, which "leave the reader suspended in mid-air, forced either to impotent irritation or else to having to invent their own outcome" (in Winn 337). She considers leaving loose or illogical ends to be cheating, believing that people read detective stories because they "must, above all things, have a definite plot" (337).

Within that plot structure, however, Mitchell gave voice to ideas and opinions that she could not address in other formats, enjoying the freedom such a strange character gave her. She certainly speaks of Mrs. Bradley as if she had a life of her own, admitting: "I am never in control of my characters. They do and say things I never intended" (Pike 251). But while Craig and Cadogan offer praise to Mrs. Bradley for her uniqueness, the praise rightly belongs to her creator, Gladys Mitchell, who, through the medium of her female detective creation, effectively explores and comments upon topics of importance to the women of her time period.

Miss Marple, Elderly Logician

Agatha Christie is the most recognized name in crime fiction. Her work has been printed more than any English author other than Shakespeare and has been translated into over 100 languages.[18] While critics disagree as to whether she is the "best" crime writer, she is certainly the most popular, perhaps the best at taking an established form like the detective story and both working within its conventions and transforming them.

Unlike Sayers, who focused specifically on creating honest and believable characters in her fiction, Christie relished the puzzle format of detective fiction, focusing on the unexpected, the game, the twist in plot. Her characters are not particularly well-drawn, and she often relies on stereotypes which are put in place simply to anchor down the puzzle format. Yet she created a number of female detectives to star in her stories, both young adventurer types, like Anne Beddingfeld and Tuppence Beresford, and elderly spinsters such as Miss Jane Marple. Her strong female characters clearly extend from Christie's own woman-centered childhood, just as her reliance on the conservative puzzle plot, where the criminal is caught and the young couple marries, reflects her traditional upbringing.

Christie was born in Devonshire in 1890 and had a typically sheltered late–Victorian childhood. Her family was quite wealthy when she was young; however, bad investments and a stockmarket crash led to severe economizing, even more so after her father's death when Agatha was ten years old.

Because she was so much younger than her siblings, Christie was alone most of the time growing up and created imaginative games and stories to entertain herself. Her sister Madge married (socially very well) only a few months after their father died; and her brother Monty lived in Africa and then France for much of his life.[19] Therefore, Christie's teenage years were spent primarily with her mother and without any strong male figures. Christie did not leave her mother's home in Torquay until after the war— she was even educated at home—and her mother's death in 1926 led to a severe depression. The other great influence on her life was the family matriarch known as "Auntie-Grannie," who she names as a prototype for Miss Marple.[20] The influence of these three strong older women—her sister

Madge, her mother, and her Auntie-Grannie—can be seen throughout her fiction, as she presents a wide variety of types and classes of women. Drawn quickly so that they are recognizable to her large middle-class readership, the disparate but largely positive female characters in her fiction reflect the complexities and ambiguities in the status of women in the early twentieth century.

Though her sister Madge was eleven years older than she, the sisters were close, and Christie felt that Madge had more artistic and literary talent. Christie says she herself had no literary ambitions, despite the publication of a poem in the local newspaper when she was eleven: "I was elated at seeing myself in print, but I cannot say that it led me to contemplate a literary career" (125). Madge introduced her to detective fiction, re-telling her Sherlock Holmes mysteries over and over at Agatha's request. Her sister also presented her with a dare that she couldn't forget: after Madge said she didn't think she could do it, Christie became "fired by the determination that [she] would write a detective story" (211).

Christie began to think about her detective story in more detail a few years later. Nervous about her new husband Archie Christie, who was fighting in World War I as one of Britain's first wartime pilots, she passed the time at the dispensary of the hospital where she was stationed as a VAD by thinking about the plot and characters for her novel (including Poirot) and the manner of death, appropriately by poisoning. *The Mysterious Affair at Styles* was duly written and published in 1920. According to Christie, that was it: "I had been dared to write a detective story; I had written a detective story; it had been accepted, and was going to appear in print. There, as far as I was concerned, the matter ended" (278). But of course, some sixty-five detective novels followed, including several with female detectives. The young adventurous type of detective, typified by Tuppence Beresford, was the star of that next book (along with her husband Tommy), and Anne Beddingfeld from *The Man in the Brown Suit* followed soon after. These were plucky, independent, curious, intelligent women who solved the crimes in which they become involved. Christie wrote several of these "thriller" types of novels in the 1920s, saying they were fun and easier to write than a standard puzzle-type detection novel.[21]

Curiously, writing *Murder at the Vicarage*, the novel which introduced Miss Marple, does not seem to have made much of an initial impression on Christie: "I cannot remember where, when or how I wrote it, why I came to write it, or even what suggested to me that I should select a new character—Miss Marple—to act as sleuth to the story. Certainly at the time I had no intention of continuing her for the rest of my life" (445). Part of the reason for Christie's uncertainty as to Miss Marple's "birth" might reside in the fact that Miss Marple did not spring fully formed from her imagination like Poirot had; the spinster character had appeared several times in Christie's fiction before 1930, in different forms.

Even Miss Marple's home, the village of St. Mary Mead, had been created previously in the novel Christie says she hated writing more than any other, *The Mystery of the Blue Train*. Miss Viner, a complaining but warm-hearted old maid, writes letters to the heroine of the novel, gossiping and providing details of village life; eventually, full of nostalgia, the heroine returns to St. Mary Mead and works as a companion to Miss Viner. Christie doesn't mention Miss Viner or *Blue Train* as an impetus for Miss Marple in her autobiography. However, that is not surprising, considering the book's negative associations for Christie—she had to finish it in order to make money following her "nervous breakdown" and divorce.[22] It is also the book that marked the beginning of Christie's life as a professional author: "That was the moment when I changed from an amateur to a professional. I assumed the burden of a profession, which is to write even when you don't want to, don't much like what you are writing, and aren't writing particularly well" (365). However, because her books sold well and because she could make money from writing them, she continued to write.

The town's name and the shrewd spinster in it ultimately survived and were transformed. Christie even attributed a particular pleasure to the creation of literary spinsters, noting that: "it is possible that Miss Marple arose from pleasure I had taken in portraying Dr. Sheppard's sister in *The Murder of Roger Ackroyd*. She had been my favourite character in the book—an acidulated spinster, full of curiosity, knowing everything, hearing everything: the complete detective service in the home" (445).

However, when the book was made into the play *Alibi* (1928), the producers wanted a young love interest added, and to make room for her, Caroline Sheppard had to be taken out. Christie says that her removal was "one of the things that saddened me most" (445) and suspects that this specific decision on the part of the play's producers caused her to create Miss Marple: "I think at that moment, in St. Mary Mead, though I did not yet know it, Miss Marple was born, [...] lined up below the borderline of consciousness, ready to come to life" (446). When creating Miss Marple, therefore, Christie was both responding to the prejudices against unromantic female characters and satisfying an existing creative necessity for that type of character, searching until she found the setting and persona which satisfied her. Her spinster detective was born not only out of her grandmother's "Ealing cronies" (447), but out of an authorial desire which demanded fulfillment.

Miss Marple herself first appeared in 1928 in six short stories that eventually became part of *The Tuesday Club Murders* (these were published along with seven more stories in 1932, two years after *Murder at the Vicarage*). She is described as wearing "a black brocade dress, very much pinched in round the waist. Mechlin lace was arranged in a cascade down the front of the bodice. She had on black lace mittens, and a black lace cap surmounted the piled-up masses of her snowy hair. She was knitting—something white and soft and fleecy" (1). The organization around which these stories form themselves is a sort of crime-solving club. The members—a former head of Scotland Yard, a clergyman, an artist, a writer (Raymond West, Miss Marple's nephew), a lawyer, and Miss Marple—decide to meet every Tuesday, with one person in the group telling the other members an "unsolved" mystery, though they themselves know the solution. Miss Marple solves every case, establishing her method of crime-solving by analogy: she is reminded of someone in her past who has acted similarly and typecasts accordingly. When people show astonishment that "little Tommy" has anything to do with the criminal in the story they just heard, Miss Marple says simply, "everybody is very much alike, really" (84). Age works to her benefit; though she is a woman and unmarried and has never left St. Mary Mead, her vast knowledge, especially of human nature, is useful in solving crimes.

Like most female detectives, she can also "read" household clues, understanding in one case that the "hundreds and thousands" in part of a letter referred not to an amount of money but to the candies sprinkled on top of the dessert trifle—hence the way the killer introduced arsenic to the victim. She knows that the man posing as a gardener isn't really a gardener because gardeners do not work on Whit Monday; therefore he must have something to do with the crime.

But Maida and Spornick suggest that the Miss Marple character from *The Tuesday Club Murders* is not quite successful because the short story format is too limiting—"Marple requires space and time to move about in a community to cast her spell" (110). When she is established as a trusted part of a community and has a more complete background and setting, such as in *Murder at the Vicarage*, she becomes a credible and complete character.

Nonetheless, in this first novel Miss Marple is not seen altogether as kindly by the other characters: the vicar's wife calls her "the worst cat in the village [...]. [S]he always knows every single thing that happens—and draws the worst inferences from it" (5). The vicar himself, who serves as narrator, has more admiration for her, or at least respect for her "powers": "Miss Marple is a white-haired old lady with a gentle, appealing manner—Miss Wetherby is a mixture of vinegar and gush. Of the two Miss Marple is much the more dangerous" (9). Miss Marple is also not portrayed very kindly by Christie. In this novel, her two hobbies are simply excuses for eavesdropping and spying, as the vicar knows: "gardening is as good as a smoke screen and the habit of observing birds through powerful glasses can always be turned to account" (11). In future novels, Christie turns gardening and bird-watching into the passions of an older lady, emphasizing how they keep her busy rather than make her a busybody.

Though her main method of detection—reading human nature—could be viewed as a branch of women's intuition, Miss Marple does not label her knowledge of humanity a particularly female trait. According to Miss Marple, intuition is knowing how people will react in certain circumstances, and such knowledge is directly related to one's age and experience in the world: "intuition is like reading a word without having to spell it out. A child can't do that, because it has had so little experience. But a grown-up person knows the word because he's seen it often before" (54). Notice the word "person" rather than "woman." For Miss Marple (and perhaps for Christie as well) there is nothing inherently feminine about intuition.[23] This description shows Miss Marple to be much more of an observer and a logician than many give her credit for.

Despite her wide array of female characters and the largely positive light in which they are portrayed, Christie would have balked at being called a feminist. Unlike Sayers, for instance, Christie does not even support the idea of women working: "the position of women, over the years, has definitely changed for the worse. We women have behaved like mugs. We have clamoured to be allowed to work as men work. Men, not being fools, have taken kindly to the idea" (129). Christie's anti-feminist stance has been both acknowledged and disputed by critics over the years; Shaw and Vanacker say that she gave "a high value to conventionally womanly attributes and habits and showed them, in the figure of Miss Marple, as the vehicles of logic, morality, and justice" (64). Marty Knepper writes that "only a writer with a healthy respect for women's abilities and a knowledge of real women could create the diversity of female characters Christie does" (401). Peters and Krause, in their generally scathing article on the sexism displayed by four main women crime writers, believe Christie offends the least.

But critical statements concerning Christie's lack of or even anti-feminism are not as important as what goes on in her fiction; it is a fact that, more than any other detective fiction writer of this time period, Christie presents an array of women working in a variety of professions—nurses, actresses, secretaries, headmistresses. She also presents a great variety of amateur detectives, creating primarily young girls during her own youth and then re-introducing Miss Marple in 1942 with The Body in the Library. She wrote ten more full-length Miss Marple novels and several collections of short stories over the next thirty years. It is perhaps significant that Christie does not have Miss Marple die in her last novel, like she does Hercule Poirot.

Christie's Vicar Clement sums up the theme of this chapter succinctly in the early chapters of The Murder in the Vicarage: "There is no detective in

England equal to a spinster lady of uncertain age with plenty of time on her hands" (20). While the vicar may not have felt that this was a particularly positive thing, Christie's readers have certainly embraced the spinster. Out of all the characters in this study, only the spinsters survive over many novels and years. Something in their sex, characterization, status, or investigative techniques have made them appealing for well over fifty years. Michele Slung may think this is a backward step, to have amateur old ladies solving crime, and certainly the "hard boiled" American school of detective fiction relegates the spinster to a school of writing both unrealistic and old-fashioned. And, as Alison Light correctly espouses, "critics of all political hues are likely to pass Christie by" (64).

However, I think it is impossible to dismiss the phenomenon of the spinster detective as some passé aspect of drawing-room fiction, or even as mere wishful thinking. There is something powerful and appealing about this literary character that made her popular for so many years, as Shaw and Vanacker suggest:

> The spinster is moral arbiter, curb of license and disorder, and image of repression; she is also what lies outside the normal expectations of a woman's life as it is lived in patriarchal society and although this diminishes her it also gives her the power of the abnormal over the normal, to threaten, to judge, to undermine and to destroy [43].

Though they refer specifically to Miss Marple, their conclusion as to the success of the spinster can be attributed to all of the authors in this chapter: these writers have the ability to "harness" the "spinster's potential as both fearsome oddity and moral force to the structures and conventions of detective fiction" (43). Women writers who created these detectives tapped into a new formula which satisfied not only their audience but themselves, returning to these characters repeatedly over decades.

Shaw and Vanacker contend that "during the years after the First World War, women made of detective fiction a genre that suited them" (95). Nowhere is this clearer than in the creation of elderly spinster detectives. Rather than continuing to depict spinsters as a despised part of society, women writers created characters who defied conventions governing sex, age and marital status. In doing so, women writers challenged those conventions which relegated certain women to lesser subsets: unmarried women, elderly women. Confronting such stereotypes and articulating responses to it served as a method of allowing women to consolidate their own authority, as they searched for ways to write about cultural issues that mattered to them on their own terms.

FOUR

Women Writers, Detectives, and Popular Culture

> If you want to write a book, study what sizes books are,
> and write within the limits of that size. If you want to write
> a certain type of short story for a certain type of magazine
> you have to make it the length, and it has to be the type of
> story, that is printed in that magazine [...]. [As a writer] one
> is a tradesman—a tradesman in a good honest trade.
> —Agatha Christie, *An Autobiography* (1977)

Chapters Two and Three examined ways in which women detective fiction writers established professional authority through creating female detectives who adapted commonly-held notions of femininity to the masculine world of work without losing social status. They accomplished this by transforming tools demarcated "feminine" by their society—knowledge of the domestic sphere and natural feminine intuition—into tools fit for the traditionally masculine world of logic and detection and by creating successful professional female detectives out of the once-despised character of the spinster. Both of these strategies expanded the sphere of feminine achievement and expertise, exposing society's limited view of the roles women could fill, though employing these devices did not result in extensive revisioning of that sphere.

But writing and being published were in themselves acts that questioned the boundaries of appropriate "womanly" behavior. This chapter looks at strategies women writers employed in their fiction *because* they had to go outside of the "private" domestic sphere, into the public marketplace, in order to consolidate their professional authority in that sphere. One particularly effective way women writers highlighted the potential difficulties of this conflict was to create female detectives who were also writers. Women writers used their detectives to discuss issues surrounding being "public" women—being paid for work—and to explore issues that might affect them specifically as women writers in a popular genre.[1] These writers were businesswomen, from Elizabeth Braddon and L.T. Meade to Agatha Christie, and they were interested in understanding the market for detective fiction and adapting their fiction to meet the needs of that market. Making their detectives writers offered them a way to confront and explore the often restrictive cultural attitudes surrounding women and the public sphere.

This strategy was further strengthened by women writers creating female detectives who were writers of detective fiction. Georgette Heyer and Agatha Christie, for instance, used their female writer-detective characters to discuss problems faced by women writing specifically in the detective fiction genre. By the 1930s, however, women's fitness and ability to write detective fiction was more firmly established, and women writers, while continuing to explore their position in the genre, were able focus on ways of adapting and reworking the genre as well. Creating writer-detectives provided them with opportunities to comment on the conventions of the genre, parodying it and themselves and re-formulating what the genre could contain, working to solidifying women's place in it.

Female Detectives as Writers and Readers

Writing is a common occurrence in these stories, as women writers show their female detectives making good use of it as part of their crime-solving adventures. However, though writing was certainly an acceptable activity, it was not supposed that middle- or upper-class women should write (or perform any job) specifically to make money, unless circumstances were so adverse that they absolutely had to. There were of course extremely successful women novelists and moral tract writers throughout the nineteenth century, but they often felt the need to temper their public success: they wrote under pseudonyms; they pleaded family poverty (an acceptable "sacrificial" motive); they created excuses based on their supposed "natural" moral authority.

But it was during this time period, from the late nineteenth to the early twentieth centuries, that the scope of women's professional writing changed. Women no longer felt the need to be as apologetic for the personal and financial success they may have achieved through their writing. Women writers of detective fiction were among these professionally and financially successful writers who benefited from—and indeed helped shape—their society's changing attitudes. In showcasing the act of writing as a fundamental aspect of their detective fiction, they could express their views on and explore women's relationship with popular formats during this transition period.

One way women writers comment on the changing literary opportunities for women is through the increased attention to newspapers in their detective fiction. Because newspapers were largely comprised of current events, women were discouraged from reading them; it was not supposed that such things would interest women (though this perception had certainly changed by the early twentieth century).[2] Yet earlier women writers show their female detectives using the popular media as a useful contributing factor in solving crime—they read the paper to keep up on public events and cut out and keep crime-related clippings.

In C.L. Pirkis' first story starring Loveday Brooke, "The Black Bag Left on the Doorstep," there appear over seven distinct references to reading, writing, or handwriting analysis, and the solution to the crime results from Brooke's ability to understand what she reads in the right way. In addition to the newspaper cutting describing the case—that 30,000 pounds worth of jewelry were stolen and that the thief wrote "To be let, unfurnished" across the door of the safe—Brooke brings into her boss's office another cutting which she takes "from her letter-case" (403). It is an account of a "Singular Discovery," a black portmanteau with a longish suicide note attached to the outside; the police suspect the note is a fake and Mr. Dyer demands to know why she is wasting his time with this unrelated event. But Loveday sees a potential clue: "'I wanted to know [...] if you saw anything in it that might in some way connect this discovery with the robbery at Craigen Court?'" (404). They are of course, as Loveday suspects, directly related.

In addition to newspapers, Brooke's knowledge of a particularly "low brow" piece of reading material, The Reciter's Treasury, enables her to see the most vital clue to solving the case. On her way to the crime scene, she re-reads a "small volume bound in paper boards" which was "published at the low price of one shilling, and seemed specially designed to meet the requirements of third-rate amateur reciters at penny readings" (405). Once at Craigen Court she uses those detecting tools which come "naturally" to women in order to finish the work she began on the train: she is sympathetic to the suspect's lover; she spends hours listening to the housekeeper, gleaning facts; she notes details of the servant's habits; she wants to know if a certain chair is always placed in the same spot. And, to the amazement of all, she discovers the identity of the thief and his location before the night is over.

When explaining to Dyer how she solved the case, she cites the newspaper account and the book she read on the train as key clues. She recognized the language of both the "suicide note" attached to the black bag and the unusual phrase written across the safe as coming from *The Reciter's Treasury*. When she was a novice detective, first getting experience, she had to attend the working-class amusement of "penny readings" in the course of her work quite often. There she heard not only the "high falutin sentences" of the suicide note for the first time but also the speech that the housekeeper told her that a former footman at Craigen Court had made the previous Christmas Eve at the servants' party. As she explains to Dyer: "With these three pieces before me, it was not difficult to see a thread of connection between the writer of the black-bag letter and the thief who wrote across the safe at Craigen Court" (413). The footman is apprehended the next day.[3]

Other early female detectives also use the newspapers to help solve crime. L.T. Meade's Florence Cusak scours the personal ads in order to find a missing link needed to solve the case. Orczy's Lady Molly, in "The Ninescore Mystery," writes a false advertisement for a newspaper to draw a witness out of hiding. In an early example of a female detective engaging in actual "journalist" activities, Beatrice Heron-Maxwell's Molly Delamere (1894) uses writing for a newspaper as a cover for her work: "'I have been going in a little for journalism, as you know. I shall give out that I have some literary employment which necessitates my staying in town'" (5). Then she takes up pearl-broking, which must be kept secret to protect her from thieves. It is during her "adventures" as a pearl-broker that she works as a detective on an amateur level.

However, Heron-Maxwell does not mention her detective's "journalism" again; it is clearly not an important part of the story's plot line. Later women writers provide more detailed examples of female detective-writers who exploit newspapers and writing to a greater extent. Agatha Christie's Anne Beddingfeld, for example, becomes a special correspondent for a newspaper, making money by writing about crime. Writing is highlighted in these stories in an even more persuasive way in the instances where women writers make their detectives writers of detective fiction who, like themselves, face problems of authorship. Georgette Heyer, Agatha Christie, and Dorothy Sayers all create "literary doubles" like this, characters who provide them with a way to challenge both the strictures of a society which had limited views of their capabilities, and the strictures of the detective fiction genre.

Women writers used their female detectives to explore and question the literary conventions and traditional modes of narrative that govern detective fiction, to effectively challenge, as Gayle Greene writes, "the cultural and literary tradition they inherit" (2). Through their female detectives, women writers worked "both within and against the dominant discourse" (20), stretching the boundaries of the detective fiction genre. Their tremendous success contributed to what became known as Britain's Golden Age of detective fiction; the ability and fitness of women to write, and in a male-oriented popular format, could no longer be questioned.

Braddon and the Professional Standards of Women Writers

But this state of achievement certainly had to evolve. In the late nineteenth and early twentieth centuries, women writers' ability to express themselves in writing and to enjoy personal and financial success from their writing on their own terms was often challenged. The situation of Coralie Urquhart, the young writer/detective in Mary Elizabeth Braddon's *Thou Art the Man* (1894) functions as an interesting bridge from the woman who writes in the private sphere—diary-keeping and letter-writing—to the more modern woman, who may keep a diary but also is well-educated and writes for a living, such as many of the later writers in this study. Cora's writing and its appropriation are indications of the difficulties women had in establishing control over their writing during the time period covered by this study, as they faced struggles of acceptance and challenges to their authority.

Braddon herself works as a bridge between genres and time periods; though solidly part of the sensation fiction subgenre of the Victorian three-decker novel, she also wrote stories which fit thematically into the detective genre and which were published in serial formats. Her control over her career as a writer during the mid-Victorian era far exceeded what most women did to ensure publication of their work. In addition to writing sensation fiction novels, she also wrote plays and short stories for magazines and worked as editor and contributor to her own magazine. She often helped publish her own books, contacting publishers and negotiating contracts; in this way she was one of the few women who had such direct control over the output and format of her writing.[4] Braddon stepped over boundaries of the appropriately feminine in her personal life too, which was considered scandalous by her society. She lived with John Maxwell for many years until his institutionalized wife died and they could marry. Despite this "irregular" lifestyle (or perhaps in part because of it) her fiction remained continually popular. E.A. Bennett, in *Fame and Fiction: An Enquiry into Certain Popularities* (1901), writes that Braddon "is a part of England; she has woven herself into it" (25) through her immense output: "you would travel far before you reached the zone where the name of Braddon failed of its recognition" (24–25).

Therefore, at the same time that detractors of mass culture railed against the sensation novel, it was making money and names for its proponents and contributors. This fact—that people (women) were writing fiction for money—was of course part of the problem with popular genres; it was unseemly that women should write for so ignoble a reason. However, rather than seeing the marketability of popular fiction as an obstacle, women writers like Braddon and others in this study embraced the market, studied its demands, and made themselves a part of it. For instance, even during Braddon's period of grief when Maxwell died, she did not cease writing or yield control of her work, and she never lost sight of market demands. Robert Wolff, author of *Sensational Victorian: The Life and Fiction of Mary Elizabeth Braddon,* points out an example of Braddon's business astuteness at this time of her life when he discusses the three one-volume novels she wrote during 1893, 1894, and 1895, but which she held back for publication until 1896, 1897, and 1898. To Wolff, Braddon's "forehandedness" at having appropriate material to meet the changing demands of the publishing market well in advance suggests "that as an artist and a business woman she had sensed, before even the first tremors shook the publishing world, that the day of the three-volume novel [...] was coming to an end. Although she would protest against the change when it came, she was simultaneously preparing to meet it with work of high quality" (353–354).

Written in 1894, Braddon's *Thou Art the Man* is itself a bridge, being neither a "typical" turn-of-the-century detective story nor a classic sensation fiction novel for which Braddon was famous. It was printed first as a newspaper serial, then released as Braddon's last three-decker novel but one.[5] Following the demands of serial publication (and in typical sensation format) its narrative lures the reader on in bits, dropping hints and secrets about the characters and their past in a manner designed to "'preach to the nerves'" (Cvetkovich 14). Its plot too is typical of a sensation novel, for it features the plights of two women caught in different ways between society's demands and expectations of them as women and their potential for inner happiness.

Yet the seeds of a detective novel are also present, as Joseph Kestner argues. Most noticeably, Braddon uses the same title as a short story by Edgar Allen Poe, which includes such early detective fiction traits as false clues, ballistics study, and the murderer as the least likely suspect (56). Braddon's transfer of the madness motif from a female (a la Lady Audley) to a male character moves the story from a typical sensation plot to "part of a larger legal/medical/detectival debate about criminality and about masculinity" (63). Lastly, the novel's use of "retrospective narration" (57) also provides some elements of a detective story. The pages from Cora's two diaries, one written for herself and one for her father, are interspersed with a third-person narrator's voice which details events of the past and current calamities, which Kestner argues is a deliberate nod to Doyle's narrative structure in *A Study in Scarlet.*[6]

Both the physical lay-out of the novel, with its chapter-by-chapter inter-weaving of voices, and its content, showing Cora's slow awakening to the truth, highlight the confusion and negotiating process a young woman must go through in finding herself and her voice. When she eventually refuses to comply with her father's plans to use her as a spy—declining her role as detec-tive—she moves from a helpless dependent to a self-assured woman, sym-bolically and literally overthrowing patriarchal rule.

The story opens with an introduction to the two main women charac-ters: Lady Sibyl Penrith, who lives comfortably but not lovingly with her hus-band and who has a secret hidden in her past; and her niece through marriage, Coralie Urquhart, who is about 18 years old when she comes to live with her aunt and uncle. Cora has been raised unconventionally, in Paris and in boarding houses and by governesses—wherever her half-hearted father felt like placing her. Yet she still holds very traditional views about her lot in life, telling Lady Penrith that her father taught her that her "mission in life is to marry": "Well, if I can, badly, if I can't; at any rate to get myself some kind of a husband, so as to take myself off the paternal hands [...]. So long as I don't worry or burden him he is satisfied" (1: 17).

Conflicting aspects of Cora's character—headstrong and intelligent, yet stolid and hemmed in by society's conventions—are seen also in her discus-sion of reading material, as she balances the traditional Lady Penrith's love of books to her own tastes:

> I never read a book when I can get a newspaper; and I infinitely prefer *Truth* and the *World* to any of the authors who are called classics. Nor do I see that book-learning is of the slightest use to any young woman who does not want to write school-books or go out as a governess. The little I have seen of mascu-line society has shown me that men detest "culture" in a woman [1: 44–45].

Cora's preference for newspapers is a sign of her unconventional upbringing; her father has not bothered to monitor her reading material. At the same time, she uses the fact that men do not like learned women as an excuse not to read books, for she cannot see the need for intelligence beyond what is required for getting a husband.

Father and daughter are not close; nonetheless, when Cora's father demands that she keep a diary to track his sister-in-law's movements, Cora does not even consider saying no:

> "Well, you will keep a diary in future, if you please, Cora; and you will keep it in such a manner as will admit of your allowing me to read it. [...] I want you to observe her closely, and to write down everything that concerns her [...].
> "Father," said Cora, looking at him with wide-open eyes and hardening lips, more earnestly than she had ever looked at him in her life before, "you want me to be a spy!"

"No, my dear; I only want you to be an observer. My interest in Lady Penrith is founded on the purest motives [...]" [1: 30–31].

Needless to say, her father's interest in Lady Penrith is by no means pure, though Cora does not discover his less-than-altruistic motives until much later. In the meantime, she throws herself whole-heartedly into her new task, out of both submission and boredom: "All the resources of my intelligence are henceforth pledged to the solution of this social mystery. I have very little to think about [...] and for want of interest in my own insignificant existence I am naturally thrown upon speculation about my aunt" (1: 61). For Cora, writing serves as little more than an intellectual exercise or a respite from loneliness. Perhaps Braddon means to show the difficulties faced by intelligent women who are given no fulfilling employment, for in this case it is certainly boredom that contributes to Cora's zealous performance of her less-than-ladylike task.

As the "author of her being" (1: 54), as Cora calls him, Cora's father has the right to demand her acquiescence in his scheme, and she does not demur. But she does not strictly comply either. In order to circumvent complete capitulation of her feelings to her father, she resorts to duplicity:

> My father honoured me by expressing a desire to read my jottings about her ladyship; I have therefore commenced a system of diary-keeping by double entry. What I mean him to read I write in one volume; my own little reveries I keep to myself in another volume [1: 38].

Her weekly updates to her father fall under chapter headings like "for paternal perusal" and "for paternal inspection." In classic spy-like fashion, she registers her letters specially with the post, using ciphers instead of real names, and sending a key to the ciphers in a separate letter. And while her father occasionally compliments Cora—"you have the pen of a ready writer, Cora. You ought to do something in literature, by-and-by" (2: 244)—he soon after returns to the "strictly paternal" voice of a father both demanding and dismissing: "Go on with your journal. It is capital practice for your pen [...]. The task is so good for you as a literary exercise that I won't even thank you for doing it. Indeed, you ought to thank me for putting it upon you to do" (2: 246).

Yet as his demands increase, Cora begins to questions her father's motives. When she asks to be let in on the true meaning of her "secret police work" (2: 86), her father upbraids her:

> "Come, Cora, I am not going to be questioned about my past life by my own daughter."
> "And I am not going to act as your spy any more unless you give me your confidence," Cora answered resolutely, looking her father full in the face.
> There was no filial love in that look [3: 72].

This decision on Cora's part to "do no more for him unless he trusts me fully" (3: 65) is a firm one, and she is filled with a sense of remorse at the potential damage she has unwittingly done. She not only refuses to send details but stops reporting altogether. Her secret police work has stopped, one half of the journal ended.

The diary she keeps for herself, however, has expanded into a friend she affectionately calls "Letts," and she spends more and more hours of the day and night writing. Though writing began as a task to relieve boredom and to please her father, she discovers she loves it and is good at it. She has even begun to contemplate writing as a career to support herself in the future, so she does not have to be one of the "thousands of women" who are "striving and wrestling to get themselves decently married for the sake of food and raiment, a shelter, and a fireside!" (1: 52). Knowing her father's disreputable character, she is certain no one will want to marry her:

> [...] here I am at a quarter to seven still scribbling the record of the day, for my own amusement only. I find an undiminishing interest in this volume, and the facility with which my pen runs along the page makes me think that I shall some day blossom into a novelist.
>
> I see myself ten years hence a spinster novelist, in a snug little house—in Mayfair. The merest doll's house would do, provided it were in a smart street [3: 110].

Unfortunately, her father's actions lead her to cease writing in her own volume of the journal as well, when she realizes that Lord Penrith's hunting "accident" was actually his murder, committed by her father, the heir presumptive: "I shall write no more in this journal. I close the book for ever this miserable night. My heart is frozen" (3: 122). For Cora, the journal was the means through which she uncovered her father's secret past: he murdered Lady Penrith's adopted sister and framed Lady Penrith's lover, actions which contributed to his present fratricide. Its guilty associations force her to abandon it, as what she thought was a semi-harmless detective game became a deadly venture in which she was used as a pawn.

Braddon's characterization works on many levels to highlight the conflicts in the story. Cora is trapped between silence and speaking; between personal tastes and society's demands; between her father and Lady Penrith ("I must be loyal to him, however disloyal I may be to my uncle's wife," she says at one point (2: 247); between self-respect and degradation in the name of familial duty. The duality of her journal, and its usurpation for her father's nefarious designs, works as a literal version of the less visible divisions in Cora's life.

Cora's personality also seems split by the changing times in which she lives. She has been taught since she was young that she must marry; yet because women outnumbered men, a fact trumpeted loudly in the 1890s, marriage was not possible for all women. She desires to be the type of woman a respectable man might want—beautiful, demure, and semi-intelligent—yet she is plain-looking, has an acerbic wit and enjoys riding horses and playing pool, active pursuits more fitting the New Woman than the traditional aristocracy. She has the standards of an earl's niece, and so even though she is poor and thinks she'll have to support herself as a spinster novelist, she wants to live in a smart street in Mayfair. The happy ending to Cora's story combines these profiles; she marries a man who loves horses and hunting as much as she does. Even so, her life as Lady Coralie Hildrop is described by Braddon in terms of contradiction: she is "liked by a good many people, and feared by the rest" and is "a good friend, a bitter enemy, and without mercy for any pretty woman who misbehaves herself" (3: 253).

Wolff mentions *Thou Art the Man* only once in his comprehensive biography and dismisses it as an "unsuccessful variation on the theme of *The Fatal Three*" (473, fn30), an earlier and more popular Braddon novel. The variation is one involving Lady Penrith and her half-sister, and Wolff does not mention Cora's storyline at all. Yet it seems to me a story equally important as Lady Penrith's; certainly the fact that Braddon chooses Cora to serve as part-narrator forces the reader to identify with Cora's ongoing self-assessment and growth, both as a young woman and as a blossoming writer. Her journal serves as a means through which Braddon challenges the propriety of men controlling women's writing and reading, a challenge which she accepted and won in her own life.

Braddon's work not only shows her creating and maintaining her personal and professional authority, but shaping an entire sub-genre of popular fiction. She is a unique example of the fortitude and business acumen that women were capable of maintaining despite cultural constraints. The increased professionalism towards women's writing, which she helped establish, added to the ways in which women writers, including detective fiction writers, could construct and explore their own professional authority, and not despite the popularity of fiction but because of it.

Christie's Literary Heroine

It was thirty years before another female writer-detective character appeared in a novel by a woman, and the changes in women's lifestyles during this time period, brought about especially because of World War I, are immediately apparent in the confidence shown in the narrative of this later character. Agatha Christie's young female detective from *The Man in the Brown Suit* (1924), Anne Beddingfeld, reflects elements of Christie's own lit-

erary ability, seen both in Anne's first-person narration and in her employment in the plotline as a newspaper correspondent. Though Anne shows
similarities to Cora Urquhart, not the least of which is their writing abilities, Christie's novel is more complex as a document exploring the role of
writing and of women writers in the early twentieth century.

The worlds of these two young writer/detectives are both widely disparate and startlingly similar. While this might be attributed in part to the
"required" themes of popular culture,[7] it says more about the scripts available to women in fiction, that after thirty years the same themes, complete
with marriage in the last chapter, must be played out. Both women are moth-
erless and are raised solely by their fathers, though Mr. Beddingfeld is much
kinder to Anne than Hubert Urquhart was to Cora. This half-hearted
upbringing from distant fathers, along with the loneliness and boredom it
entails, contributes to their unconventional tastes and behavior.

A more notable similarity is their roles as writers, one of a (semi-) private journal, the other of a published book (Anne "writes" *The Man in the
Brown Suit*) and of newspaper articles. Anne has the fields of both popular
fiction and journalism open to her, two areas that in Cora Urquhart's day
would not have been thought entirely appropriate. Christie's decision to
include these elements in her novel shows the expansion in her day of the
limits which once contained women, an expansion from which Christie herself benefited: she received 500 pounds from the *Evening News* for allowing
them to run it as a serial.[8] These developments in women's opportunities
provide more chances for women—like Christie and like Anne—to succeed
as writers.

Unlike Cora then, Anne can tell her story with assurance and self-
confidence, as her society provides greater scope for her intelligence.
Christie's initial image of Anne—a "gay, adventurous young woman, an
orphan, who started out to seek adventure" (*Autobiography* 315)—fits solidly
into a traditional fictional pattern for young heroines. But from the beginning of Anne's narrative it is clear she is made of different stuff; a mere three
paragraphs in she is effortlessly, and with a good deal of humor, espousing
her late father's penchant for Primitive Man, in the process showing a scientific knowledge few people (much less women) possess: "Papa did not care
for modern man—even Neolithic Man he despised as a mere herder of cat-
tle, and he did not rise to enthusiasm until he reached the Mousterian
period [...]. Frankly, I hate Palaeolithic Man, be he Aurignacian, Mousterian, Chellian, or anything else" (6–7).

Moving to London after her father unexpectedly dies, Anne is soon
bored and disgusted with the women she meets at her new friends' home;
though rich, they never seemed satisfied, and their lives, ringed by servants,
milk, and sick children, seemed endlessly dull to her. Furthermore, she

writes, "they *were* stupid—stupid at even their chosen job: most of them kept the most extraordinarily inadequate and muddled housekeeping accounts" (16). Anne's inquisitiveness and intelligence soon provide relief, however, after she witnesses an accident at the tube station, the action which starts the mystery. Having worked in a hospital during the war (like Christie), she realizes that the "doctor" who appeared to take care of the accident victim was a fake by his awkwardness when handling the man. She goes to the police station to convince Inspector Meadows that the doctor wasn't really a doctor and that he was wearing a disguise, but he clearly doesn't believe her theory and dismisses her politely. Anne gets angry and rises to leave.

> "Nothing more you can tell us about him?" he demanded as I rose to depart.
> "Yes," I said. I seized my opportunity to fire a parting shot. "His head was markedly brachycephalic. He will not find it so easy to alter that."
> I observed with pleasure that Inspector Meadow's pen wavered. It was clear that he did not know how to spell brachycephalic [25].

Like most people well-versed in a specific topic, Anne assumes that her obscure knowledge is commonplace; here her scope of knowledge is even more impressive because it is part of a scientific and usually masculine area of expertise. But she is not even aware of her question's peculiarity when she asks the housekeeper at Mill House, where another murder occurred, "what kind of head" the last visitor had, trying to ascertain whether the two crimes were connected. "Just the ordinary kind, miss" (33), the housekeeper replies.

Anne's intelligence is also reflected in her writing ability. For instance, Anne serves as secretary to her father, having typed and revised her father's book on primitive peoples. But Anne contemplates taking this oft-neglected women's contribution to published scholarly work a step further. When her father angrily refuses to write a series of popular articles on humanity's relationship to monkeys for a newspaper, Anne thinks of running after the offending reporter and telling him that her father would send in the articles to the paper after all, for as she says, "I could easily have written them myself, and the probabilities were that Papa would never have learnt of the transaction, not being a reader of the *Daily Budget*" (7–8). Christie condenses Anne's abilities into one sentence here, but it is worth separating out these ideas: Anne not only has ample scholarly knowledge, but she is able to "popularize" that knowledge for a newspaper-reading public. Neither of these areas had in the past been considered particularly customary for women.

Anne does not take her chance with the newspaper this time, believing that the possibility her father might find out it makes it "too risky" (8). However, after her father's death, she does take the chance; indeed, she makes her chance. After being rebuffed by Inspector Meadows at the police station, Anne brazenly walks to the house of Lord Nasby, owner of the *Daily Budget* newspaper, tricks her way into his presence, tells him she has secret information about the Mill House Mystery, and asks to be given a job on the paper to investigate the matter. Lord Nasby recognizes Anne's intelligence—"well, you seem to have a head of some kind upon your own shoulders, young woman" (27)—and tells her to keep working on her line. If she uncovers anything she should send it along; if it is publishable, she'll be put on the payroll.

Anne uses this opportunity to provide herself with a reason for staying in South Africa, where she can keep a close eye on the Man in the Brown Suit. While there she sends lengthy cables to Lord Nasby, and thanks to Anne,

> the *Daily Budget* had the scoop of its lifetime. "Victim of the Mill House Murder identified by our special reporter." And so on. "Our reporter makes voyage with the murderer. 'The Man in the Brown Suit.' What he is really like."
> The main facts were, of course, cabled to the South African papers [...]. I received approval and full instructions by cable at Bulawayo. I was on the staff of the *Daily Budget*, and I had a private word of congratulation from Lord Nasby himself [143].

Using writing, Anne not only finds a cover for her detective work but is also able to make money and support herself. This increased role of newspapers as a form of women's writing within her detective fiction provides Christie with a way to emphasize women's ability to write in different popular formats.

Anne's voice in *The Man in the Brown Suit* is interspersed with that of Sir Eustace Pedlar's "private reminiscences," and Christie represents him as a member of the typical "masculine" and "old-fashioned" world. Not surprisingly, his descriptions of Anne's work for the *Daily Budget* are decidedly different and negative. Though he admits Anne is clever, he can't imagine "how she ever got on the staff of the *Daily Budget*" (138). She is full of "coaxing ways that mask an invincible determination" (138). Her determination to track down the Man in the Brown Suit makes her "cold blooded": "I hinted to her that it was an unwomanly action. She laughed at me. She assured me that did she run him to earth her fortune was made" (139). Furthermore, he scoffs at her "deduction" as to the identity of the victim at Mill House: "Women have these intuitions—I've no doubt that Anne Beddingfeld is perfectly right in her guess—but to call it a deduction is absurd" (138). By alternating young with old, female with male, new viewpoints with faded ones, Christie can, without one word from an omniscient narrator's point of view, make Anne's world (and her own) the desirable one, the world that must be ushered in. The time for Sir Eustace's old-fashioned stereotypes is gone.

Through Anne, Christie is able to comment upon the social debates going on around her, especially society's limitations of women, which, with great fun, she shows Anne supremely able to overcome. Though she would not describe herself as a feminist, Christie's female characters are never limited by traditional notions of their intended sphere or by what others think they could or should be able to do. Miss Marple, an elderly logician, is the consummate example of this. Thus Christie, through the numerous female detectives she created to challenge the stereotypes surrounding women, actively engaged in expanding these limitations, discovering in the process a way to establish her own authority in the genre.

But Christie was able to take her fiction a step further. Her self-conscious play with aspects of the detective fiction genre, writing stories which continually extended its limits while remaining within an established form, speaks not only to her investment in the popular marketplace—she wanted to write books that would sell—but identifies a strategic way in which later women writers were able to establish their authority in the genre. The self-referential nature of several of her novels is one example of Christie's literary self-consciousness. Christie's characters make constant references to the detective fiction genre, showing a belief in its plausibility and treating it seriously. In *The Man in the Brown Suit*, Anne plays the role of "young detective" very consciously from the beginning, when trying to figure out what to do next: "Of course! I must visit the 'scene of the crime.' Always done by the best sleuths!" (30). When she gets to the house, she is disappointed that she cannot find anything: "there was not so much as a pin lying about. The gifted young detective did not seem likely to discover a neglected clue" (35). And in her analysis of suspects, she immediately reverts to the tropes with which she is familiar: "'if you've read any detective stories, Suzanne, you must know that it's always the most unlikely person who's the villain'" (124).

Christie's second novel featuring Tommy and Tuppence Beresford, *Partners in Crime* (1929), is completely dedicated to her fellow authors of detective fiction, and she pays her homage to them by following the adage that imitation is the sincerest form of flattery. In each chapter of the book, Tommy and Tuppence take on the personas of a different detective of the day, imitating their habits and attempting to follow their methods in solving the various crimes. They begin with Holmes, naturally, and then move to the more contemporary Dr. Thorndyke (Austin Freeman), and Orczy's Old Man in the Corner; even Christie's own Poirot is caricatured in one of the final chapters of the book. Confident in her own work and style, Christie begins to play with the styles of others. H. Douglas Thompson writes of this book that "it is almost as if she had set herself to learn all she could about the methods and technique of 'How to Write A Detective Story for Profit'—and then proceeded to pull legs" (in Bloom, *British* 22). His analysis highlights both the parodic aspects of her craft and its money-making nature, both of which are self-conscious displays of her professional authority.

Alison Light writes that the signs of modernity in Christie's fiction are clearest in her "dabbling in available popular forms throughout the 1920s, and the ironised use of earlier literary conventions" (66). I see this "modernity" in part as a by-product of the authority that she worked to consolidate during this time period, as her ability to "dabble" in and "ironise" earlier literary conventions speaks to a control and self-assurance that earlier women writers in the genre did not have. Christie's varied means of deliberately emphasizing the generic components of detective fiction in her novels is at the very least a sign of the genre's pervasiveness in the 1920s and 1930s. Christie consciously contributed to the widespread dissemination of detective fiction with an earnestness that furthered not only the genre's popularity but her own popularity as well. In the process, she embraced the chance to create fictional female characters that belied her society's narrow view of women.

Female Detectives as Writers of Detective Fiction

In yet another more pointed narrative strategy used by women detective fiction writers during this time, we find fictional female detectives who are writers of detective fiction. In effect, these writers put their fictional creations in the same role as themselves. Georgette Heyer in *A Blunt Instrument* creates Sally Drew, a writer of murder mysteries whose sister is implicated in the crime. Agatha Christie creates Ariadne Oliver, a clear spoof of herself who works in several novels in tandem with Hercule Poirot. Finally, Dorothy L. Sayers and her detective fiction novelist, Harriet D. Vane, whom I discuss in the next chapter, emerge as the most complete examples of this strategy.

We can see the strategic examination that can occur when detective fiction writers create fictional detective fiction writers who also work as detectives as part of the plots of their stories. These women writers are able introduce a subplot into the main plot which allows them to thematize and examine more closely what it means to become a professional writer. These women were able to define their own roles in part by using characters who mirrored themselves. In this way, they explored what it meant to be women writers in their society.

The outcome of this layering works on two levels. On the most basic level, their self-referential characters work as parodies, both of themselves as writers of detective fiction and of the genre itself, which by the 1930s was ripe for parody. Their portrayals of these women, who are so clearly meant to represent themselves, add an element of humor to their novels, largely at their own expense, as they caricature the work they do and the way their society sees them as Lady Mystery Novelists.

A more important outcome of using their characters as reflections of themselves is the way they use their "alter-egos" to thematize issues of their writing difficulties. What they choose as authors to say through these characters—about the way they shape their fiction and the characters within their fiction—reveal, as Maida and Spornick say of Christie, "as much about creator as creation" (143). It serves as perhaps the most potent example of the way women writers used their female detective creations to question the limitations that their society's gender ideology placed upon women and the ways it affected their own work as women writers. Their decision to engage their material in this way—exposing both the challenges of writing and the inherent fictiveness of their work—shows a mastery of and authority in the detective fiction genre that earlier women writers had not exhibited.

Sally Drew: Heyer's Serious Parody

Though Georgette Heyer, like many of these women, was a prolific writer, she created only twelve detective novels (the same number as Sayers). She was better known for her forty or so meticulously researched romance novels set in London's Regency era.[9] Educated at seminaries and briefly at Westminster College, Heyer wrote her first novel in 1919 when she was only seventeen; it was published two years later. She published twelve more Regency-era romances before writing her first detective novel, *Footsteps in the Dark* (1932), and she continued to write both types of novels for the rest of her career. Though she and her husband lived in both East Africa and Yugoslavia, her novels are particularly London-based, and her detective and domestic romance novels both center around the enclosed spaces of country houses or London flats. She wrote nearly sixty novels in all before her death in 1974.

Heyer's works of detective fiction do not star a female detective proper but usually two policemen from Scotland Yard, Hannysade and Hemingway. In many of these mysteries, however, including *A Blunt Instrument* (1938), one or more of the central female characters, usually young, sarcastic, and eccentric, do detective work of some kind, either trying to clear their own or a loved one's name or, as is the case in this novel and in *Death in the Stocks*, "helping" the police think of additional motives for murder. In *A*

Blunt Instrument, the police try to discover who killed Ernest Fletcher and how. Among the suspects are several of these flippant young people Heyer is known for creating: Ernie's nephew Neville, his neighbors John North and Helen North, the latter of whom Ernie was blackmailing, or Helen's sister Sally Drew, a writer of mystery novels.

Though Sally Drew is not officially involved in the case, she is interested in investigating the crime for two reasons: one, because she wishes to help clear her sister of any involvement, a motive consistent with that of many amateur female detectives from this time period; and two, because she is anxious to learn ways she can improve her fiction through being involved with this "real" murder case. In this overlap of fictional and "real" crime-solving, Heyer parodies detective fiction writers and the seriousness with which they view themselves and their fiction, which was seen by their contemporaries as anything from essentially escapist to "merely" popular. In the post-war years, when readers wanted entertainment more than anything else and found it in detective fiction, Heyer especially gives her readers what they want. Sally Drew functions both as a commentator on the process of crime writing, as through her Heyer discusses some of the technical difficulties of constructing a novel, and as a symbol of a genre which was seemingly without limits, in popularity and sales and in elaborateness of narrative, in which murder itself is reduced to a plot for the next novel. In their mention of Heyer's "ironic treatment of character" in the preface to this novel, critics Barzun and Taylor clearly have not only the "sardonic beaux" Neville in mind, but Sally as well.

Sally's characterization also exposes at its roots a more serious situation, as much parody does. Throughout this novel Sally exhibits great ignorance about what can and should be done to further along a police investigation, which is not surprising since she is not a detective. But in trying to "use" her fiction as a blueprint to help solve the crime (which, like Anne Beddingfeld, many amateur detectives do), it becomes apparent that she is ignorant about even those elements which in her *fiction* help solve the crime. Since Heyer herself went to great lengths to ensure accuracy in her fiction (as did Christie and Sayers), her creation of a character who is unable to create realistic scenarios in a genre that depends to a great extent on the plausibility of the events speaks to a greater purpose. It is true that Sally's ignorance of "real life" is humorous; the parody works on that level. However, it is also true that there were few opportunities for women in detective work and that the reputation of women police in the 1930s was very low. Thus, Sally's "stupidity" is also very much related to her society's belief about what women should be allowed to do. While Sally is not literally confined to the home, she is nonetheless confined to her fiction and has little opportunity of experiencing those circumstances which occur in her fiction. In poking fun at women writers who double as amateur detectives, these authors expose an underlying problem and the reason the joke exists. They show how so few women have the opportunities open to them to be able to contribute to their professions in a meaningful way.

Sally's narrow and indeed shallow outlook towards the murder is apparent from the outset. After Ernie Fletcher is found murdered in his study, Neville, his nephew, walks over to their neighbors' house, where Jerry and Helen North and her sister Sally Drew live, to tell Helen that he failed to retrieve her gambling I.O.U.s from Ernie's safe. He then adds, offhandedly, that Ernie has just been killed. Sally Drew, interested mildly because her sister might be implicated (because Ernie bought up her gambling debts), is more seriously attracted to the details of the murder because she is a writer and "it might be good copy" (26). When Neville tells them that Ernie had his head smashed in, Helen is disgusted, but Sally nods her head comprehendingly, "with the air of a connoisseur. 'A blow from a blunt instrument,' she said. 'Any idea who did it?'" (27). From this point on, Sally slips completely into the conventionalities of detective fiction, with her inability to see past the obvious in reconstructing the murder resembling something akin to writer's block.

Indeed, Sally is hampered in her desire to help find the murderer because she cannot see any way of thinking about the crime except for how she would have written it, continually comparing real life to her crime fiction. The best example of this occurs when these three players—Sally, Helen, and Neville—try to think of a way to get the implicating I.O.U.s out of Ernie's safe. Neither Neville or Helen succeeded through mere talking and cajoling; but Sally, who knows that "'there are ways of opening safes'" because characters in her books do it all the time, wonders why they just don't make a "soup" to blow it up. When questioned, she exhibits an ignorance that would make any serious crime fiction writer wince: soup is "'the stuff you blow open safes with. I forget exactly what it's made of, but it's an explosive of sorts'" (39).

Though she claims that her interest in the murder is "'purely academic'" (83), she is upset with their inability to act, to do something definitive: "'We can't open the safe, and we don't know how to get by the policeman. In fact, we're futile. But if I created this situation in a book I could think of something for the book me to do. Why the devil can't I think of something now?'" (40). Neville tells her its because her characters are always "'rather more than life-size'"; in her fiction they should have both more nerve and more brains. He says to Sally:

> "You, for instance, would know how to make your soup—"
> "And where to buy the—the ingredients, which actually one just doesn't know," she interpolated.

"Exactly. Helen would go and scream blue murder outside the house, to draw the policeman off while you blew up the safe, and I should put up a great act to regale him with on his return, telling him I thought I heard some-one in the study, and leading him there when you'd beaten it with the incrimi-nating documents. And can you see any one of us doing any of it?" [40].

When Sally complains about Helen's obviousness as a decoy, Neville glibly continues the patter of detective fiction: "'Helen would never be seen. She'd have merged into the night by the time the policeman got there'" (40).

Heyer presents several such opportunities to parody detective fiction, and specifically detective fiction writers, in this novel. For Sally, what hap-pens in her work is more real than "real life," to the point where the two get switched around. As Sally points out to Sergeant Hemingway, a real life murder is much more difficult to accommodate than one supplied by detec-tive fiction. In discussing her "plans" to blow up the safe, she believes that:

"If I'd had my criminal notebook with me, and time to think it out, I believe I could have had a stab at it. [...] if I'd been writing this story, I should have thought up a perfectly plausible reason for the fictitious me to have the means at hand of concocting the stuff you call soup. I should have turned myself into a scientist's assistant, with the run of his laboratory, or something like that" [181].

When Neville comments upon what has by this time become obvious, that "'whoever killed Ernie disposed of the weapon with such skill as to pro-vide this case with its most baffling feature,'" Sally responds, "'Very nice [...]. You've been reading my books'" (153), as if such a thing as a blow with a blunt instrument had been invented in the pages of detective fiction. And, not surprisingly, her deductions as to the method and means of the mur-der are all wrong, since she can only go by what she's written. For instance, Sally is "'not a believer in these sudden flashes of brilliance of the part of murderers'" and therefore thinks the murder must have been well planned, because, as she says, "'when I think out a bit of dazzling ingenuity for my criminal to indulge in, it usually costs me several hours of brain-racking thought'" (153). Of course, in this case, the murder *was* done in a "sudden flash"—of brilliance and anger—with little foresight. But for Sally, who must ponderously think out elaborately-laid plots and examine every detail, such an action is impractical and highly improbable.

Detective fiction's popularity is also parodied in a conversation Miss Fletcher, Ernest's sister, has with Sally. Upon meeting her at her brother's house during the murder investigation, Miss Fletcher, in the manner of an out-of-touch upper class spinster/household manager, says, "'I expect you must find this all *most* interesting. I always think it so clever of you to write books. So complicated, too. Not that I've read them, of course, because I find I'm too stupid to understand detective stories, but I always put them down on my library list'" (155).

Heyer herself was very knowledgeable about everything in her books and would never have included details about a procedure—such as how to blow up a safe—about which she knew nothing. But in creating such an inept amateur detective, Heyer perhaps is also poking fun at and distinguishing herself from her fellow detective fiction writers, who create amateur detectives with the ability to solve crime regardless of their place in life. Detective fiction critics too receive Heyer's sarcasm, for, as Sally reminds Neville, even though her novels are "'improbable,'" the critics consider her "'one of the six most important crime novelists'" of her time (29). In the 1930's world of detective fiction mania, this is high praise indeed.

Clearly in Heyer's case, her "detective" work lies elsewhere; in this, perhaps, she agreed with those who said that women would not make good detectives though they might make good detective fiction writers. But again, this characterization is also a function of society's still-limited roles for women in the work world, especially detective work. Heyer's portrayal of Sally Drew, while nominally providing a venue for discussing the craft of detective fiction, works also as a general parody of detective fiction of the genre and of writers like herself who cashed in on the craze; within that parody is the seed of a larger issue surrounding society's limitations of women.

Christie in Disguise? Mrs. Ariadne Oliver

With Christie's Ariadne Oliver, the portrait of a "detective fiction writer" grows a bit more, extending beyond obvious parody to include an obvious self-portrait as well. Ariadne Oliver is more clearly an effort at self-portrayal than Sally Drew is of Heyer; she is indeed, as Maida and Spornick claim, an "artistic projection of self" (141) and therefore provides insight into Christie's writing habits, her values, and possibly her own relationship to her writing and to her public. Furthermore, in exploring the difficulties of writing through a fictional surrogate, Christie is able to address more fully the problems faced by literary women.

Ariadne Oliver does not begin her career as an obvious stand-in for Christie but first appears as a "writer of sensation fiction" in *Parker Pyne Investigates* (1934). Mr. Pyne is not a detective so much as a sort of "happiness broker." After customers tell him their problem, he classifies the cause of their unhappiness and then constructs an elaborate ruse around them, designed to fulfill their wishes. Each of Pyne's employees has a specialization that he or she brings to the job of "making people happy." Ariadne Oliver's job is to script tales of danger for people to star in whose cause of unhappiness stems from boredom. She creates model sensation plots for

house, to keep her childhood home, to support herself and her daughter after her divorce. Similarly, Mrs. Oliver admits that money motivates her: "'Some days I can only keep going by repeating over and over to myself the amount of money I might get for my next serial rights. That spurs you on, you know. So does your bank book when you see how much overdrawn you are'" (127).

They are also similar in their knowledge of the popular marketplace and the necessity of giving readers what they want. Mrs. Oliver debunks the "glamour" of the writing profession when she acknowledges the difficulties of writing in a pre-determined literary form for a demanding public: "'I always think I've finished and then when I count up I find I've only written thirty thousand words instead of sixty thousand and so then I have to throw in another murder and get the heroine kidnapped again. Its all very boring" (128). Similarly, Christie says that the only criticism she will give to other writers is about the proper length for a book—that one must be business-like and match the story to its market. One wonders what "additional" murders appear in Christie's works in order to satisfy this demand; as Mrs. Oliver says, just add another body when things start to get dull— "'some more blood cheers it up!'" (56).

Christie was never comfortable as a best-selling author, being both a terribly shy woman and one raised to avoid the limelight. And while writing was certainly an acceptable pastime, it was not considered a career, either by society as a whole or by Christie, as a product of her society. She writes that even as late as 1930, though she had been a best-selling author for years, she would never have dreamt of saying that her occupation was "anything but the time-honoured 'married woman'" (442). Christie hated publicity, rarely gave interviews, and did not like to discuss the private details of her life or work. Through Mrs. Oliver, however, Christie discusses some of the difficulties faced not only by herself but by women writers in a popular genre as a whole: they often had to write for money, an essentially un-feminine act; they had to manipulate plots to match an "ideal" length, limiting their freedom to write as they chose; and, once they became famous, they were indebted to a sometimes unforgiving and rapacious public, which demanded both quantity and quality.

As in Heyer's novel, there exists in *Cards* an uncertain relationship between the "real world" and the world of fiction, with women's place in both commented on by the authors. As portrayed by Heyer and Christie, women writers of detective fiction are naive and inexperienced in the ways of the world. For instance, Mrs. Oliver, like Sally Drew, speaks of the "inadequacy" of the real crime in which she is involved when compared to the crimes which occur in her novels, and she is vocal about the way she would have planned it better. Thus she is disappointed when Superintendent Battle of Scotland Yard interviews first the man she "knows" is the murderer, pointing out that she would have kept him to the end:

> "In a book I mean," she added apologetically.
> "Real life's a bit different," said Battle.
> "I know," said Mrs. Oliver. "Badly constructed" [27].

The supposed superiority of fiction to reality is also discussed between Mrs. Oliver and Superintendent Battle when they compare the merits of murdering with an untraceable poison, which Mrs. Oliver says fiction-readers prefer, to the more traditional arsenic, which Battle says most murderers use, since they are generally a class of people not very subtle. But the conversation turns to the merits of women as crime-solvers over men. Mrs. Oliver states her belief that many murderers use obscure poisons, but since men—who are also not subtle—are responsible for solving crimes, the murders go undetected:

> "That's simply because there are lots of crimes you people at Scotland Yard never find out. Now if you had a woman there—"
> "As a matter of fact we have—"
> "Yes, those dreadful policewomen in funny hats who bother people in parks! I mean a Woman at the Head of things. Women *know* about crime" [14].

Battle picks up on Mrs. Oliver's comments later when they discuss how to go about interviewing the four potential murderers. Mrs. Oliver, who guesses immediately that Dr. Roberts has killed Mr. Shaitana, opts for arresting him at once. Battle says good-naturedly that if perhaps a Woman were at the Head of things they could proceed in that way, but since "'mere men'" are in charge they have to "'be careful'" and "'get there slowly,'" a procedure which Mrs. Oliver finds annoying: "'Oh, men—men,' sighed Mrs. Oliver and began to compose newspaper articles in her head" (26). Mrs. Oliver's creation of newspaper articles not only shows her preference for fiction and invention over reality (the articles presumably are about the suspect's capture, which has not yet occurred), but it also shows women's greater comfort in the public sphere represented by newspapers, compared to women's more ambivalent status earlier in the century.

Mrs. Oliver's dismissive comments about policewomen reiterate society's popular perception of them as unnecessary. As Chapter One pointed out, policewomen had very little authority when they were finally "officially" appointed as part of the force; Mary Allen's history of women police notes that after taking away the title of Metropolitan Police and any powers of arrest they may have had, the "duties" of policewomen were "correspondingly curtailed" (Allen 130)—thus Mrs. Oliver's impression that they did nothing but "bother people in parks." It is quite possible that women were given little else to do beyond patrol work, thus bearing witness to the literal truth of that statement. Regardless of their true status on the force in 1936, it is important to note that they were portrayed negatively in the pages of popular fiction.

Mrs. Oliver seems to reject that limited role for women, arguing that they should have more power, significantly, because they "know about crime." She seems to imply that it is only from lack of training and opportunity that they are not in greater positions of power; as women, inherently, they belong in the "unwomanly" realm of crime. Thus she rejects the outdated conception that a woman's place is the home—it can be in Scotland Yard as well.

At the same time, however, Mrs. Oliver's comments are clearly supposed to be funny; the idea of a Woman at the Head of Scotland Yard is not taken seriously by the other characters in the story, nor seemingly by Christie. Christie's professed view of working women was low. She called women "mugs" for wanting the same work as men. Her portrayal of Mrs. Oliver, a mere writer who clearly has no idea what the job of Head of Scotland Yard actually entails or how to go about solving a crime, highlights the apparent absurdity of women wanting men's jobs.

Yet Christie's novels as a whole belie this negative view of women's capabilities, containing as they do a multitude of strong positive working women. This includes women writers of detective fiction, and this includes Christie herself, as she was one of several women who changed the way the world viewed women's role as "detective fiction writer" during the Golden Age. Christie perhaps more than anyone else helped prove conclusively that if women do not have a place as crime-solvers in the "real" world, then they have at least made their presence indubitably felt in the world of crime fiction.

Christie developed Mrs. Oliver over thirty-eight years, ending with *Elephants can Remember* (1972). It is clear that she took care in creating this character and meant her to be more than a mere spoof of herself. Sylvia Patterson, in "Agatha Christie's Alter-Ego" concludes that while Christie "never took herself too seriously—witness her self-parody—she did in her self-portrait take her writing seriously" (227). Through Ariadne Oliver, Christie presents both an enjoyable fictitious character and an insightful look into the problems and motivations of being a successful mystery writer. In doing so, she more completely examines in her fiction the relationship between women writers and popular fiction.

In light of women's uneasy relationship with popular fictional media at the beginning of the century, it should not seem odd that women writers would choose to create a character whose own relationship to the public reflects that uneasiness. Portraying female detectives entering the public sphere gave women writers an opportunity to create something more in their fiction than entertainment, without forgetting, of course, that this is the main reason they wrote in this genre. Coward and Semple argue convincingly that women writers throughout the history of the genre "have used the form to raise and explore social issues affecting women" and that "women's concerns, far from being alien to this genre, are often the very stuff of the crime novel—violence, sexual violence, conflict between individuals, and conflict between men and women" (54). This being so, one can hardly wonder at their attraction to or success in the genre.

Female detectives who pursued their work by reading daily newspapers, as well as those who became newspaper reporters and those who wrote professionally in the detective fiction genre, provided a way for women writers to talk about the issues facing them as "public" women. These characterizations worked in many ways: as a way of showing women's ability to maintain their lady-like status in the public sphere, as a humorous alter-ego, and as a doubling technique to give women writers a place for the exploration of their craft. These characters also provided ways for women writers to comment on the limitations faced by women as they attempted to enter other professions or gain experience in the world of work.

As women concerned with the scripts available to women (both in real life and in their fiction), these writers of detective fiction portrayed a unique brand of female character who combined intelligence and self-confidence with the standards of middle-class gentility. By retaining the moral authority granted to them as women by their society, and combining it with a professional authority in the work force gained over time (especially after the War), female detectives served as a means through which women writers could articulate a response to their society and challenge its strictures at the same time.

FIVE

Dorothy L. Sayers and Professional Authority

> To combine the novel of mystery with the novel of manners was the great achievement of English writers in the past, and is increasingly their ambition today. After the divorce of plot from psychology had been made absolute in the first quarter of the century, attempts at reconciliation began to be made from both sides, but the difficulties were, and still are, acute. [...] No one has yet perfectly resolved the problem.
> —Dorothy L. Sayers, *Sunday Times* (1933)

Dorothy L. Sayers, while not nearly as prolific a novel-writer as Christie, Allingham, or Marsh (often labeled the "Big Four" of the Golden Age), did more to advance and solidify the detective fiction genre than these others by her thorough and scholarly approach to the craft of writing. She also expressed more strongly in her fiction and non-fiction the desire to see women's opportunities in her society increase, by opening wider the doors of higher education and increasing the avenues of fulfilling employment. Her questioning of gender roles and her exploration of the options for women are most thoroughly delineated through her own mystery fiction writer, Harriet Vane. Like the characters created by Georgette Heyer and Agatha Christie, Sayers' Harriet Vane at times both parodies detective fiction and articulates concerns about women writing in the detective fiction genre.

However, Sayers' characterization of Harriet Vane is much more complete than that of these other characters and thus serves as a more convincing and comprehensive example of the argument posed in this study: that women writers have used their female detectives as a means of negotiating their own professional authority. Sayers uses the character of Harriet Vane to articulate some of the problems she encountered as a writer of detective fiction, as well as to discuss several issues of importance to women, especially women and work. Over the novels in which she appears—*Strong Poison, Have His Carcase, Gaudy Night*, and *Busman's Honeymoon*[1]—Harriet Vane helps Sayers dispense with standard conventions of the detective story and make it a more complete, less-formulaic tale, ushering in changes Sayers wanted to see in the detective story, including making it more of a novel of manners (as the epigram states). By intelligently discussing some of the social problems of its time, particularly the problems faced by women juggling higher education and the workplace with love and marriage, and re-introducing growth of character and thematic structure, Sayers takes an established genre and creates out of it something new.

Equally important is the way Harriet Vane provides Sayers with a venue for discussing one of her most cherished beliefs: that every person, including and especially every woman, must have meaningful work in order to be satisfied. Chapter Three looked at how she expressed this idea through the character of Miss Climpson; this chapter looks at the way that Harriet Vane as a writer emphasizes the particular dilemmas of women detective fiction writers. And, though Lord Peter Wimsey and Harriet Vane both help Sayers address issues of evil, power, and morality—issues very important to the future religious playwright and translator of Dante—only through Harriet Vane can Sayers explore the equally important issues of women's work, marriage, and higher education. Thus the Harriet Vane character is most effective in helping Sayers negotiate the parameters of her own role as a writer, by giving her greater scope to question the gender constructs of her society.

Sayers began carving out a path for herself in the literary world in her girlhood, though it was not until her late twenties that she had finally decided to make her living by writing. She was an only child, born in Oxford-shire in 1893. She had lessons in French and Latin while just a child and was educated at home until she was fifteen. She was largely unhappy at the Godolphin School, where she attended until she was eighteen, because she did not fit in. She was much farther ahead of her class in many subjects and showed off her knowledge; she was uncoordinated and tall and wore thick glasses; she did not care about typical "girl" subjects like hair ribbons and boys.[2] Her final semester was actually spent at home, where she was tutored by mail and studied for her qualifying exams for Oxford.[3]

There seemed to be no doubt in her teen years that she would attend college, as her parents avidly supported her intellectual and literary pursuits. In October 1912, she began at Somerville College, receiving one of Oxford's most honored scholarships, the Gilchrist scholarship. She sat for qualifying exams in June 1915 and earned a first-class honors in French, specializing in the medieval period.[4] After graduation, she held various teaching posts (including one from 1919–1920 at a school in France), punctuated by working as a reader for Blackwell's from 1917–1918. Her first works were volumes of poetry published by Blackwell's, Op I (1916) and Catholic Tales and Christian Songs (1919). She lived in London, trying to make a living from freelance writing, but was primarily supported by her parents and small translating jobs. She was just about to give up London and writing to take another teaching post when a job at Benson's advertising agency came through in the spring of 1922. She stayed with Benson's until 1931, only the second woman copywriter to work for the company.

Yet the most influential circumstance in her life was not literary but highly personal. Sayers had an affair in 1923 and gave birth to a son in 1924. The pregnancy was kept entirely secret: she left Benson's for an "illness" for several months, told none of her friends or relatives, and after the baby's birth, gave it to her cousin Ivy Shrimpton to raise, since Shrimpton and her mother made their living taking in foster children. She did not tell Shrimpton that the boy was her own until after all the arrangements were made, writing in letters only that she "was very personally interested in the matter" (in Reynolds 205), and Shrimpton did not even tell her own mother. Sayers married Oswald Arthur "Mac" Fleming in 1926, a journalist and gourmet cook, but the marriage was not a happy one. Mac, who got gassed during the war, became increasingly sick and clinically depressed, and then, largely unemployable, became resentful that Sayers' writing had to support them both. When John Anthony was of school age, they "unofficially adopted" him, using the name Fleming. Sayers did such a good job keeping her son's birth a secret that it was not until Janet Hitchman's biography (the first) came out in 1975 that their relationship was disclosed.

Though most people know her only as a writer of detective fiction, much of her work lies elsewhere: she wrote over ten plays, most of them on religious themes, and several books of essays; she wrote countless pieces of criticism on detective fiction for newspapers and magazines over a 15-year span; she gave many addresses to various organizations and over the radio for the BBC during World War II; she edited four volumes of detective fiction and co-edited three volumes of poetry; and she translated The Song of Roland (released after her death in 1957), Tristan in Brittany (1929), and Dante's Divine Comedy (Paradisio was finished after Sayers' death by Barbara Reynolds). She was president of the British Modern Language Association from 1939–1945 and was president of the Detection Club from 1949 until her death in 1957.

Sayers' first detective novel, *Whose Body?*, came out in 1923, followed shortly after by *Clouds of Witness*. Today Lord Peter Wimsey is seen as the epitome of the British interwar amateur detective—aristocratic, suave, intelligent, and carefree—and he made Sayers famous as a detective fiction novelist. She also became renowned as a writer who dared to produce good writing in a field not known for its literariness and as a learned detective fiction critic. Her introduction to *The Omnibus of Crime* (1928) is considered the first (and one of the best) thorough background descriptions of the genre and is included or at least mentioned in many collections of detective fiction criticism.[5]

By 1930, however, Sayers, was "getting a bit weary of Lord Peter," as she wrote to a friend: "there are times when I wish him the victim of one of his own plots!" (in Reynolds 310). She had already introduced detective fiction writer Harriet Vane in *Strong Poison* (1929) with the avowed intention of marrying Peter off in order to end his career. Sayers, however, did not marry Peter off at this time, for reasons that this chapter will discuss; her desire to complete her "love story," coupled with the fact that fans in larger numbers were beginning to read her books, forced Sayers to delay terminating Lord Peter's career for several more years.

Sayers' Harriet Vane is more than just a self-projection, though like Agatha Christie and her literary "double" Mrs. Oliver, there are distinct similarities between Sayers and Vane in both major and minor character traits: both are mystery writers who create a male detective; both attended Oxford when it was unusual for women to do so (Harriet gets a first in English; Sayers in French); both sang in the Bach choir in Oxford and have beautiful voices; both had lovers before marriage. Janet Hitchman writes about the ways Harriet resembles Dorothy: Harriet was "tall and dark-haired, not by any means beautiful. She had 'a nice throat' with 'a kind of arum lily quality.' She wrote detective stories, and always signed her name Harriet D. Vane, an echo of Dorothy's insistence on her 'L.' Like Dorothy she had a beautiful speaking voice" (75).

However, these surface features are important only in that they more firmly establish the strong correlation between Sayers and Vane. Valerie Pitt says that, despite their similarities, Harriet is not so much a "proxy" for Sayers as she is a literary character "made out of Sayers' experience of [her] culture and her understanding of its various phenomena" (173). Joyce Watts delineates the qualities she sees in Sayers which are spread out over both Wimsey and Vane, and believes that putting aspects of herself into both characters accounts for their "fascination and completeness" (1).

While Hitchman contends that there is no doubt that "Harriet is Sayers as she saw herself" (75), I think it rather more important to look at what Sayers could accomplish through the character she created. When Sayers introduces Harriet Vane in *Strong Poison*, she begins to examine in her fiction technical and artistic difficulties which in 1929 she had just begun to recognize. Though she writes in "Gaudy Night" that she tried to write "something 'less like a conventional detective story and more like a novel'" (208) beginning with her first book in 1923, she does not reach this goal (as she herself admits) until she creates Vane.

Perhaps because the two share so many traits, Sayers inadvertently fell into the trap she warned against in her introduction to *The Omnibus of Crime*, the "difficulty of allowing real human beings into a detective-story. At some point or other, either their emotions make hay of the detective interest, or the detective interest gets hold of them and makes their emotions look like pasteboard" (40). Harriet, who "had been a human being from the start" ("Gaudy Night" 212), made Lord Peter and the standard puzzle-plot detective story look flimsy. Therefore, though she began *Strong Poison* with the intent of marrying Peter off and ending his career, she found that she could not write the planned ending and "force" them to marry "without shocking [her]self" (211).

Sayers was then forced to dig beneath the caricature of her main character and come up with a human being instead. In the process, she provided herself with a medium through which to discuss and transform her detective fiction. Thus Harriet Vane from the outset furthers Sayers' goal for her detective fiction; by humanizing the characters, she also creates a more literary standard for the detective fiction genre.

Strong Poison opens with a thirty-page summation from the judge's point of view of Harriet's trial and supposed crime: the murder of her lover with the same method used in her latest book—arsenic poisoning. The judge's speech, full of platitudes about women and reflective of middle-class morality, makes it clear how he (and society) feel about Harriet Vane. She was left alone to "make her own way in the world," and it is "very much to her credit" that she has made herself independent "in a legitimate way" (4). And yet her road to independence is suspect: not only is Harriet a "novelist by profession," but as the judge reminds the jury, she writes "so-called 'mystery ' or 'detective' stories, such as deal with various ingenious methods of committing murder and other crimes" (3).

She and Philip Boyes met in "artistic and literary circles where 'advanced' topics are discussed" (3). Though she had a "strictly religious upbringing" (4) she eventually gave in to Boyes' repeated requests to live with him "outside the bonds of marriage" (4).[6] The jury, the judge reminds them, can make "allowances for this young woman's unprotected position" (4) but still does not have to accept Harriet's "social outlawry" (5) for anything but an "ordinary vulgar act of misbehavior" (4). Through examples such as these, it becomes clear that Harriet is on trial for many things: not only for murder, but for being an unmarried sexually active woman, and to compound her problems, for being a writer of popular fiction.

Setting out Vane in this way, on the dock with public sentiment against her, forces Sayers immediately to establish Harriet's main trait, her honesty, though her brand of it seems at odds with society's expectations. For example, the judge is not convinced by Harriet's reason for breaking up with Boyes *after* he had proposed marriage. She said during her trial that she had consented to live with him because he had told her he did not believe in marriage; therefore, when he proposed—writing to his clergyman father that he had decided to "do the thing properly" (62)—Harriet felt she had been "'made a fool of'" (7). She tells Peter, "I quite thought he was honest when he said he didn't believe in marriage—and then it turned out that it was a test to see whether my devotion was abject enough. Well it wasn't. I didn't like having matrimony offered as a bad conduct prize" (43). Though this shows Harriet's honesty to her own principles, it confounds the judge and jury looking at the evidence in the case, who, assuming that marriage is the culmination of women's experience, cannot understand her refusal to let Boyes make an "honest woman" of her.[7] Harriet's honesty lies elsewhere.

This is merely the first and perhaps most telling way that Sayers establishes the importance of honesty to oneself in this novel, and it remains throughout as Harriet's most telling feature and the most important facet of the Wimsey-Vane trilogy. Wimsey, in *Gaudy Night*, admits that it is her honesty which attracted him to her and the reason he fell in love with her; in this novel Sayers more fully explores "the themes of the almost sacramental importance of work and of intellectual honesty" (James in Reynolds xiv) which she herself struggled with and tried to follow.

But *Gaudy Night* did not appear for six more years. In the meantime, Sayers wrote books designed to flesh out her main detective a bit, including another one with Harriet Vane, *Have His Carcase* (1932). And, having created a detective fiction writer very much like herself, Sayers used Vane in this novel as a more noticeable double, articulating many of Sayers' own views on writing detective fiction and on the role of women in that fiction.

Like many of her contemporaries in the 1920s, Sayers believed in ground rules for the detective tale, most of all so that its development would be fair to the reader. This hallmark of the Golden Age established one of the biggest changes in way the detective story was told, one that still holds true today. The novelist must provide the same clues to the reader that are provided to the detective, taking the reader down the same path to enlightenment, as opposed to a surprise solution on the final page.

As these rules make clear, the writers from the Golden Age were anxious to distinguish their detective fiction from earlier models, which they felt as a whole leaned too much towards the fantastic. Many elements of detective fiction's questionable cousin, the romantic thriller, seemed out-dated and irrelevant to the fiction which Sayers and fellow Detection Club members wanted to write. For instance, two of Ronald Knox's rules included "Not more than one secret room or passage is allowable" and "No China-man must figure in the story" (in Haycraft, Art 194). Such scenarios seemed too absurd to fit into the deliberately plotted "realistic" murder mysteries that these authors were trying to create.[8]

One way that Sayers uses the Harriet Vane character is to discuss the items Sayers wanted to see removed from the detective fiction of her day and which she did dispense with in her own detective fiction: using female intuition as a way to solve crime, including a love interest as part of the plot, and creating unrealistic romantic plot lines which not only disrupted the authenticity of "fair play" detective fiction, but perpetuated outmoded and negative stereotypes of women as passive and illogical creatures.

Though using female intuition as a crime-solving technique was accept-able in earlier fiction and was embraced by many writers as a means of inte-grating women's specialized ways of knowing into the male-dominated genre, many post-War women writers abandoned it as the genre gained in popu-larity, and as some of the cultural limitations surrounding women began to diminish. As Chapter Three shows, even authors who created dowdy grand-motherly spinster detectives (in whom such a female trait might be expected and excused) do not allow their detectives to rely on this trait. For one, female intuition went against logic; it could not be considered "playing fair" with the reader if the solution to a crime was discovered to be based in part on a feeling. However, the more deeply embedded social consequence of this "unfair" tenet was its unfairness to women as a whole, the fact that the use of female intuition placed women's intelligence or the bases of women's knowledge not on education or job training—that is, not on something they could learn—but on something they "couldn't help" having. Women's knowl-edge, if based purely on intuition, was something recognizable and, because it was "merely" a feminine trait, could therefore be more easily dismissed. Witness Sir Eustace Pedlar's interpretation of Anne Beddingfeld's guess as to the murdered woman in Christie's The Man in the Brown Suit: he has "no doubt" that Anne is right in her guess, but "to call it a deduction is absurd" (138).

Sayers was similarly against using female intuition in her novels, as it was both an unfair plot device and an unfair limitation placed upon well-educated, well-trained women. In Have His Carcase, Wimsey and Vane work side by side in solving this case, but the police inspectors of the small sea-side town where the murder occurs have no explanation for Harriet's intel-ligent contributions to the investigation except "female intuition," and thus place her suggestions, in this case about one woman's motive for murder, under that rubric. When Harriet tells the three men working on the case that their solution is impossible, this commonplace is put forward again:

> "Miss Vane's intuition, as they call it, is against it," said he.
> "It's not intuition," retorted Harriet. "There's no such thing. It's common sense. It's artistic sense, if you like. All those theories—they're all wrong" [323].

Harriet realizes, as can the reader of the novel by this point, that they are simply abandoning facts that won't fit into their notion of what must have happened. She tells them their case is like a "bad plot, built up round an idea that won't work" (323). Her training as a detective fiction writer allows her to recognize their struggle to fit in facts coherently and to see the bigger picture of the crime, and she is able to see practically—with her artistic sense—what the others passed over in order to reach their desired conclusion. The men's vague language—"this feminine intuition and all that" (113) and "intuition, as they call it" (323)—reveals their uncertainty as to the source of Harriet's knowledge. But it is the only answer they have. And while earlier women writers of detective fiction vacillate as well in deciding upon a proper label for their female detectives' knowledge—Orczy's interchangeable "knowledge of human nature" and "knowledge of psychology" come to mind—Sayers labels her character's practical contributions to solving the crime as a learned and cultivated attribute based on the training she receives in the course of doing her job.

Sayers was also an avid proponent of ridding detective fiction of the "love interest," as was Christie and several other members of the Detection Club.[9] Sayers devoted an entire section of the introduction in her *Omnibus* to denouncing the love interest as a "fettering convention" of unknowing publishers, who "labour under the delusion that all stories must have a nice young man and woman who have to be united in the last chapter" (38). She believed that it ruined the logical development of a story to include "heroes who insist on fooling about after young women when they ought to be putting their minds on the job of detection" (*Omnibus* 38–39). Thus Lord Peter's telegram to Harriet, when both are working on *Carcase*, reads: FOLLOWING RAZOR CLUE TO STAMFORD REFUSE RESEMBLE THRILLER HERO WHO HANGS ROUND HEROINE TO NEGLECT OF DUTY BUT WILL YOU MARRY ME—PETER (76). Needless to say, Harriet refuses.

But the "fettering" love interest does worse damage than get in the way of detecting. Often the love story was only introduced as a way to bring a pretty woman into the plot, to serve as a distraction for the detective or the detective's (male) friend. In these cases the plot line for women consisted almost entirely of falling in love and marrying—depicted as the completion of women's goals—and thus this fiction continued to place women in traditional secondary and passive roles. To emphasize her displeasure with this element, Sayers shows a frustrated Harriet having difficulty writing a love story into the plot of her *Fountain Pen Mystery*, though she has arrived at the point in her novel where, according to the current tenets of serial detective fiction, the detective's friend was "expected in indulge in a spot of love-making" (179) with the lovely heroine. Sayers writes out several of Harriet's false starts in her attempt to deal competently with "two innocents in a rose-garden" before the venture fails:

> "As if there was anything in the world I wouldn't try and do for you—
> Betty!"
>   "Well, Jack?"
>   "Betty—darling—I suppose you couldn't possibly—"
> Harriet came to the conclusion that she couldn't—not possibly [180].

Thus an indignant telegram to her agent ensues, in which she writes she "absolutely refuse[s]" to introduce a love interest.

Hilary Schor has noted how the term "love interest" can refer "to both the heroine and her plot in the conventional hero's narrative" (14). Harriet, dissatisfied with both the plot she is supposed to write and with the place of her heroine in that plot, refuses to conform to convention. Thus Harriet inhabits two levels, both as an author within the text, struggling for her right to refuse to conform to conventionality in her work, and at the level of Sayers' heroine, struggling to refuse her role as an object of desire within Sayers' text.

Sayers' method of doubling (or in this case tripling) the plot questions, on an initial level, the centrality of the love interest to women's narratives, and on a broader level, the limited roles of women in society. She questions, in Schor's words, the right for a woman "to confront the fictions that write her life" (15). In creating Harriet Vane, Sayers introduced a love interest who did not conform to convention and marry Lord Peter Wimsey at the end of the book. Their eventual engagement in a later novel comes about not so much as a means of conforming to convention or fulfilling a publisher's ideal, but as a re-visioning of what occurs for women in what was still the largely male-centered plot of detective fiction.

Sayers herself was a woman who refused to conform to the script written out for women in her society. She introduces a character whose questioning of her "plot" within the text serves as a means through which her author can do the same. Both Sayers and Harriet Vane confront issues of professional authority and re-construct that authority along lines more suitable for themselves as professional women writers.

It may seem contradictory that a writer who was in theory against a love interest would write several books trying to marry off her detective. But

Sayers was not against love in a story in general, just when it seemed perfunctory and reductive. She praised Collins' *The Moonstone* and Bentley's *Trent's Last Case* for the skillful and necessary way the love element forms and moves the plot. She recognized that her own *Gaudy Night*, in which the love story is an integral part of the book's detective element and to its theme of integrity, nonetheless breaks the established rules for a detective story. She says it is "not really a detective story at all, but a novel with a mild detective interest of an almost entirely psychological kind" (in Reynolds 354). Recognizing its contradictory elements, she writes to her publisher that he can promote *Gaudy Night* however he sees fit: "whether you advertise it as a love-story, or as educational propaganda, or as a lunatic freak, I leave to you" (in Reynolds 357).

One final way Sayers elevates detective fiction above romantic fiction, distinguishing it from this "lesser" genre, is by having Harriet and Peter use the narrative strategies found in the detective fiction genre to help solve a crime that has its roots in the romantic thriller genre. Sayers places the two side by side within the narrative of *Have His Carcase*, continually weaving the implausible narratives of romance fiction in with Harriet's—and Sayers' own—rational world of detective fiction. From the outset, Sayers shows Harriet relying on her own knowledge of detective fiction to help her solve the case of Paul Alexis' murder, a murder which in its execution depends on the predictability of the elements in romance novels. Set up in this way, Sayers nearly forces the reader to view detective fiction—which follows rules, which values ratiocination, which in her novels at least explores the roles of women—as superior to the truly escapist thriller romance, in which women more commonly play passive roles as objects of desire.

The underpinnings of *Have His Carcase* consist almost entirely of the world of popular fiction, both the thriller romance and detective fiction, as a brief plot outline makes clear: Paul Alexis, a young Russian émigré turned professional dancer, is engaged to the wealthy widowed middle-aged Mrs. Weldon. Her son, Henry Weldon, is a gentleman farmer very badly off; he and his accomplices murder Alexis so that Mrs. Weldon is not able to leave Alexis her money (which they will then split upon Mrs. Weldon's death, a death which they will undoubtedly hasten). Having learnt that Alexis was very fond of thriller romance books, they build up a plot for him to star in over a period of several months. Their elaborate ruse is cleverly designed to make Alexis believe that he is next in line for the Russian throne through a morganatic marriage on his mother's side (a "rumor" upon which Alexis had himself been raised, making their job easier), and that Mother Russia is waiting for his return to free them from the oppressive Soviets. Part of the reason they are able to convince him of his supposed apotheosis is because he has read so many thriller romance books, in which such unrealistic happenings happen all the time. And part of the reason Harriet can understand the background of the case and help solve it is that as a writer herself she is able to recognize the elements of fiction that keep appearing.

Throughout this novel, Sayers shows Harriet continually relying on the tenets of detective fiction when confronted with Paul Alexis' murder. Harriet finds the body lying on a flat rock with a slit throat when she is on a walking tour about a year and a half after her trial. Upon finding the corpse ("How—how appropriate!"), Harriet turns to her own detective creation to help her decide how to proceed: "Robert Templeton, she felt, would at once ask himself, 'Is it Murder or Suicide?'"(8).[10] Having written detective fiction, she realizes that she knows what she should do. The fact that the tide is coming in wakes her up to the fact that she is all alone with the body—there are no people around, much less the police—and that she must examine the body to try to create a record of what happened. She takes photos of the footprints, the body, and the surroundings. She pulls off a shoe, noticing that it is sandy but not wet, and makes sure it fits the only set of footprints she sees. She searches for and finds a razor at the foot of the rock; she tries to take items which will identify the man from his pockets. When she finally does find the police, she tells the surprised Inspector that she knew what to do because she wrote mystery novels, though her feeling that the Inspector must think it "an idle and foolish occupation" (32) shows that she realizes the hollowness of fiction when compared to the real thing.

Unfortunately, knowing what to do because she has written about it goes both ways: the extent of Harriet's knowledge only reaches as far as Templeton's in her own fiction, and sometimes not even that far. Templeton has a thermometer and can judge from the temperature and rigor mortis of a body how long it has been dead. Harriet realizes she has no idea how to measure those two things. She cannot determine how long it will take before the sea washes the body away because Robert Templeton has never had to investigate a mystery by the sea (thus releasing Harriet from the laborious duty of studying times and tides). That night, retreating into the safety of her own fiction, Harriet tries to convince herself that her own forthcoming "absorbing" mystery novel is much more interesting than what has occurred earlier in the day, preferring her own neat set of problems over which she has control, to the problems of a murder/suicide over which she has none. Ironically, Harriet is beset with problems of alibis and the time of the murder in her *Fountain-Pen Mystery*, the same problem she and Peter are faced with in *Have His Carcase*, trying to solve Alexis' murder.

As the plot unfolds, Harriet and Peter begin to see more and more clearly all of the unnatural ways that the murdered man's life was a case of life imitating art—in this case, the cheap thrillers that Alexis loved. Throughout the early part of the novel, their presence seems to be hovering in the background: other characters in the novel confirm his fascination with them; his room is full of various cheap copies, and plots of stories like *The Trail of the Purple Python* are told to Harriet in detail. Much to her (and our) delight, its plot is perfectly ridiculous. But these books give Harriet the first clue as to the method the murderer used to lure Alexis to his death on the shore, and as she and Peter get closer to solving the crime, the obvious characteristics stand out. Letters are written to Alexis in a code (which Peter manages to crack), and Alexis is instructed to write back in similar code. Secrets surround the murdered man as to his uncertain past (was he really a product of a morganatic marriage, and is he related to the Romanovs?). A photo of Alexis' supposed Russian bride-to-be is found on his dead body, a beautiful woman eagerly anticipating his return so they can take the Imperial throne together. Lines in the translated missive like "silence, secrecy imperative" and "burn all papers all clues to identity" are, as Peter realizes, lines which inhabited the pages of the romance novels Alexis constantly read (376). These sorts of novels fed into Alexis' mania that he was of noble birth, if only he could prove that Nicholas I married his great-great-grandmother.

Since most of the novel is seen through Harriet's consciousness, we are shown the workings of her detective mind when confronted with such "literary" problems. When they find the coded letter on Alexis' dead body and wonder why Alexis didn't burn it like he did the rest of his personal papers, she turns to her own books and guesses that the "villain" of this plot requests that the victim "bring this letter with you" for the same reason: "'The idea is, from the villain's point of view, that he can then make certain that the paper is destroyed. From my point of view, of course, I put it in so that the villain can leave a fragment of paper clutched in the victim's stiffened hand to assist Robert Templeton'" (356).

When they do decipher the letter and are still unable to understand how its clichés and pat phrases coincide with what they know of the crime, Harriet again is able to come up with the answer, based on her writing and reading knowledge: "It's like the kind of thing I should put into a detective story if I didn't know a thing about Russia and didn't care much, and only wanted to give a general idea that somebody was a conspirator" (375). They realize soon after that this is exactly what the murderers are: people who don't know much, but who are able convince a young impressionable Russian, who has himself been brought up to believe that he is related to the Romanovs, that the plot *is* real. Thus they are able to lure him to the shore, where the "Rider from the Sea," instead of bringing him the crown to his country, slashes his throat. And its precisely because the situation is so clichéd that Alexis believes it so completely; as Christie's Mrs. Oliver says, "'knowing about it beforehand gives it an extra thrill when it happens to oneself.'"

Harriet's line that she would put it into a detective story if she didn't care much about Russia is telling. While it is good enough to form the entire plot of a "lesser" thriller, in her own books it would only be used as a lure, as a ruse. Detective fiction, which relied on facts and timetables and the "rational and scientific," would not stoop to the level of insincerity displayed by these Ruritanian romances and other books of its kind.

It is certainly true that the lines between the two genres of popular fiction cross, with several elements appearing in both types of works: the "bring this letter with you" line, and of course, the supposed necessity of a love interest. It follows that since Harriet can recognize so many of these elements of romance books, she must be familiar with them and their clichés because she has read many of them herself. Indeed, when she gets stuck with *The Fountain Pen Mystery*, she reads these thrillers instead of writing, justifying it to herself by saying she's letting her work "clear": "When she ought to have been writing, Harriet would sit comfortably in an armchair, reading a volume taken from Paul Alexis' bookshelf, with the idea of freeing the subconscious for its job" (282–283). This is one example, says Gayle Wald, of the way that Harriet's use of Alexis' books "asserts the literariness of detective fiction while positing romance as the true escapist literature" (104). Harriet uses such fiction to "escape" her own more difficult writing task, one much more demanding in its requirement to "play fair" and retain verisimilitude, and one which requires more skill and intelligence.

Sayers portrays romance thrillers condescendingly in *Have His Carcase*, as non-logical fantasies which exaggerate men's supposed masculinity and women's supposed femininity. Her portrayal of the murder victim who reads and believes these romances is also described in unfavorable terms: he is weak, frail, effeminate, romantic. Even more belittling, he is duped by a plot come straight out of a romance novel, an act of willful blindness and romantic fantasizing that leads to his murder.

Though Alexis loved these romances—in which governments rose and fell heedless of the outside world and where heroes arose from nowhere to save the day—none of his co-workers are able place him in the role of a swashbuckler come to rescue a princess. One says that "'poor dear Paul wasn't really a bit like a hero'" (185); another calls him a "'regular namby-pamby'" (82). Peter calls Alexis' belief in the plot a "'poor boob's monomania'" (375). Right after he gets his last coded letter, his landlady describes his manner as "'hysterical, I should call it, if he'd been a girl'" (193).

As John Cawelti has divided them, male-directed romances such as the ones Alexis reads revolve around the relationship of the hero to the villain (as opposed to women's romances, wherein the major relationship is between the hero and the heroine).[11] But reading romances, despite one's actual sex, was, like novels generally or sensation fiction specifically, aligned with femininity. Novels were for those who had time to waste, and men were supposed to be active. As an ex-girlfriend of Alexis' put it, when explaining why she got sick of him: "'A girl could not help preferring manly men, who had *done* something'" (406). The implication is of course that Alexis would not be reading these if he were more manly, if he were not prone to the fantasizing and romanticizing done by women. Thus, despite Alexis' sex and the action-oriented novels he read, he is aligned through his reading material with weakness, illogic, and fantasy. Sayers seems to emphasize this with her physical description of the murdered man.

Not only was thriller/romance fiction lesser in its cultural status than detective fiction (according to Sayers), it was lesser because it portrayed women in stereotyped ways, a harmful trend that both Sayers and other women writers who created unusual female detective characters were trying to check. Certainly the clichés encompassed the roles of both men and women, but women were more ill-treated than men by the perpetuation of the stereotypes contained within these stories because they afforded so little scope for women's abilities: while men act, women wait. Cultural perceptions about the ways women could and should act and how they are portrayed in popular fiction are forcefully displayed at the scene of Alexis' inquest, where detective fiction is shown by Sayers as portraying women in a more favorable light. Harriet, as a detective fiction writer, is more closely aligned with the logical, the "masculine," throughout the novel. At the inquest Sayers writes that Harriet is able to give expert testimony about the way she found the body because as a mystery writer she knew how "to assemble details of this kind coherently" (264). Henry Weldon, on the other hand, questions Harriet's ability to give evidence. Based on his experience of women and their fiction, he can't understand how "'a girl'" like Harriet can know anything about the reality of crime or murder: "'Women always get that idea of blood running about all over the place. Always reading novels. "Wallowing in gore." That kind of stuff'" (276).

Weldon's study of female psychology taught him that in books women think in clichés and in formula, and thus are not to be trusted to think logically in real life either—that they see "'what they think they ought to see'" (276). His beliefs, which attached little importance to women's abilities and activities, were merely those which also appear in the popular fiction of his time. No wonder Sayers attempted to elevate her detective fiction above the "thriller" genre: not only was its critical reputation dreadful, but the stereotypes in these stories relegated women to passive, traditional roles. Sayers, who actively worked to make something more "literary" out of detective fiction, also worked to expand the view of women's limited roles within that fiction.

It is impossible to overlook the deliberate and repeated efforts of Sayers to draw the reader's attention to the elements of fiction and of fiction-making which form the basis of *Have His Carcase*. I think her use of clichés and rules is partly tongue-in-cheek; like Heyer and Christie, she is able to parody detective fiction and some of its "well-worn gadgets." But it works on other levels as well, some of which have already been noted: she can talk about the methods and problems of writing detective fiction through her alter-ego; she can talk about the difficulties of being a writer beholden to a fickle public; she can help solidify some of the standards of her fiction and elevate its status over other popular genres.

At the same time, this novel plays with those established tenets. By this point, Sayers realized that Peter's career as a cardboard character had to end, now that he was paired with a "real" character. Sayers therefore took this opportunity to address where detective fiction was going next and where else she wanted to take it. Though Sayers and her fellow Detection Club members were committed to these rules throughout much of the decade, they came to realize that some of them at least had to be broken in order to advance their craft. Harriet Vane, while she works as a double for Sayers to uphold some of these rules, also breaks those rules, ushering in changes in the style and format of the detective novel, as much as the Detection Club's own rules had changed detective fiction into a genre that differentiated itself from the style and format of the thriller romance.

But this is only the first of the dilemmas that Sayers both introduced and addressed through Vane. In attempting to move the detective fiction genre forward, Sayers uses this opportunity to discuss what had become for her a topic of supreme importance: the theme of work and its place in the lives of human beings. P.D. James does not exaggerate when she calls the subject of work one of "almost sacramental importance" to Sayers; Sayers felt that it was vital for everyone to have a proper job not only so that they could contribute to society in a meaningful way, but so that their lives could be fulfilled. This idea of the importance of work is expressed most thoroughly in Sayers' nonfiction essays, but she begins dealing with the subject in her detective fiction. Therefore, Harriet Vane as a character not only helps Sayers create a type of detective fiction more like a character-based novel of manners, but she also presents Sayers with a means of expressing the importance of work for people as creative beings. This is especially true for women, whose roles in society were not well-defined and who were often unfulfilled in the realm of work.

These ideas about art and work—and often their relation to Christianity—are the subjects of many of Sayers' non-fiction essays and addresses.

Sayers (who, as a clergyman's daughter, had, like Harriet Vane, a "strict religious upbringing") wrote often about her understanding of Church doctrines, fundamentally "explaining" them as best she could. At the same time, she chastised the Church for its failure to take more responsibility towards society in matters such as work. She felt that it is when human beings create that they are most like God, the Creator of all things, and thus in striving to be like God, human beings must view work as an expression of creativity and as a service to God.

She called "revolutionary" the ideas that she felt naturally arose out of this doctrinal assumption: one, that work is not "a thing one does to live, but the thing one lives to do" (53); two, that the Church should recognize work as something sacred for humanity; and three, that "the worker's first duty is to *serve the work*" ("Why Work?" in *Creed* 59). Sayers felt that humanity would always remain unhappy with the role of work in their lives, seeing it only as a means to an end instead of as a fundamental part of existence, until they took this sacramental attitude towards it.

In essays such as "Are Women Human?" and "The-Human-Not-Quite-Human," she makes it clear that when she talks about man and his work she means "humans" and "their" work. Although the essay "Are Women Human?" was originally an address presented to a Woman's Society, who asked her to talk about her feminist views, she publicly disassociated herself from the feminist movement, saying she preferred to think of people not in terms of "men" or "women" as groups, as feminists tended to do in asserting that "women are as good as men," but as individuals, as human beings with "individual preferences, and with just as much right to the tastes and preferences of an individual" (in *Unpopular Opinions* 130).

Thus, she answers the "cry" that went up upon women being admitted to universities: "'Why should women want to know about Aristotle?'" in this way:

> The answer is NOT that *all* women would be the better for knowing about Aristotle [...] but simply: "What women want as a class is irrelevant. *I* want to know about Aristotle [...] and I submit that there is nothing in my shape or bodily functions which need prevent my knowing about him" [131].

Further, Sayers claims that there are no traits particular to men or to women as a whole which fit them for certain occupations; she believes that regardless of one's sex, the job should be done by the person who best does it. In both of these essays she berates those who say that they wish women would stick with the work they did in "the good old days," say, the Middle Ages, and not compete with men in today's workforce, because she contends that men have taken those jobs which in the Middle Ages belonged to women: "spinning, weaving, baking, brewing, distilling, perfumery, preserving, pickling—in which [women] worked with head as well as hands [...]. But now the control and direction—all the intelligent part—of those industries have gone to the men, and the women have been left, not with their 'proper' *work* but with *employment* in those occupations" ("The Human-Not-Quite-Human" in *Unpopular* 145–146). The distinction, as we have seen, is vital to Sayers. She doesn't complain that such jobs have been taken over by men—if they can do them better—but the rule must be applied universally: "once lay down the rule that the job comes first and you throw that job open to every individual, man or woman [...]" ("Are Women Human?" in *Unpopular* 134).

Sayers' biographer Ralph Hone calls these "satirical" pieces (137), especially "The Human-Not-Quite-Human," though I see it more as an angry piece, especially in its closing paragraphs. So too, obviously, did the BBC, which originally commissioned the piece and then refused to air it, stating that their "'listeners do not want to be admonished by a woman'" (Hitchman 142).[12] The essay begins with recognition of the fact that both men (*Vir*) and women (*Femina*) are human beings (*Homo*); however, Sayers argues, "Man is always dealt with as both *Homo* and *Vir*, but Woman only as *Femina*" (142), and thus they are not fully human. She then reverses what she sees as the status quo—that women are judged only as *Femina*—and provides pages of very funny examples of men being "unrelentingly assessed in terms of [their] maleness" (143), wondering if any man has ever imagined "how strange his life would appear to himself [...] if from school and lecture-room, Press and pulpit, he heard the persistent outpouring of a shrill and scolding voice, bidding him remember his biological function" (143). It ends with a characteristic criticism of the Church for perpetuating such injustices against women, noting that though Jesus treated women as human beings, His successors in the faith have not.

These essays, written during the 1930s and 1940s, articulate most clearly the themes of work and women's roles, themes also explored in her detective stories during this time, though less deliberately detailed. It is a fact, however, that in nearly all of her mystery novels, the culprit is someone who, in the course of whatever other crime, has been false to his job, the great sin in Sayers' eyes. In *Murder Must Advertise* (1933), Mr. Tallboys uses the advertisement agency where he works as a cover for a drug ring, providing clues to where the next drug deal will take place through the newspaper. Mary Whitaker in *Unnatural Death* (1927) is a nurse who kills her great aunt in order to inherit her money before an inheritance law changes. Even in Sayers' first novel, *Whose Body?* (1923), the murderer is someone who abused his position as a doctor and head of a laboratory to cover up murder. Kathleen Gregory Klein speaks at length about Sayers and work in her contribution to Bargannier's *10 Women of Mystery*, writing that the subject is the "most important subject which Sayers chooses to consider in the detective stories" (29).

I showed in Chapter Three how Sayers used the spinster character Miss Climpson in her detective fiction to uphold her belief that women are human beings who must have access to satisfying work in order to feel a useful part of society. The Wimsey-Vane novels add another vital element to Sayers' exploration of this doctrine; here the necessity of doing one's work honestly both propels the story and shapes it. On a very basic level, for instance, Harriet's job as a mystery writer helps her solve the crime, or at least helps her understand the motives behind the crime, in *Have His Carcase*. Sayers' attitude about women's roles in the workplace (and in higher education as well, as we see in *Gaudy Night*) is more specifically detailed through Vane's character, as Sayers explores the avenues both open and closed to women, especially women who work independently as writers.

Maintaining a good reputation is one such concern; this was a more demanding task for women, since their actions were scrutinized more carefully than men's. A woman's reputation, as Sayers well knew, rested to a large extent on fulfilling society's expectations of what a woman should be, especially when one was only the second woman copywriter for one of the largest advertising firms in England. Sayers knew she could not return to her job with her child born out of wedlock. And while in the long run it many not have ruined her writing career, she felt she had to give her son to someone else to raise in order to return to work and to make enough money to pay for his keep, all the while knowing, as biographer Alzina Stone Dale sympathetically writes, "that at any moment she might suddenly find herself, as her character Harriet Vane actually does, before the bar of public opinion, with the press having a field day discussing her morals in print" (64). As Dale points out, even Vanessa Bell, a woman much less conservative than Sayers, brought up her illegitimate daughter with her husband's name, so as to avoid complications of illegitimate children.[13]

Sayers' concern for her reputation in the professional realm is well-known. She made sure that details of her novels were scientifically correct, regularly requesting advice from experts in the field. These range from the medical advice on the optical properties of synthetic muscarine, upon which rests the murder in *The Documents in the Case*,[14] to the exact nature of "haemophilic blood when copiously shed (as by throat-cutting)," a vital part of *Have His Carcase* (in Reynolds 311). She apologizes to one reader who wrote to her about a mistake she made concerning the musical instruments needed for a Bach piece, writing that she was very sick and couldn't correct her proofs (in Reynolds 340).

As her talk "Aristotle on Detective Fiction" makes clear, in which she humorously applies the principles in *Poetics* to detective fiction, she did not see the genre as something a writer should dash off to make money, but as a medium which required the same planning, control of plot and character, and verisimilitude that went into all works of art. She regularly went to the British Library when her proofs were near completion to look up newspapers and add into her books bits of news that had actually occurred at that time (Reynolds 258, fn1).[15]

Sayers also depicts the difficulty of establishing and maintaining a good reputation through Harriet. Though Harriet's personal reputation was perhaps permanently stained in the public eye by her "immorality," her lawyer insists at the end of *Strong Poison* that all implication of Harriet committing murder must be removed; she must be acquitted "'not only at this bar, but at the bar of public opinion'" (260). Vane is also a businesswoman, and, despite the un-womanly connotation of controlling one's money, knows she must capitalize on her popularity while she can, potentially adding to her infamy and negative reputation. While in prison, therefore, she corrected the proofs of the novel she had been writing when she was arrested—the one in which a lover is poisoned with arsenic—while her agent procures her the most profitable contracts he can during this time (*Strong Poison* 68).

When *Have His Carcase* opens, Harriet has become a successful author. Having been exonerated of murder, her books sell madly; she makes lots of money, and she is indeed a notorious person, both because she lived with her lover and because she was on trial for murdering him. As an intelligent independent writer, she understands both the hazards and necessities of publicity. Sayers begins *Have His Carcase* from Harriet's point of view, and we are in her consciousness when she wonders if what she sees on top of a flat rock in the distance is lump of seaweed or, if she "had any luck," a corpse. Then she could report it to the newspapers and get the publicity:

> "Well-known Woman Detective-Writer Finds Mystery Corpse on Lonely Shore." But these things never happen to authors.
> Harriet's luck was in.
> It was a corpse [7].

Right after she calls the police, she calls the *Morning Star* newspaper to give them her story exclusively, provided that they give her "a good show" (29). Even Peter, though noting that she is a "'woman of business,'" submits that calling the Press "'with all the gory details'" suggests "'a coarsening of the fibers'" (42). But as Harriet reminds him, she had no choice but to be "brazen" and to get publicity out of the murder, even though it might appear unseemly: "'Would it have been better to wait till the papers dragged the juicy bits out of the dust-bin for themselves?'" (165). Because she lives by her name, she realizes that she must capitalize on that fact.

The situation is brought up in an even more personal way in *Gaudy*

Night. When asked why she continues writing detective fiction, rather than something less sensational (in light of her own past), Harriet pushes aside personal feeling in favor of looking at the question from a business point of view: "writers can't pick and choose until they've made money. If you've made your name for one kind of book and then switch over to another, your sales are apt to go down, and that's the brutal fact" (31). Sayers knew something of this situation herself, feeling that she couldn't stop writing Lord Peter books, since he "seem[ed] to pay pretty well" (in Reynolds 310), even though she also wanted to work on other projects.[16] Living by one's name, as Sayers knew, was difficult for women, and she shows Harriet encountering the same problems.

Harriet, as a woman of business, as an Oxford graduate, as a member of the Bloomsbury set trying to survive in London in the 1930s through writing detective fiction, provides Sayers with a medium to discuss the issues facing women in her society. In these novels, the questions raised are not just of job or husband but the extent to which women can ascertain for themselves which of their society's written and unwritten rules are right for them as individuals, finding their place in a culture which in Sayers' eyes treated women as not fully human. Women's difficulties, as well as their opportunities, in balancing the things which might make them happy—motherhood, education, profession—are explored in these novels in light of their culture's biases.

As a whole, the women portrayed in *Strong Poison* represent those who have tried to make opportunities for themselves and, in questioning what society has said is right for them, have come up with more satisfying answers. Most of them, from the young artists and writers in Harriet's Bloomsbury crowd to the "Cattery" headed by Miss Climpson, have jobs and support themselves. Such independence is not without its problems, however. Harriet's friends tell Wimsey that part of the problem Harriet and Philip Boyes had when they were living together was that Harriet made four times as much money, and Boyes deeply resented it. Despite their so-called nontraditional relationship, he felt that she should have been "ministering to his work, not making money for them both with her own independent trash" (94). Boyes' friend, on the other hand, holds Harriet completely at fault, saying to Peter that he believes "'that bitch of a woman'" killed Boyes out of spite:

> "Harriet Vane's got the bug all these damned women have got—fancy they can do things. They hate a man and they hate his work. You'd think it would have been enough for her to help and look after a genius like Phil, wouldn't you? Why, damn it, he used to ask her advice about his work, her advice, good lord!"
>
> "And did he take it?"

"Take it? She wouldn't give it. Told him she never gave opinions on other authors' work. Other authors! The impudence of it!" [85–86].

Indeed, Harriet is dangerous not just as a potential murderer but as an economically independent women whose independence raises male anxieties about women's freedom—anxieties ranging from the decline of the institution of marriage to the more topical concern of job competition. Thus, her decision to live with Boyes outside of marriage is read by her society simultaneously as immorality and as a warning to society at large about the hazards of women working and supporting themselves.

The women portrayed by Sayers in *Have His Carcase*, on the other hand, represent the other end of the spectrum. Unlike in *Strong Poison*, which portrays economically independent women, *Have His Carcase* portrays women who do not have satisfying jobs of their own, whose lives revolve around their husbands, or lack thereof, and their subsequent attempts to procure them. Harriet is disgusted by the hypocrisy of the courting game going at Wilvercombe, noticing that in order to attract men, women are imitating both in dress and in manner the "womanliness" of the 1870's. Seeing a girl flirting shamelessly with a group of men, Harriet prophesies that "if she doesn't find something to occupy her mind" she will turn into "a predatory hag like the woman at the next table" (39). And watching that woman— older, "pathetically made up" (38), continually checking a pocket mirror and clearly waiting for her "gigolo"—makes Harriet feel even more disgusted: "Did it come to this then, if one did not marry? Making a public scorn of one's self before the waiters? [...] Single, married, widowed, divorced, one came to the same end" (39).

Harriet Vane is the only woman in this book who retains a sense of her own worth arising from her perception of herself and not through another person's. Sayers shows here the side of life that exists for a woman in her society who does not have a job, a proper outlet. In Harriet's eyes, all the women in this novel are pathetic; in Sayers' fiction, they serve as an exploration of the failure of society to allow women to pursue their own interests, for insisting upon "rules of the game" which state that a woman should exist merely as *Femina* and not as *Femina* and *Homo*. Even Mrs. Weldon, who admits that she "'lived for [her] emotions'" and is "'all heart,'" believes that she could have gotten more out of life than the experience of husband and child if she had "'painted pictures or ridden a motorcycle or something'" (61).

As further confirmation of Sayers' feelings on this topic, it is worth noting that in these two novels, and in *Gaudy Night* as well, the crimes that occur are related to or involve in some way cultural restrictions on women.[17] For example, in *Strong Poison*, Harriet is accused of both murder and "social outlawry"; and though her lawyer insists that she leaves court "'without a stain upon her character'" (259), only the stain of "murderer" can truly be removed. In *Have His Carcase*, Mrs. Weldon's fiancé, a much younger man, is murdered by her son to prevent her re-marriage, so that she cannot make a will in her new husband's favor. Thus Mrs. Weldon, Harriet's "predatory hag," is an example of what can happen to a woman who plays by society's rules and is then abandoned by those rules. She lives for and through a man and feels incomplete without one, as her society expects of her, but her son refuses to allow a re-marriage to occur, thus preventing the one important aspect of his mother's life.

In *Gaudy Night*, both types of women are depicted: women who work as scholars and teachers, performing the jobs for which they are best fit, and women who have not cultivated their own interests but have made other people their jobs. One of these women, Annie Wilson, is responsible for the disturbances at the College which Harriet helps investigate, forming the detective part of the novel. The implication is that women who "play by the rules," as Annie and Mrs. Weldon do, can become pathological if they do not have another appropriate outlet for their intelligence and their needs as human beings. It is not one of the dons who has become unbalanced, though their society maintains a belief in the maladjustment of working and scholarly women, but a "normal" married woman.

For Sayers, the decision to have the novel take place at Oxford was more lucky coincidence than intense planning. It wasn't until she received an invitation to speak at her own Oxford Gaudy (an alumni dinner) in 1929 that she realized that she could use that setting in her fiction as a way to tie together all of the strands on which she was still working: the love story between Harriet and Peter, the transformation of the detective story into more of a "novel," and a serious thesis on the subjects of women, work, and their place in society.

Sayers had written two novels in between *Strong Poison* and *Have His Carcase*, and two more between that one and *Gaudy Night*. While she had been avidly working on making Peter more human, giving him a past and a consistent psychological outlook, she had let lie the situation between him and Harriet. Since Harriet's consciousness and outlook so closely matched her own, she was having difficulty finding a solution. In a letter to musicologist and composer Donald Tovey, who wrote to her about how much he enjoyed her work, she explained her feelings in more detail:

> You are one of the very few people with intelligent sympathy for Lord Peter and his Harriet. Most of them beg me not to let him marry "that horrid girl." They don't understand the violent conflict undermining her obstinacy—I'm glad you do. There's stuff in Harriet, but it isn't the conventional heroine stuff, you see. My only reason for holding her up is that the situation between her and Lord P. is psychologically so difficult that it really needs a whole book to examine and resolve [in Reynolds 340].

Gaudy Night was to be that book. In figuring out a way to help Harriet get over her "inferiority complex," Sayers realized that it was on the intellectual level alone that Harriet could be equal with Peter, "since in that sphere she had never been false to her own standards" ("Gaudy Night" 213). In making Oxford the setting of her story, Sayers could make the theme of intellectual integrity, which she thought of as the one "great permanent value" in the world, mesh with the plot: "I should be saying the thing that [...] I had been wanting to say all my life. Finally, I should have found a universal theme which could be made integral both to the detective plot and to the "'love-interest'" (213).

Sayers considered *Gaudy Night* her most deliberately-planned book, noting with irony that a common complaint lodged against it was its lack of construction. But in uniting the "love-problem" with the "detective-problem, so that the same key should unlock both at once" ("Gaudy Night" 215), Sayers had to go beyond the usual mechanics that occurred in the construction of a detective novel. In addition to this careful restructuring of the detective novel, she takes the opportunity to examine in detail the cultural standards which surround and constrict women, especially women like Oxford dons, who were in such an unusual profession and often "'cursed with both a heart and a brain'" (*Gaudy Night* 190).

The plot is briefly this: Miss de Vine, the newest scholar at Oxford, had at her previous post exposed another scholar's dishonesty (he suppressed evidence contrary to his thesis), and eventually, having lost his job and degree, he committed suicide. His wife (of a lower class and not college-educated), after finding out that Miss de Vine had come to Oxford, got a job there as a scout (a servant), and begins to wreak revenge on Miss de Vine and the college, blaming educated women as a whole for destroying her family. Most of the disturbances are vicious poison-pen letters sent to various scholars, but the actions increase in severity until Harriet herself is attacked. Annie felt that scholars like Miss de Vine and Harriet were unnatural women who took jobs away from men, who cared more about a "dirty bit of paper" (485) than they did about human beings; they were women who, by valuing scholarship and professional interests above private ones, "killed" her husband. In this way, Annie's misguided loyalty to another human being becomes pathological. In Sayers' view, she made another person her job instead of finding one which was right for herself. In being what her society told her she should be—a wife and mother, living in and through her husband and children—she denied herself any other outlet.

Harriet sees on several occasions what happens in a marriage when one lets one's own interests slide in favor of another's. One old friend returns to haunt Oxford every year at the Gaudy, in remembrance of her glory days, but, having married, does nothing herself anymore. Another former student, a top scholar of her class, married a farmer and spends all of her time working with her husband on the land. Harriet sees this woman's life as a "damned waste," and tells her that she is "'all wrong'" for not pursuing her own interests: "'I'm sure one should do one's own job, however trivial, and not persuade one's self into doing somebody else's, no matter how noble'" (48). But, Harriet is reminded, often one marries a job; often for women, marriage *is* the job. Miss de Vine tells Harriet that she herself just escaped making this mistake, but broke up with her fiancé when she realized that she "'wasn't taking as much trouble with him as I should have done over a disputed reading. So I decided he wasn't my job'" (192). Only one of Harriet's former friends has married an equal, a history major who married an archeologist, but Harriet thinks their relationship must be unique.

On the other side of the coin are the women who have chosen to spend their lives teaching and working for the college, most of whom have chosen not to marry. They discuss the question of work from the standpoint of their scholarship, a question difficult for women scholars on two levels: to those doing manual labor such ethereal work was, to begin with, "'mere beating of air,'" as the farmer's wife tells Harriet (48). Further, women in academia had the additional dilemma of justifying woman's fitness for higher education; Chapter One shows some of the difficulties that women in the previous generation had to face. But Sayers shows that they have the same dedication to learning, intellectual pursuits, and principles of scholarship that men in similar positions have.

Harriet, having broken "all her old ties and half the commandments, dragged her reputation in the dust and made money" (3), is nervous on her way to Oxford, aware that her own reputation reflects upon the College and that she did not have the "kind of career that Shrewsbury expected of its old students" (2). But she soon remembers that amongst the Oxford dons it is one's work "'that really counts'" (10), and Harriet's books are well-researched, well-written, and interesting, and the entire Senior Common Room reads them (despite the fact that they are best-sellers and have made money). Harriet has not stopped growing intellectually, the gravest sin among these scholars. Even Miss Lydgate, the most charitable of the dons, demands a high quality of scholarship before anything else: Harriet remembers "only one time" she heard Miss Lydgate speak with "unqualified disapproval" about someone, a former pupil who had written a popular book about Carlyle: "'No research at all,' had been Miss Lydgate's verdict, 'and no effort at critical judgment. She has reproduced all of the old gossip without troubling to verify anything. Slipshod, showy, and catchpenny. I am really ashamed of her'" (15).

But it is when Harriet is called to defend her own work as a detective fiction writer that she must put into words for the first time what her work means to her. She is called upon to defend herself, not for being popular or for making money, but because someone thinks that it is inappropriate for her to write books about murder after having been through what she has, that her work reduces the sufferings of others to intellectual exercise. She defends herself admirably: "I know what you're thinking—that anybody with proper sensitive feeling would rather scrub floors for a living. But I should scrub floors very badly, and I write detective stories rather well. I don't see why proper feelings should prevent me from doing my proper job" (31). Harriet does not display proper "feminine" feelings in her choice to continue working in her line, and her feelings as a "human being," as one who enjoys her work and does it well, get overlooked.

Harriet comes to realize that the intellectual side of her life is the one thing she hasn't made a mess of: despite personal mistakes,

> she had stuck to her work—and in the face of what might have seemed over-whelming reasons for abandoning it and doing something different [...]. She had written what she felt herself called upon to write; and, though she was beginning to feel that she might perhaps do this thing better, she had no doubt that the thing itself was the right thing for her [38].

Sayers, in writing some of herself into Harriet Vane, justifies the rightness of finding and doing the work that one is meant to do. Sayers too—in light of her affair, her pregnancy, and her marriage to a man with whom she was incompatible—felt a great attachment to her work, believing that it was the one part of her life she had not made a mess of.

And, as Sayers herself does, Harriet wonders whether her books, which were good, could be better. This problem is discussed throughout *Gaudy Night* in a way similar to *Have His Carcase*, wherein Sayers shows Harriet having problems with her latest detective novel on several occasions. In *Death 'twixt Wind and Water*, Harriet has conceived of an intricate plot that she feels should be working itself out perfectly—five people with motives and alibis for murder all trapped in an old water-mill. Even though "there seemed to be nothing fundamentally wrong with the thing" (230), Harriet is stuck, realizing that "the permutations and combinations of the five people's relationships were beginning to take on an unnatural, an incredible symmetry. Human beings were not like that; human problems were not like that" (230). When Peter suggests some ways to give Wilfrid, her main character, some more realistic and life-like motivation, Harriet answers:

> "Yes—he'd be interesting. But if I give Wilfrid all of those of violent and life-like feelings, he'll throw the whole book out of balance."
> "You would have to abandon the jigsaw kind of story and write about human beings for a change" [332].

This is, of course, exactly what Sayers herself desired to do in her detective fiction, and does do, beginning with *Strong Poison*, when Harriet comes on the scene and throws the "whole book out of balance" (Heldreth 124) with her inherent humanity. And though Sayers speaks of this as if it were a mistake—creating too life-like a character that wouldn't do her bidding— she successfully transforms that mistake into the answer to her problems in later novels. Harriet's determination to "knock the sawdust" (333) out of her Wilfrid is a version of Sayers' own realization that her Lord Peter had to become less of a puppet and more of a human being, so she "chipped away at his internal mechanism through three longish books" ("Gaudy Night" 211) until he seemed in balance with Harriet, "humaniz[ing] him for her benefit" (212). Thus Harriet becomes the means, though unintentionally at first, through which Sayers tackled one of her most important writing tasks.

However, Sayers felt even more strongly about the book's message of intellectual integrity. In a letter to Muriel St. Clare Bryne she writes vehemently about her feelings on this subject, after Bryne had suggested to her that the "average reader" did not want to read about "'the real Oxford.'" But Sayers recoils at the idea of writing about Oxford in such a way as to falsify its image, merely to suit their tastes. To do so, she writes,

> you would be asking the writer to commit that ultimate and unforgivable
> sin whose unforgivableness is the whole theme of the book—the sin against
> intellectual integrity. To make a deliberate falsification for personal gain is the
> last, worst depth to which either scholar or artist can descend in work or life:
> which, as it happens, is what *Gaudy Night* is about [in Reynolds 352].

The places in the book which draw the most complaints are precisely those pages which establish how the Oxford dons feel about this subject. Peter, during a rather tense (and yes, long) conversation in the Senior Common Room, gets them all to admit that they would never sacrifice professional honor over personal desires; this re-establishes what they all already knew about each other, but in the madness of the disturbances at their college had forgotten.

In such scenes Sayers again highlights the difference between what is expected of men and women, even on a topic so "human" as intellectual integrity. Men can sacrifice private loyalties to public ones and they are called honorable; but when women make such sacrifices, they are called unnatural. Sayers makes this point most dramatically in the penultimate scene, when Annie is confronted with her crimes. She shouts at all the dons as a whole and then turns on Miss de Vine, accusing her of murder:

> "You broke him and killed him—all for nothing. Do you think that's a
> woman's job?"
> "Most unhappily," said Miss de Vine, "it was my job" [485].

To Annie, who believes that a woman's job is "'to look after a husband and children,'" this stance is inconceivable and unforgivable: "'I wish I had killed you. I wish I could kill you all. I wish I could burn this place down and all the places like it—where you teach women to take men's jobs and rob them first and kill them afterwards'" (486). But to Sayers, who wrote that it was the only book she had ever written "which embodies any kind of a 'moral'" and that she felt "passionately about this business of the integrity of the mind" (357), a life of academic and intellectual honesty is the only fulfilling life possible.

Many critics dislike the book; most of them mirror Janet Hitchman's complaint that one picks up a detective story to read a detective story, not a "treatise on ultimate truth" (86). She thinks it Sayers' worst book, one comprised mostly of "a series of conversations" that "go on interminably, with, intermittently, a flurry into detection as if Miss Sayers had suddenly remembered what kind of book she was supposed to be writing" (90). Symons, in his famous *Bloody Murder*, calls it "a 'woman's novel' full of the most tedious pseudo-serious chat between the characters" (118). George Grella, in an essay called "The Formal Detective Novel," calls it an "academic comedy devoted to a rather repellent intellectual-feminist thesis" (in Winks 100).[18] Q. D. Leavis came out very strongly against it, accusing it of the worst kind of snobbery and "vicious presentation because it is popular and romantic while pretending to realism" (in McDiarmid 125).

Sayers was well-aware of the book's faults from a "detective fiction" standpoint, having broken many of the Detection Club rules in writing it. "There is not even a corpse!"(86), Hitchman points out, a fact that breaks S.S. Van Dine's Rule #7: "no lesser crime than murder will suffice" (in Haycraft, *Art* 190). But as Sayers wrote in a *Sunday Times* review in July 1935, she felt that the time had come for the detective fiction genre to move forward, as her fiction from this time also shows:

> A technique is not perfected all in a moment; it has taken some hard work to reach this point, and we are to be congratulated on having got so far. But now comes the moment when, having made our rules and got them by heart, we can begin to experiment and play about with them. And this will bring us face to face with a whole set of new problems, most of which will turn out to be questions of balance and treatment [in Hone, "Critic" 48].

She speaks of *Gaudy Night* in particular as a novel which needed to be balanced in order to succeed, and she was proud of its construction and the way that the detective and love problems were both unlocked by the same key. But as the theme of intellectual integrity was one about which she felt passionately, the novel in many ways sprung from her mind already completed; she speaks of it both as a novel with thoughtful construction and as a novel over which she had little control. As she wrote to Muriel St. Clare Byrne on the subject: "surely one can only write the book that is there to be written. If I seem to be obstinate about it, it is just that I couldn't write the book any other way. It came like that [...]" (in Reynolds 353). She writes in a similar vein to Donald Tovey, who wrote to her about how much he enjoyed the book even though the characters developed along slightly different lines than the way they had talked about previously: "I find that characters have a way of taking hold of the situation and working it out for themselves, regardless" (in Reynolds 361).

Her publisher liked the book and presented it to the British public as "a novel—not without detection," thus admitting in a forthright manner the terms of the debate Sayers was having with herself (in Wald 99). Reviewers in turn picked up on the distinction between the definition of a "novel" and a "detective story" and therefore assisted, though perhaps unwittingly, in portraying the book as a "literary" achievement, one more novelistic, to use Wald's term, than detection-oriented. Sayers herself seemed resigned to the book's fate, whatever it happened to be, stating that she felt she could not write something to be popular if it meant falsifying what she knew; she washed her hands of the debate when she sent it on to her publisher: "But there it is—it's the book I wanted to write and I've written it [...]. It may be highly unpopular, but, though I wouldn't claim that it was in itself a work of great literary importance, it is important to me, and I hope it won't be a ghastly flop" (in Reynolds 357).

Laura Ray, in her article on "The Mysteries of *Gaudy Night*," points out rightly that if a novel is to be considered a "criticism of life," which Sayers increasingly came to want from her own fiction, then it must accurately "concern itself with the conditions under which life is actually lived" (276).[19] The Harriet Vane novels contain within them many of those problems which women writers like Sayers did or could have encountered, and through Harriet Vane, Sayers was able to address the personal and professional problems of an educated woman, exploring them in her fiction as women of her culture faced them. She cannot do this through Peter Wimsey alone, nor through Miss Climpson.

It is doubtful whether Sayers could have completed the work she wished to and created for herself the authority which she thoroughly achieved and maintained had she not created the Harriet Vane character. It becomes easier to understand why Sayers didn't make her primary detective a woman, believing that for a "novel of manners" to emerge from detective fiction, the characters had to be both human and realistic, and female detectives, in her society, were not.

Thus in *Gaudy Night* Sayers completes the mission she set out to perform on all levels: narratively, artistically, aesthetically. In doing so, she broke many of the old rules she and her cohorts had set for themselves, discovering a much richer and satisfying writing career. *Busman's Honeymoon* (1937), her final detective novel, began as a detective play, and writing it ushered in a new era in Sayers' career, one that she remained with the rest of her life, the stage. Subtitled "A Love Story with Detective Interruptions," *Busman's Honeymoon* focuses on the balance of opposing forces—between heart and mind, man and woman, emotion and intellect—as they relate to Peter and Harriet's marriage. Honesty and integrity in one's actions must still be the cornerstones of one's being, but here they become personal as well as professional. There is, by the way, a corpse.

Sayers had quit working at Benson's in 1931 and was making a living solely from writing. She worked as a critic of detective fiction and as a religious dramatist for the BBC and the Canterbury Cathedral, pulling out Peter and Family only during a series of short papers for *The Spectator* during the War. Her greatest work, as a translator, was yet to come: she was determined to create a translation of Dante's *Divine Comedy* that revealed its humor and its exuberance, its joyfulness, aspects of the work she felt had been left out by earlier translations. Though she did not know mediaeval Italian when she began, she had already translated *Tristan in Brittany* and *The Song of Roland* from the old French, and she knew enough Latin to make up for the rest; by the time she had finished the *Inferno* she discovered a richness that she had never imagined the *Comedy* could contain. A deeply religious woman, in Dante she found a beauty and honesty she had found nowhere else and dedicated the rest of her working days to him, trying to better explain to the rest of the world his vision of truth.

But detective fiction was not separate from that world of truth and beauty for which Sayers was searching; it is a mistake to imagine that she wrote detective fiction to make money and then abandoned it for something else more meaningful, as the "stages" of her career might suggest. Sayers threw herself whole-heartedly into becoming a detective fiction writer, establishing the first authoritative critical background for the genre, and then working to take it to its next logical level, always trying to uphold a scholarly and serious ideal. Detective fiction, like the religious drama to which she later turned her hand, has always been concerned with good and evil, as Sayers well knew. It is merely a different form of exploration. As Peter quips to his sister-in-law in *Strong Poison*, proclaiming Harriet innocent of murder: "'Damn it, she writes detective stories, and in detective stories virtue is always triumphant! They're the purest literature we have'" (132).

Surely this is Dorothy L. Sayers speaking.

Conclusion

The women writers in this study emerged out of a society which as a whole held rigid beliefs about the roles of women, including women writers. These women writers worked largely within those recognizable pillars of thought. They created young professional detectives, ready to take on male work in a male world when the possibility of such employment actually occurring was very slim; and they created older, more conventional women detectives when women working in male jobs became a reality. Yet in both of these cases, one can read an element of dissension in their writings, as they wrote stories which played within the "rules" of their society while simultaneously working to expand those rules. Like many feminists of their time, who sought to redefine women's roles but not necessarily to dismantle the culture which created those roles, women writers created womanly, feminine heroines who did not often jolt readers' sensibilities, but who subtly demanded a change in philosophy. They negotiated for recognition and greater possibility within an accepted and expected place. In doing so, they worked to define professional authority for themselves as women in the detective fiction genre.

The ways in which women's professional authority has been problematized, constructed, and explored in their detective fiction thus forms the central part of my study. As such, it is a particularly gender-based critical discussion. However, some of the issues about authority that I raise in this study could be transferable to male writers of popular fiction as well: they might feel the need to do whatever it takes to stay popular; to bow down to demands of a fickle audience; to have to continue with a series character, even if they don't want to. Similar frustrations might arise as to how to stand out among the myriad of writers all striving to make names for themselves, and even among writers not striving to make a name but merely writing to make money. Raymond Chandler, in "The Simple Art of Murder," writes about the voracious detective fiction-reading public which allowed publishing houses to print anything that came across their desk and make a best-seller out of it: "the average detective story is probably no worse that the average novel, but you never see the average novel. It doesn't get published. The average—or only slightly above average—detective story does" (in Haycraft 225). The frustration of having one's "art" so indistinguishable from everybody else's, even those writers and publishers who did not conceive of detective fiction as art, is a concern for those writers, male or female, trying to accomplish something "literary" in their work.

But men writing in this genre did not face the additional dilemmas that women did, based purely on their sex and the cultural restrictions placed upon them because of their sex. A later study desiring to fill in a blank in the current study might look more closely at the female detectives who were created by men from this time period as well, to see what narrative strategies male writers employed to give their female detectives the tools to solve crime and to examine the ways they portrayed their female detectives. A cursory examination (reading the collections by Kestner, Slung and Marcus) shows that male writers did create female detectives who use household clues and "natural" female intuition to solve crimes, and there were a few elderly spinster detectives.

Yet Barbara Lawrence, in "Female Detectives: The Feminist–Anti-Feminist Debate," argues that such female detectives, though they resembled those created by women writers, were not designed to highlight the skills of women but rather their inability to succeed without male help: "female writers create female detectives who rely on their skills as logical, thinking people" while male writers "cynically create detectives whose unconscious, intuitive efforts must be interpreted by men, or worse yet, one who is little more than an American private-eye type with a woman's name" (38). Her point about spinster detectives is a case in point: she compares the capable intelligence shown by Miss Marple and Miss Climpson to the "patronizing, belittling" (38) characterization of little Heron Carvic's Miss Seeton, a "figure of ridicule, bumbling about, incredibly naive but possessing intuitive powers which emerge in her sketches, drawn at the request of her male employers and interpreted by them" (43).

Furthermore, it is highly improbable that male writers would have used the character of female detective as a way to discuss problems of establishing their own authority, as I have argued women writers did. While providing female detectives with knowledge emanating from the domestic sphere seems common, I could not find one male-created female detective who is a writer, and certainly not one who is a writer of detective fiction; yet this, as I have shown, was a particularly potent strategy on the part of women writers to successfully negotiate their entrance into the detective fiction genre. These representations seem to have come about only in women writers, in response to the limited ways they had to establish their authority through their fiction. The authority of men to speak on any subject, in any genre, has rarely been questioned; nor was it questioned in detective fiction, a genre which, as most histories will relate, began with men: either with Edgar Allan Poe or Vidocq's memoirs and reaching its zenith in Sherlock Holmes.

A similar "woman's" history in detective fiction might be set up alongside this one, extending from its roots in the gothic novel and sensation fiction, both associated with women writers. But it is for precisely this reason that early women's detective fiction has been overlooked: it was more easily dismissed by their society because it was "merely feminine." While female detectives as a whole were popular, in part because of their oddity, women writers who created these detectives were largely ignored. Even in current studies, they have often been viewed only as stepping-stones to the Golden Age, when women's contributions could no longer be overlooked.

But how did Agatha Christie and Dorothy Sayers get there? What did they draw upon when forging out a place for female detection, and, more importantly, for women detective fiction writers? This is one reason why my study of professional authority in early women's detective fiction is valuable. As a male-dominated genre, the manner in which women solidified their presence in detective fiction extends from the particular narrative strategies employed by these early women writers; and, as writers in a male-dominated genre, they had more to gain in attempting to make a name for themselves in it, extending the boundaries which limited not only their fiction but their roles as women in their society as well.

At the same time, I see the work done by these women writers as valuable in itself, not merely as the necessary precursor to later and greater things. It is a record of women's struggles to maintain their own sphere of influence while expanding what that sphere could contain. More importantly, it is an example of the way women extended the scope of their authority, from a moral authority arising from the domestic sphere to a professional authority in the public sphere.

It is only recently that serious academic attention has been given to the detective fiction genre. But it seems to me an important area of study; the popular literature of a time period offers great insight into the particular issues facing the populace at that time. Certainly the roles of women during the late nineteenth and early twentieth centuries constituted one such issue. Women writers who created female detectives were able to engage in hotly contested cultural and social debates through them, thereby adding to the ways in which women could create their own authority in response to the dominant male culture. Over their one hundred years of existence, female detectives have consistently contributed to the ways in which women envisioned, and therefore constructed, their present and future place in society.

Chapter Notes

INTRODUCTION

1. For example, Sally Munt's *Murder by the Book?* (New York: Routledge, 1994) and Maureen T. Reddy's *Sisters in Crime* (New York: Continuum, 1988), both of which are subtitled *Feminism and the Crime Novel*, frame their discussions of what they consider feminist crime fiction with brief looks at early female detectives, but they focus on more recent characterizations and developments in the genre. Kathleen Gregory Klein's *Women Times Three: Writers, Detectives, Readers* (Bowling Green: BGSU Popular Press, 1995) looks at the ways the "contemporary crop of detecting women" presents a critique of earlier female detective models, whose stereotypes, she claims, have "never been easy to maintain" (12). I am not suggesting that these works fail in some way based on what they do or do not discuss; rather, I am trying to point out the general tendency in feminist critical discourse to pass over of the sub-genre of early women detectives in favor of later ones.

Similarly, essays in collections such as Glenwood Irons' *Feminism in Women's Detective Fiction* (Toronto: U of Toronto P, 1995) often compare an earlier writer/detective with a more modern writer/detective; the latter receives more favorable feminist comment. Thus, SueEllen Campbell's "The Detective Heroine and Her Hero: Sayers to James" concludes that Sayers cannot bring her characters to a satisfactory conclusion, but P.D. James, using her female detective Cordelia Gray, can: "the detective heroine and the possibility of a hero are at last not presented in problematic terms" (26). Glenwood Irons' and Joan Roberts' essay, "Spinster to Hipster: the 'Suitability' of Miss Marple and Anna Lee," looks at how Liza Cody "reinvented" the spinster and moved the character well beyond what Christie was able to accomplish. Implicit in these formats is the suggestion that earlier women detectives (and their writers) leave something to be desired and that later women detectives and writers rectify the situation.

2. Michelle Slung's *Crime on Her Mind: Fifteen Stories of Female Sleuths from the Victorian Era to the Forties* (New York: Pantheon, 1975), is one of the first collections about female detectives, and many excellent studies on women detectives have followed. These include Kathleen Gregory Klein, *The Woman Detective: Gender and Genre* (2nd ed. Urbana: U of Illinois Press, 1995); Patricia Craig and Mary Cadogan, *The Lady Investigates: Women Detectives and Spies in Fiction* (London: Victor Gollancz, 1981); and Joseph Kestner, *Sherlock's Sisters: The British Female Detective, 1864–1913* (Hants, England: Ashgate, 2003). All of these studies focus on one half of my question: the female detective. However, their studies cover fiction by both male and female authors. Other sources discussing late nineteenth and early twentieth century women detectives are Fay Blake, "Lady Sleuths and Women Detectives," *Turn of the*

Century Woman 3.1 (Summer 1986): 29–42; Laura Marcus, *Twelve Women Detective Stories* (Oxford: Oxford UP, 1997); and Kathleen L. Maio, "'A Strange and Fierce Delight': The Early Days of Women's Mystery Fiction," *Chrysalis* 10: 94–105.

There are also several collections that look at mystery and detective stories written by women; however, these cover both male and female detective creations. They include Kathleen Gregory Klein, *Great Women Mystery Writers: Classic to Contemporary* (Westport: Greenwood Press, 1994); Jean Swanson and Dean James, *By a Woman's Hand: A Guide to Mystery Fiction by Women* (New York: Berkley Books, 1994); Jessica Mann, *Deadlier Than the Male: An Investigation into Feminine Crime Writing* (London: David & Charles, 1981) which focuses specifically on women writers of the Golden Age; Earl Bargainnier, ed., *Ten Women of Mystery* (Bowling Green: BGSU Popular Press, 1981); and Jane S. Bakerman, *And Then There Were Nine ... More Women of Mystery* (Bowling Green: BGSU Popular Press, 1985).

Feminist studies of women's crime writing in general (either writers or characters) include Sally R. Munt, *Murder By the Book?*; Maureen T. Reddy, *Sisters in Crime*; Glenwood Irons, ed., *Feminism in Women's Detective Fiction*; and Kathleen Gregory Klein, *Women Times Three: Writers, Detectives, Readers*. Victoria Nichols and Susan Thompson, *Silk Stalkings: When Women Write of Murder* (Berkeley: Black Lizard Books, 1988) is a useful survey of series characters created by women writers.

3. Many critics, seeking to problematize the decidedly narrow term "Golden Age," insert the phrase "so-called" before it. This is especially true of those critics who wonder why, if it was such a "Golden Age," didn't the women writers who anchored the time period (women such as Sayers, Allingham, Marsh, Tey and Christie) create female detectives as their main character? See Kathleen Gregory Klein, for example, in *The Woman Detective*, ch. 5. However, throughout this book I will refer to the period simply as the Golden Age, recognizing that critics have increasingly questioned this simplistic designation.

4. In using a cultural studies approach to help illuminate this project's goals, I am relying on the definitions (and debates) provided by Grossberg, Nelson, and Treichler in their landmark *Cultural Studies* collection (New York: Routledge, 1992). Cultural studies can be broadly defined as the attempt to recognize and articulate the processes which shape society (4); for these editors, "culture is understood *both* as a way of life—encompassing ideas, attitudes, languages, practices, institutions, and structures of power—and a whole range of cultural practices: artistic forms, texts, canons, architecture, mass-produced commodities, and so forth"(5). Because it insists that all forms of cultural practices be studied, it often concerns itself with the tensions that arise when one sets larger societal forces which compose a way of life next to the cultural practices, of all forms, which that way of life engenders.

Within this larger critical approach comes the study of popular culture, "the beliefs and practices, and the objects through which they are organized, that are widely shared among a population" (Mukerji and Schudson 3). Though cultural studies often concerns itself with popular forms, it insists that we look at not only *what* is produced but how and why such popular forms are produced. Hence, a discussion of women and their relationship to popular forms must examine not just the works themselves but also the cultural attitudes which swirled about the production of such works.

5. The Woman Question, as its name implies, became the common term for the society-wide debate about women's roles, from about the mid-Victorian era to World War I. Questions of education and employment for women, as well as their legal rights (or lack thereof), pervaded British society, as men and women, liberals and conservatives alike, strove to define woman's place in a rapidly changing world. The three-volume work by Helsinger, Veeder and Sheets is the most complete and thorough at charting the implications and ramifications of these debates. See Elizabeth K. Helsinger, Robin Lauterbach Sheets, and William Veeder, *The Woman Question: Society and Literature in Britain and America, 1837–1883*, 3 vols. (New York: Garland, 1983).

6. Reynolds and Humble write about the gendered discourse in which "the masculine (positive) term was reserved for work that offered itself as the unique expression of individual genius" (31). They quote Andreas Huyssen: "'The notion [...] gained ground during the nineteenth century that mass culture is somehow associated with women while real, authentic culture remains the

prerogative of men'" (31). Kimberly Reynolds and Nicola Humble, *Victorian Heroines: Representations of Femininity in Nineteenth-Century Literature and Art* (New York: New York UP, 1993).

7. See Howard Haycraft's *Murder for Pleasure: The Life and Times of the Detective Story* (New York: Appleton-Century, 1941), 158, for a list of these changes, which also includes a discussion of the increased "literariness" of the genre. Most single-author general histories of the detective novel discuss the genre's changes during this time. In addition to Haycraft, see Leroy Lad Panek: *An Introduction to the Detective Story* (Bowling Green: BGSU Popular Press, 1987) and *Watteau's Shepherds: The Detective Novel in Britain 1914–1940* (Bowling Green: BGSU Popular Press, 1979); A. E. Murch's *The Development of the Detective Novel* (New York: Philosophical Library, Inc., 1958), which discusses nineteenth-century detective fiction in depth; and T.J. Binyon's *'Murder Will Out': The Detective in Fiction* (Oxford: Oxford UP, 1989). I did not find Julian Symons' popular *Bloody Murder: From the Detective Story to the Crime Novel: A History* (1972; New York: Viking, 1985) particularly useful as a history. Symons himself says in his preface to the second edition that he is an "addict not an academic" and is not interested in presenting a history except through those authors he likes; thus it is not particularly comprehensive.

Most information about the detective fiction genre, including its changes or shifts, I found in collections of essays: Howard Haycraft, ed., *The Art of the Mystery Story: A Collection of Critical Essays* (New York: Simon and Schuster, 1946) which contains some of the now-classic discussions of the genre, including Sayers' introduction to *The Omnibus of Crime*, Raymond Chandler's "The Simple Art of Murder," and R. Austin Freeman's "The Art of the Detective Story." Other good collections include: Clive Bloom, ed., *Twentieth-Century Suspense: The Thriller Comes of Age* (New York: St. Martin's, 1990); Robin Winks, ed., *Detective Fiction: A Collection of Critical Essays* (Woodstock, VT: The Countryman Press, 1988); Ronald G. Walker and June M. Frazer, eds., *The Cunning Craft: Original Essays on Detective Fiction and Contemporary Literary Theory*, Essays in Literature (Western Illinois University, 1990); and Barbara Rader and Howard G. Zettler, *The Sleuth and the Scholar* (New York: Greenwood Press, 1988).

8. On the whole, writers of the Golden Age stood by these rules; the oath taken by members of the Detection Club sprung from the desire to ensure members' complicity. Though such rules were primarily tongue-in-cheek, there was often a controversy if a writer was thought to have abandoned them. One of Agatha Christie's works can serve as an example.

Christie was notorious for "breaking the rules." Carl Lovitt, in "Controlling Discourse in Detective Fiction, or Caring Very Much Who Killed Roger Ackroyd," looks specifically at Christie's supposed lack of fair play in *The Murder of Roger Ackroyd* (1926), wondering how "an author whose name is virtually synonymous with the genre" could have "repeatedly violated the rules without alienating that audience" (in Walker and Frazer 69).

Yet the fact that there is an argument about whether Christie played fair in this novel admits conflicting viewpoints. Lovitt writes that many readers and critics were furious that Christie would have the narrator, the Watson-character whom one implicitly trusts, be the murderer (69–70). Sayers defended Christie's maneuver in *Ackroyd*, saying she felt readers were mad primarily because they got tricked—in other words, because Christie did her job so well. She argues that Christie's use of a murder-narrator does not break the "fair play" rule because there is nothing in a narrator's status (his "Watsonity") that inherently vouches for his moral worth. But note that Sayers' defense nonetheless revolves around the primacy of the rules—its not that Christie abandoned them, but that she didn't break them ("Aristotle and Detective Fiction" in Winks 25–34).

Lovitt himself concludes that Christie simply showed her expertise at expanding the rules, that creating Sheppard showed "ingenious accommodation of an inviolable generic restriction" (83). Yet he believes that Christie's "infraction" in this novel helped consolidate the tenets of Golden Age dogma, tracing two of the rules in Ronald Knox's Decalogue, written in 1929, to this novel. Thus in breaking the rules, she solidified them.

9. In general, in the late eighteenth and early nineteenth centuries, both men and women engaged in those tasks which made the large households of landowners run smoothly; while men were primarily responsible for public and "outside" tasks and

women for indoor or household tasks, neither sex was so firmly cemented in these roles. Women managed large-scale brewing and baking operations, for example, which contributed to the estate's income, and men often took an avid interest in the management of household affairs.

See the introduction to the collection edited by Vanessa D. Dickerson, *Keeping the Victorian House: A Collection of Essays* (New York: Garland, 1995) and Jessica Gerard's essay "The Chatelaine: Women of the Victorian Landed Classes and the Country House" in that collection, 175–205. The study edited by historians Leonore Davidoff and Belinda Westover, *Our Work, Our Lives, Our Words: Women's History and Women's Work* (Totowa, New Jersey: Barnes & Noble, 1986) centers primarily on working-class women, but it discusses in its introduction this same general shift in men's and women's employment after industrialization. See also Dorothy Sayers, "The Human-Not-Quite-Human," *Unpopular Opinions: Twenty-One Essays* (New York: Harcourt, Brace, 1947) 142–149.

10. Lynda Nead provides a description of the "'perfect ideal of an English wife and mother'" by Dr. William Acton, a prominent mid-Victorian authority on prostitution and women's sexuality: she is "'kind, considerate, self-sacrificing, and sensible, so pure-hearted as to be utterly ignorant of and averse to any sensual indulgence, but so unselfishly attached to the man she loves, as to be willing to give up her own wishes and feelings for his sake.'" In *Myths of Sexuality: Representations of Women in Victorian Britain* (Oxford: Basil Blackwell, 1990) 19.

11. See Laura Faisik, "God's House, Woman's Place" in Dickerson for a discussion of the spinster in the fiction of Charlotte Yonge, Elizabeth Sewell, and Dinah Mulock Craik, 75–103; see also Laura Doan, ed., *Old Maids and Radical Spinsters: Unmarried Women in the Twentieth Century Novel*, foreword by Nina Auerbach (Urbana: U of Illinois P, 1991). Nina Auerbach's *Woman and the Demon: The Life of a Victorian Myth* is an illuminating discussion of the spinster's representation in fiction, in which she argues that the spinster character could be seen as both empowered and (because of her power) potentially threatening (Cambridge: Harvard UP, 1982). Studies by Sheila Jeffreys, *The Spinster and Her Enemies: Feminism and Sexuality 1880–1930* (London: Pandora, 1985) and Martha Vicinus, *Independent Women: Work*

and Community for Single Women, 1850–1920 (Chicago: University of Chicago Press, 1985) look primarily at spinsters in "real life" but acknowledge the ways she is present in fiction.

12. Sandra M. Gilbert and Susan Gubar, *The Madwoman in the Attic* (New Haven: Yale UP, 1979); Elaine Showalter, *A Literature of Their Own* (Princeton: Princeton UP, 1977).

13. Light's study is particularly useful as an examination of British culture between the wars and the "conservative modernity" that several women writers created through gendered narratives, locating both conservatism and modernism in domestic sites. Her analysis of Agatha Christie as a "modern" writer is truly ground-breaking, arguing that her fiction, rather than evoking an "England gone by" is instead a record of new kinds of social anxiety about English life. Alison Light, *Forever England: Femininity, Literature and Conservatism between the Wars* (London: Routledge, 1991).

14. Two female detectives appeared in the 1860s: Mrs. Pascal, created by W.S. Hayward, and a woman simply known as "The Female Detective," created by Andrew Forester, Jr. Both women took up detective work to escape "genteel poverty" (Craig and Cadogan 15).

15. David Mitchell puts it most succinctly when he writes: "Like many other employers, the police hastened to put back the feminist clock when the emergency was over." In *Monstrous Regiment: The Story of Women in the First World War* (New York: MacMillan, 1965) 220.

16. See Chloe Owings, *Women Police* (New York: Frederick H. Hitchcock, 1925), who writes: "In Parliament there were many debates, conferences, and discussions, while outside of Parliament, women's societies organized public protest meetings and delegations to visit government officials" (32). See pages 23–39 for a complete discussion. See also Joan Lock, *The British Policewoman: Her Story* (London: Robert Hale, 1979) and Mary S. Allen, *The Pioneer Policewoman* (London: Chatto and Windus, 1925) for general histories of early women police.

17. I find it surprising that so few critics comment directly on this connection between these two subgenres. Most do not recognize the influence of the former upon the latter, or if they do, do not consider it worth discussion. The exception to this is A.E. Murch's *The Development of the Detective Novel*, which, as its title suggests, devotes

much space to the relationship of gothic and sensation fiction to detective fiction. Other critics who touch upon the subject include: Winifred Hughes, *The Maniac in the Cellar: Sensation Novels of the 1860s* (Princeton: Princeton UP, 1980) ch. 6; and Maureen T Reddy, *Sisters in Crime* conclusion.

18. General characteristics of a *Bildungsroman* usually include a boy leaving home to search for himself, undergoing painful lessons which become learning experiences (his "apprenticeship"), and ultimately finding his place in society, signaling his maturity. For ways in which women's growing experiences differ, see Elizabeth Abel, Marianne Hirsh, and Elizabeth Langland, *The Voyage In: Fictions of Female Development* (Hanover: UP of New England, 1983); Susan Fraiman, *Unbecoming Women: British Women Writers and the Novel of Development* (New York: Columbia UP, 1993); and Penny Brown, *Poison at the Source: The Female Novel of Self-Development in the Early Twentieth Century* (New York: St. Martin's, 1992). The collection edited by Suzanne W. Jones, *Writing the Woman Artist: Essays on Poetics, Politics, and Portraitures* (Philadelphia: U of Philadelphia P, 1991) contains essays that examine the way women portray the woman artist figure in their fiction.

19. See Theresa Freda Nicolay, *Gender Roles, Literary Authority, and Three American Women Writers*, The Age of Revolution and Romanticism Interdisciplinary Studies (New York: Peter Lang, 1995); Vineta Colby, *Yesterday's Woman: Domestic Realism in the English Novel* (Princeton: Princeton UP, 1974); Mary Jean Corbett, "Feminine Authorship and Spiritual Authority in Victorian Women Writers' Autobiographies," *Women's Studies* 18.1 (1990): 13–29; Margaret Dickie, "The Maternal Gaze: Women Modernists and Poetic Authority," *Alternative Identities: The Self in Literature, History, Theory*, Ed. Marie Brooks, Wellesley Studies in Critical Theory, Literary History, and Culture (New York: Garland, 1995).

For other studies of women's authority concentrating on a specific genre or type of writing, see Elizabeth C. Goldsmith, ed., *Writing the Female Voice: Essays on Epistolary Literature* (Boston: Northeastern UP, 1989); Betsy Erkkila, *The Wicked Sisters: Women Poets, Literary History and Discord* (Oxford: Oxford UP, 1992); Susan Sniader Lanser, *Fictions of Authority: Women Writers and Narrative Voice* (Ithaca: Cornell UP, 1992); Lyn Pykett, *The "Improper" Feminine: The Women's Sensation*

Novel and the New Woman Writing (London: Routledge, 1992); William J. Scheick, *Authority and Female Authorship in Colonial America* (Lexington: UP of Kentucky, 1998); Sherry Lee Linkon, ed., *In Her Own Voice: Nineteenth Century American Women Essayists* (New York: Garland, 1997); Sydney Janet Kaplan, *Feminine Consciousness in the Modern British Novel* (Urbana: U of Illinois P, 1975); Martha Cutter, *Unruly Tongue: Identity and Voice in American Women's Writing* (Jackson: UP of Mississippi, 1999); Elsie B. Michie, *Outside the Pale: Cultural Exclusion, Gender Difference, and the Victorian Woman Writer* (Ithaca: Cornell UP, 1993); Belinda Edmondson, *Making Men: Gender, Literary Authority, and Women's Writing in Caribbean Narrative* (Durham: Duke UP, 1999); Wendy Wall, *The Imprint of Gender: Authorship and Publication in the English Renaissance* (Ithaca: Cornell UP, 1993).

Carolyn Heilbrun's *Writing a Woman's Life* (New York: W. W. Norton & Company, 1988) is an excellent general discussion of women's authority in fiction and the impact gender has on authority.

20. This idea will be discussed in greater detail in Chapter Two.

21. I am basing my claim that a diverse audience read the work of early female detective fiction writers primarily on the ubiquity of the magazines which printed these stories. Alan K. Russell, in his collection of early detective fiction, lists several monthly "famous and popular" magazines in which detective stories, including those written by women, were published: *The Strand Magazine, The Windsor Magazine* ("An Illustrated Monthly for Men and Women"), *Pearson's Magazine, The Ludgate Monthly,* and *The Harmsworth Magazine,* to name a few. Such magazines "virtually monopolized" creative talent, he writes, and were "as keenly read and talked about as a new television series is today" (viii). in *The Rivals of Sherlock Holmes* (Secaucus, NJ: Castle Books, 1978).

Reginald Pound, in *Mirror of the Century: The Strand Magazine 1891-1950* (New York: A. S. Barnes and Co., 1966) writes that "the middle-classes of England never cast a clearer image of themselves in print than they did in *The Strand Magazine*," which was among those that published detective stories by women (7). He notes that Queen Victoria herself helped complete an article on the dolls of her infancy. Judging from the type of articles printed in this magazine and the fact that in Pound's estimation it "attained the status of a national institution" (9), it is safe to say that both men and women read it and other monthly publications like it.

22. Angela Woollacott's article, "From Moral to Professional Authority: Secularism, Social Work, and Middle-Class Women's Self-Construction in World War I Britain," offers a model for this discussion in looking at women's professional authority. She examines the ways that three groups of women workers during World War I—YWCA social workers, women police officers and patrols, and women industrial welfare supervisors— adapted traditional views of female authority to their newly established professional activities. *Journal of Women's History* 10.2 (Summer 1998): 85–111. Similarly, I suggest that women writers too searched for ways of transferring traditional aspects of female authority to help establish their professional authority in detective fiction.

CHAPTER ONE

1. Several excellent accounts of the beginning of women police in England exist, including Mary S. Allen, *The Pioneer Policewoman* (London: Chatto and Windus, 1925), Lock's *The British Policewoman*, and Chloe Owings, *Women Police*. Mary Allen delves into the specific issue of maintaining a standing police force after the war in the most detail and with the most bitterness.

For general accounts of the various types of work women did during the war, see Helen Fraser, *Women And War Work* (New York: G. Arnold Shaw, 1918); Gilbert Stone, ed., *Women War Workers* (New York: Thomas Y. Crowell Company, 1917); Arthur Marwick, *Women at War, 1914–1918* (Fontana Paperbacks in Association with The Imperial War Museum, 1977); and Mrs. Alec Tweedie, *Women and Soldiers* (London: John Lane, The Bodley Head, 1918). David Mitchell, *Monstrous Regiment* is a more modern account of women's work during the war and the way it was seen by their society; though published in 1965, it is not out-dated.

2. Ellery Queen, *The Female of the Species* (Boston: Little, Brown, 1944) predates Slung's collection; however, he offers no analysis of the phenomenon of the female detective or of the sociological influences behind her formation. His collection is not exclusively about female detectives, by the

way, but also includes stories which "star" female criminals.

3. For further discussions of the variety of feminist beliefs and actions during this time, see Philippa Levine, *Feminist Lives in Victorian England* (Oxford: Basil Blackwell, 1990) and *Victorian Feminism* (London: Hutchinson, 1987); Sheila Jeffreys, *The Spinster and Her Enemies: Feminism and Sexuality 1880–1930* (London: Pandora, 1985); and Barbara Caine, *Victorian Feminists* (Oxford: Oxford UP, 1992).

4. Jobs within the police force for which Hamilton thinks women are well-suited include patrol work, fingerprinting, working with children, and, interestingly, "The Policewoman as a Detective." She calls detective work "one of the most logical branches of the service for which the sex it fitted." See Mary E. Hamilton, *The Policewoman: Her Service and Ideals* (New York: Frederick A. Stoles, 1924) 77.

5. Holcombe 11.

6. Billie Melman, *Women and the Popular Imagination in the Twenties* (New York: St. Martin's, 1988) 5.

7. This idea was first proposed in an 1862 article by journalist W.R. Greg, entitled "Why Are Women Redundant?" Martha Vicinus, in her introduction to *Independent Women: Work and Community for Single Women 1850–1920*, names Greg's article as "one of the best-known solutions to 'the woman question'" (3). The other suggestion Greg made in his rather notoriously famous proposal was that women should learn how to make themselves more agreeable so that men will want to marry them.

For information on the establishment of schools to provide office training see Leonore Davidoff and Belinda Westover, eds., introduction. Edith J., Morley, ed., *Women Workers in Seven Professions: A Survey of their Economic Conditions and Prospects* (London: George Routledge & Sons, 1914) gives several first-hand accounts of women in offices, 235–297.

8. For the establishment of teaching as a profession see Erna Olafson Hellerstein, Leslie Parker Hume, and Karen M. Offen, eds., *Victorian Women: A Documentary Account of Women's Lives in Nineteenth-Century England, France, and the United States* (Stanford: Stanford UP, 1981) 283–284; Francis Widdowson in Davidoff and Westover (99–123), and Morley 2–37.

9. While in theory the SDRA satisfied

the need for legal reform, its terms often proved unsuccessful when put to the test, as historian Harold Smith notes: "its deficiencies as an instrument for change are suggested by the unsuccessful efforts to use it to remove sex-based barriers" (52). He cites several examples of the Act's failure, including Lady Rhondda's attempt in 1922 to enter the House of Lords. Even though her father drafted his will in such a way so that she would inherit his title and be eligible to take his seat in the House, she was barred from doing so. "British Feminism in the Twentieth Century," Harold L. Smith, ed., *British Feminism in the Twentieth Century* (Amherst: U of Massachusetts P, 1990) 47–65.

10. In Marwick ch. 6.

11. Teaching was often more than just a "common career path" for women after college; claiming teaching as a vocation was often only way they could get to college. Edith Morley, for example, laments the fact that for young intelligent girls who want to attend college, "it is still the line of least resistance to say that she wishes to become a teacher" (11). In a paragraph unto itself she writes: "There should be other paths from elementary and secondary school to the University than that which leads to the teacher's platform" (12). She reiterates in several places that teachers need to have a "true calling," since they are badly-paid, over-worked and face "inevitably severe" physical and mental strain (2). Many girls, however, either to gain parental consent in order to attend college or to be eligible for scholarship money, trained to become teachers.

It is interesting to note that the two women detective fiction writers in this study who attended college (and got degrees), Gladys Mitchell and Dorothy L. Sayers, taught at the secondary school level.

12. See Carol Dyhouse, *No Distinction of Sex? Women in British Universities 1870–1939* (London: UCL Press, 1995) 11–13.

13. Sally Mitchell, *The New Girl: Girl's Culture in England 1880–1915* (New York: Columbia, 1995) ch. 3.

14. Davy discusses this in particular with female typists, but it held true for other professions as well that became "feminized." See Teresa Davy, "'A Cissy Job for Men; A Nice Job for Girls': Women Shorthand Typists in London, 1900–1939." in Davidoff and Westover 126.

15. Harold Smith writes that enforcing the "marriage bar" became standard practice

in the civil service, local government, and in the teaching professions during the 1920s, though it had always been a regular part of employment philosophy earlier in the century. One of the roadblocks that the SDRA was supposed to remove was the marriage bar, which allowed employers to dismiss women once they got married. The Act's inability to protect married women workers was yet another aspect of its inadequacy. Smith 52–54.

16. I have split governessing off from teaching in its own separate category because my decision concerning what jobs to discuss in this chapter is based solely on those jobs mentioned in detective fiction during this time. In this case, Miss Silver is described distinctly as an ex-governess, not a teacher, though the two are often thought of as a single category.

17. Holcombe 12.

18. Holcombe 14.

19. Vicinus, in *Independent Women*, cites the founding date for the GBI as 1841 (23), as does Holcombe (14). However, Alice Renton, *Tyrant or Victim? A History of Governesses* (London: George Weidenfeld and Nicolson Limited, 1991), gives the founding date as 1843 (90).

20. Katharine Leaf West, *Chapter of Governesses: A Study of the Governess in English Fiction, 1800–1949* (London: Cohen & West, 1949).

21. Renton 139–141.

22. Davy in Davidoff and Westover 125.

23. in Davidoff and Westover 124.

24. Nicola Diane Thompson's discussion of mid-Victorian women literary reviewers illustrates some of the difficulties of women writing for the public sphere. On the one hand, it was certainly true that several magazines employed women reviewers, most notably Geraldine Jewsbury at the *Athanaeum*. At the same time, the potential disruption of employing women writers was mitigated by the standard practices of the day (true for both men and women): employing anonymity in reviews, using the pronoun "we" instead of "I" in order to further submerge the journalists' identity, and consciously or unconsciously adopting the "voice" of the organ for which they were writing. (12). Thompson suggests that such sexless conditions were favorable to women reviewers who "would want to consolidate their precarious hold on literary authority and respectability, and would desire to be

taken seriously and accepted as part of the patriarchal establishment" (12). In other words, removing the fact of their sex from their reviews allowed women to perform their jobs as writers. In *Reviewing Sex: Gender and the Reception of Victorian Novels* (New York: New York UP, 1996).

25. L.S. Hearnshaw, *A Short History of British Psychology, 1840–1940* (New York: Barnes & Noble, 1964) 30.

26. Lisa Appignanesi and John Forrester's chapter, "Joan Riviere and Alix Strachey: Translating Psychoanalysis," gives a complete account of women's roles in translating Freud's theories into English. in *Freud's Women* (New York: BasicBooks, 1992) ch. 12.

27. Naomi Loughnan, "Munition Work," in Stone 25–45.

28. Sheila Rowbotham, in *A Century of Women*, relates the following account, acknowledging this fact: "When a young VAD managed to get transferred to the Ambulance Corps, the major to whom she reported teased her about her desire for adventure: 'I doubt one half of you VADs and others are doing your bit just out of patriotism'" (New York: Viking, 1997) 71.

29. However, it might be a misnomer to consider the WAACs or other women's paramilitary attachments "military." Mitchell for one writes explicitly that the WAACs did not have "full military status." They enrolled, not enlisted; they were punished for any crimes in civil courts, not military courts; and saluting was "neither officially authorized or officially forbidden." In other words, at least in military circles, they were seen as civilians. See D. Mitchell, *Monstrous Regiment* 223.

30. See also D. Mitchell 222 and Woollacott, *On Her* 196.

31. D. Mitchell 222.

32. Keep in mind that by 1916 there were very few men available to be nurses—they had all been recruited as soldiers. This doesn't change the fact that the VADs were in theory at least supposed to have both male and female members.

33. Summers, for one, writes extensively about the outdoor and masculine-oriented activities of VAD work that cut across its more traditional domestic aspects. These activities could provide leadership positions for women who otherwise may not have been given opportunities to take charge (253–263). She writes that "improvisation and spontaneity were the key words of the movement." In *Angels and Citizens: British Women as Military*

Nurses 1854– 1914 (London: Routledge & Kegan Paul, 1987) 258.

34. Barbara McLaren writes: "The employment of women for police service, in vogue for some years on the Continent and in the United States of America, has been developed in this country [England] only by the outbreak of war." in *Women of the War* (London: Hodder and Stoughton, 1917) 62.

35. Angela Woollacott, "'Khaki Fever' and its Control: Gender, Class, Age and Sexual Morality on the British Homefront in the First World War," *Journal of Contemporary History* 29 (1994): 325–347. Levine and Bland also come to this conclusion; Bland's article especially looks at the double-bind women patrols fell into: "in their attempts to protect women and girls, the protection provided by the women police and patrols tended to slip into surveillance" (23). See Lucy Bland, "In the Name of Protection: The Policing of Women in the First World War," *Women-in-law: Explorations in Law, Family, and Sexuality*, eds. Julia Brophy and Carol Smart (London: Routledge & Kegan Paul, 1985) 23–49. See also Philippa Levine, "'Walking the Streets in a Way No Decent Woman Should': Women Police in World War I," *Journal of Modern History* 66 (1994): 34–78.

36. In fact, Nina Boyle, one of the original founders of the Women Police Volunteers (which became the WPS after she left), split off from the group for this very reason. She believed that the newly enacted Defence of the Realm Act (DORA), like the earlier Contagious Disease Acts, gave power to men at the expense of the basic human rights of women—it allowed women's homes to be entered and searched, with women getting arrested if soldiers were found on the premises. She was furious that women police patrols would participate in carrying out this "law," but only two other members agreed with her, and so they were forced to leave the group. Ultimately, this did the WPS a world of good, since the Home Office and Chief Constables wanted nothing to do with suffragettes or people who they saw as militant feminists. See Levine 52–53.

37. Allen remarks that since "a Chief Constable is a power in his own district" (21), he could deal with women recruits as he saw fit. Thus the status of women recruits varied, depending upon what the Chief Constable

felt they were capable of and what he wanted to do with them (47).

38. Owings spends some time discussing the legality of this swearing in, since women were not considered "persons" for the purposes of the law. The Home Office eventually decided that this was *not* a legal swearing-in. See Owings 13.

39. Joan Lock, writing more evenhandedly, points out that most of the first recruits were trained patrols from the NUWW, which was seen as much less threatening than the WPS, as the former was supposedly not connected to the suffragettes. She also reports that "class and education" took "prime place" in selection of women, at least in theory, and that the second 25 women chosen to patrol the streets contained a few WPS-trained women.

40. Patrols from the NUWW were often married; as a whole women who joined this group were not trying to make a career out of their work but went patrolling only "one or two evenings a week" (Fraser 238). See also Levine 46.

41. See Alison Light for an apt discussion on why this became true for male detectives— the once brash hero had gone out and gotten himself blown up and had wrecked society; now the effeminate, less manly-man had to be heroic, since brawn didn't pay off. Hence types such as Wimsey and Poirot appeared (72–73).

42. Moylan, for instance, merely notes that women have long been "associated with" the police to help search female prisoners or to work as a matron (222). I have not checked Scotland Yard's archives; these papers might provide some more specific information on the "unofficial" detective work women performed, as well as insights into why their work was not recognized publicly.

43. Lock's version of things is less ecstatic: she says that "present day survivors of those early women detectives recall that their work was largely clerical and secretarial with the occasional indecency statement, pickpocket observation at markets and races, and decoy duty during spates of sexual attacks" (101). From this account, these women seem to have been detectives in little more than name. Nonetheless, they did perform work more varied than most other women police, and the steps that the Chief Constable took in attempting to make them equal with their male counterparts—at least in name and in theory—count for something.

CHAPTER TWO

1. In Mary Elizabeth Braddon's *Aurora Floyd*, for example, the heroine accidentally commits bigamy and is framed for murder, but eventually is redeemed and remains happily married. In Wilkie Collins' *No Name*, Magdalene Vanstone resorts to lying, stealing, manipulating and disguise in order to have revenge, but eventually she falls ill and then in love with a sea captain, whom she marries at the end of the book.

2. Fay Blake in her excellent article finds four examples of working class female detectives appearing in the 1890s, but all of these were created by men, suggesting perhaps that women writers had a different agenda. Of these four, one is a twelve-year old girl (which places her out of the range of a study of female detectives) and one is a gypsy who runs a pawn shop. That two of these four are not traditional British women again implies some limitations of what was acceptable. Fay Blake, "Lady Sleuths and Women Detectives," *Turn of the Century Women* 3.1 (Summer 1986): 29–42.

3. Mary Poovey, *Uneven Developments*, ch. 3.

4. See also the recent collection *Rewriting the Victorians*, which contains several chapters arguing "for the strength of the female, while allowing for the cultural constraints placed on her" (preface xi). Linda M. Shires, ed., *Rewriting the Victorians* (London: Routledge, 1992).

5. See B.A. Pike, "In Praise of Gladys Mitchell," *The Armchair Detective* 9 (1976): 250–260.

6. I am using Cvetkovich's terms here, p. 15. But the debate about "high" and "low" literature had been going on well before the time frame Cvetkovich discusses. Since the mid- to late eighteenth century—indeed, since the rise of the novel—there had been sometimes fierce debates about what should and should not be considered literature, coinciding with the rights of authors to copyright their work as their own. See Martha Woodmansee, *The Author, Art, and the Market: Rereading the History of Aesthetics* (New York: Columbia UP, 1994) for a discussion of copyright and "authorship" in this broader sense. See also Peter Stallybrass and Allon White, *The Politics and Poetics of Transgression* (Ithaca: Cornell UP, 1986) on the "high/low" split and its aesthetic implications.

7. Lynn Pykett, *The "Improper" Feminine:*

The Women's Sensation Novel and the New Woman Writing (New York: Routledge, 1992) 6.

8. Sayers, for one, chose to pin hopes on her first detective story, despite her belief that it would not get published, because she desperately needed an income. She writes to her parents: "there is a market for detective literature if one can get in, and he [Lord Peter] might go some way towards providing bread and cheese" (in Reynolds, *Letters* 181).

9. Miller's other story starring Valeska, "The Murder of Lawrence Drummond," also contains some examples of "social" knowledge, including recognizing the distinct type of paper found on trans–Atlantic steamships. See Elizabeth York Miller, "Valeska, Woman Detective: The Murder of Lawrence Drummond," *London Magazine* 21 (1908/9): 666–672.

10. Again, this is an invented position; Moylan (as I pointed out in the previous chapter) specifically cites Orczy's fiction as an example of what did *not* exist.

11. Though male authors include "natural female intuition" as a resource for their female detectives, it often appears in a very superfluous way, minimizing the strategic function of it as a deliberate tool for detection. For example, in one of Dorcas Dene's cases, "The Man with the Wild Eyes," George Sims introduces Dorcas' intuitive skills in a completely gratuitous manner. A retired colonel comes to consult Dorcas because he fears something more happened to his daughter than the fainting fit story she has given out to the doctor and himself; the doctor, he says, has given him information that makes him uneasy. That there is more to the story is fairly obvious; or why else would he have come to a private detective? But when Dorcas rhetorically asks if this is true, the Colonel seems amazed:

"He didn't believe in the fainting fit?" said Dorcas, who had been closely watching the Colonel's features.

The Colonel looked at Dorcas Dene in astonishment. "I don't know how you have divined that," he said, "but your surmise is correct" (in Slung 40).

Better uses of Dorcas' "intuition" come later in her investigation, especially in assigning motives for the daughter's subterfuge. Yet these more applicable uses of knowledge of human nature, examples upon which female authors would certainly have commented, pass by unmentioned. George

Sims, "The Man with the Wild Eyes" in Slung 35–61.

12. A classic example of this confusion appearing in one's language occurs in Hugh C. Weir's "The Man with Nine Lives," starring Madeline Mack (in Slung 113–151). A male onlooker to the case Mack has just solved says to her: "'Allow me to present a problem to your *analytical skill*, Miss Mack,' I said humbly. 'Which man does your *knowledge of feminine psychology* say Muriel Jansen will reward [...]?'" (in Slung 151; emphasis mine). Though here this "knowledge" is talked of as a skill, it is clearly one ordered on gendered lines, one which she is expected as a woman to know. A male detective would never have been asked this question; nor would Miss Mack ever have been asked a question about masculine psychology.

13. Mudie's Circulating Library, for example, guaranteed that subscribers could be sure "they were getting wholesome fiction, fit reading for 'the Young Person'" (Ardis 39). This policy excluded from circulation the books of many authors—including George Moore, Thomas Hardy, and several New Woman novelists—who wanted to portray a "realism" in their novels that they felt was lacking in British fiction. Interestingly, Linton was originally for this new realism, though she very shortly afterward spoke out heatedly against the New Woman novel as a whole. See Ann Ardis, *New Women New Novels* (New Brunswick: Rutgers, 1990) ch. 2.

14. There are several male/female pairs in which this occurs: for example, George R. Sims' series on Dorcas Dene is narrated by a friend and dramatist Mr. Saxon; L.T. Meade's tales about Florence Cusak are narrated by Dr. Lonsdale; and Grant Allen's Hilda Wade, a nurse turned detective, marries her recorder and admirer, Hubert, at the end of her adventures.

CHAPTER THREE

1. In Shaw and Vanacker *Reflecting on Miss Marple (Heroines?)* (London: Routledge, 1991) 35.

2. This doesn't mean that all single women in this fiction were spinsters; within this study, in addition to the classic definition of a spinster as a never-married woman, there are two widows, one secretly married sleuth, one divorced sleuth, and four women who get married at the end of the novels,

ending their spinsterhood and, with the exception of Tuppence Beresford, their sleuthing activities as well.

3. I feel I should reiterate that these proscriptions against women working applied to middle-class women only. Lower class women worked throughout this time period, even when cultural condemnation of women working was at its height, without provoking any social commentary.

4. This idea will be discussed fully in Chapter 5. Sayers devotes an entire section to the "love-interest" and her dislike for it in the introduction to The Omnibus of Crime 38–40.

5. By 1910, "Books for Girls," according to Sally Mitchell, had become a "standard category in the lists of British publishers." in The New Girl: Girl's Culture in England 1880–1915 (New York: Columbia, 1995) 1. Judging from the amount of fiction and number of magazines aimed at this age group during this time period, it is clear that these writers and their stories held immense fascination for teens, that their fictional heroines tapped into a vein of the nation which needed exploring.

There has been a recent outpouring of critical attention focused on British girlhood and its attendant fiction. In addition to Sally Mitchell, see Kimberly Reynolds, Girls Only? Gender and Popular Children's Fiction in Britain, 1880–1910 (Philadelphia: Temple UP, 1990); and Claudia Nelson and Lynne Vallone, eds., The Girls Own: Cultural Histories of the Anglo-American Girl, 1830–1915 (Athens: U of Georgia P, 1994). Other useful critical works on this subject include: Patricia Craig and Mary Cadogan, You're A Brick, Angela! A New Look at Girl's Fiction from 1839–1975 (London: Gollancz, 1976); Judith Rowbotham, Good Girls Make Good Wives: Guidance for Girls in Victorian Fiction (Oxford: Basil Blackwell, 1989); Kirsten Drotner, "Intensities of Feeling: Emotion, Reception and Gender in Popular Culture," Dolphin , 17 (1989): 76–100; and Kirsten Drotner, "The Modern Girl and Mass Culture," Ethnologia Scandinavia (1988): 95–101.]

6. Mitchell 11. She also points out that the heroine rarely marries in Meade's extensive catalogue of girl's fiction; nor is there "usually any romance" in these books (21). Such divergence from the usual plot suggests Meade's desire to create new models for girls' lives.

7. Lonsdale's presence as narrator, as well as the medical solutions upon which some cases rest, are generally believed to be Eustace's influence on and contribution to the stories. See Sayers, The Omnibus of Crime 31 fn2. The same Robert Eustace, by the way, collaborated with Sayers herself on The Documents in the Case. Craig and Cadogen also suspect that it was Eustace who "helped to inject some vigor" into these stories (31).

8. Mitchell cites another Meade short story called "Ruffles" which features a girl sleuth but I have not been able to locate it (Mitchell 15).

9. Kestner notes that Meade and Eustace did write one final story for Harmsworth Magazine (June 1901) that appears to finish the series; however, "The Great Pink Pearl" features only Dr Londsdale, and Cusack does not appear at all. It is hard to say, therefore, whether this story was written merely to fulfill a contract and is not truly an ending, or if, as Kestner optimistically suggests, Meade and Eustace use this story to show what Londsale "has learned from Florence Cusack, that far from undercutting Florence Cusack's saga, it confirms her ability to teach the physician/narrator Lonsdale about her profession and its similarity to his own" (157).

10. It might be useful to point out that Pirkis herself did not marry until she was thirty-three, past what might be considered a marriageable age (Slung, Introduction xiii). Having "escaped" spinsterhood herself, I find it interesting that her female detective, created twenty years after her own marriage, is so comfortably ensconced as a working spinster.

11. An exception is Klein's The Woman Detective, which contains a brief discussion of Joan Mar and mentions Lucile Dare, but the criticism focuses on the detective and not the writer herself. Klein's otherwise thorough Great Women Mystery Writers does not, however, contain an entry on Leighton, suggesting perhaps that she was not primarily known as a detective fiction writer. Interestingly, The Arno Press's Literature and Detection Series reprinted her Michael Dred, Detective (1899), which she wrote with her husband, but not either Joan Mar, Detective or Lucile Dare, Detective, copies of which are consequently rare in this country. They are available on microfilm.

The British Museum lists around sixty works for Leighton, but this may not be a definitive number. The general pattern of many of her novels is that of a secret or a falsehood, a woman in trouble because of it, her great courage and fortitude, and her eventual redemption and marriage. Leighton may certainly have written more books that have women working as detectives, perhaps as amateurs, but none are titled, as the above are, with such clear clues as to their content. From their titles, though, it is obvious that many are crime-related. Among the titles listed: *Convict 100*, *The Missing Miss Randolf*, *Marked Woman*, *Silent Clue*, and *Mystery of the Three Fingers*.

The Arno Press has reissued two other books (in addition to Leighton's *Michael Dred*) by other women authors in this study— both Orczy's *Lady Molly of Scotland Yard* and Meade's *Stories from the Diary of a Doctor*.

12. I chose the end of the classic Golden Age period (roughly 1939) as a stopping point for this book; therefore, this discussion includes only the first few books written by these women, though three out of the four wrote well into later decades. Most of the novels I do discuss in this chapter were written in the 1930s.

13. In addition to "Why Work?" in *Creed or Chaos?* (New York: Harcourt, Brace, 1940), Sayers wrote the essays "Are Women Human?," "The Human-Not-Quite-Human," and "Living to Work" in *Unpopular Opinions* (New York: Harcourt, Brace, 1949) and "The Worth of Work" in *The Mind of the Maker* (New York: Harcourt, Brace, 1941). *The Mind of the Maker* and *Creed or Chaos?* discuss the subjects of work and creativity in general.

14. See Nina Auerbach, *Woman and the Demon*, Chapter V. She provides many convincing examples from both Victorian fiction and artwork which expresses the "intense alliances between the old maid and the fallen woman" (150).

15. I have used the bibliography by Kathleen Gregory Klein in John Reilly, ed., *Twentieth Century Crime and Mystery Writers*, 2nd ed. (New York: St. Martin's, 1985) for these dates. There seem to be a few discrepancies in publishing dates for some of these works.

16. As Chapter Two pointed out, women writers may or may not have subscribed to the idea of "natural female intuition," but whether they thought of it as a learned behavior or as a natural attribute, they often emphasized it in their female detectives. However, Mitchell makes fun of many common tenets of detective fiction in this first novel and especially of female detectives, like showing Mrs. Bradley knitting or using female intuition.

17. Compare this to the actions of Agatha Christie's famous detective. Poirot ends his career in *Curtain* (1975) by killing a murderer who he knows cannot be brought to justice. He dies shortly afterwards, having written a confession to his "Watson," Captain Hastings. This was considered a shocking thing. Mitchell's detective, on the other hand, murders her first time out and in 1929—certainly a more daring move on Mitchell's part.

18. See Patricia D. Maida and Nicholas B. Spornick, *Murder She Wrote: A Study of Agatha Christie's Detective Fiction* (Bowling Green: BGSU Popular Press, 1982) 1.

19. Monty was a family scapegrace, a classic example of the loveable "ne'er-do-well" who got away with anything. The sisters basically provided for him, and eventually, to keep him happy and out of trouble, they bought him a cottage on the coast and provided household help to take care of him.

20. "Auntie-Grannie" was Mrs. Margaret Miller, the second wife of Nathaniel Miller and maternal aunt to Christie's mother. Christie's mother was raised by Nathaniel and Margaret Miller rather than by her own mother because of financial reasons. Christie's mother eventually married Frederick Miller—Nathaniel Miller's son by his first marriage, her step-cousin. Therefore, Auntie-Grannie played a triple role in Christie's mother's life: as guardian, aunt and mother-in-law, which may account for her unusual title.

21. She says this specifically about *The Seven Dials Mystery* (1929), a sequel to *The Secret of Chimneys* (1925), both of which feature Lady Eileen "Bundle" Brent, as amateur sleuth; she writes that *Seven Dials* was "one of what I called the 'light-hearted thriller type.' These were always easy to write, not requiring too much plotting and planning" (*Autobiography* 423).

22. Maida and Spornick are the only critics who discuss this book in detail as a potential forerunner of Miss Marple, which is surprising since it seems so relevant (Shaw and Vanacker do mention it in their study, p. 37). Maida and Spornick also present the most detailed discussion of Christie's breakdown, an episode which Christie herself overlooks entirely in her own autobiography. See Maida and Spornick 108–9.

23. Michele Slung makes a similar observation in "Let's Hear it for Agatha Christie: A Feminist Appreciation." Rader and Zettler 68.

CHAPTER FOUR

1. Angela Woollacott uses this definition of a public woman when she discusses the difference between "'ladies' fulfilling their 'womanly mission' and women stepping into the realm of masculine work and authority" during World War I and the ideological upheaval associated with crossing over this line. She continues: "Middle-class women who took paid jobs entered the masculine public sphere of commerce, and thus blurred the line of sex segregation that insisted upon a separate private sphere of feminine refinement and purity [...]. In taking a paid job, Kelly and others made themselves public women" (100). In "From Moral to Professional Authority: Secularism, Social Work, and Middle-class Women's Self-Construction in World War I Britain," Journal of Women's History, 10:2 (1998) 85–111.

2. Even as late as the 1910's papers were considered unfit reading for young "ladies." Vera Brittain, looking back at her days at school, recalls the forwardness of her headmistress in letting students "read the newspapers, which were then quite unusual adjuncts to teaching in girls' private schools." She continues: "We were never, of course, allowed to have the papers themselves—our innocent eyes might have strayed from foreign affairs to the evidence being taken by the Royal Commission of Marriage and Divorce or the Report of the International Paris Conference for the suppression of the White Slave Traffic—and the carefully selected cuttings invariably came from The Times or the Observer unmodified by contrary political opinions, but the fact that we had them at all testified to a recognition of the importance of current events far from customary at a time when politics and economics were still thought by most headmistresses to be no part of the education of marriageable young females" (Testament of Youth [New York: Seaview Books, 1980] 39). Newspapers are one of the most prevalent ways early women detective fiction writers show their female detecives plunging into the "common" world, highlighting the lessening rigidity between private and public spheres occurring during this time period.

3. This story is also unique in that Brooke's knowledge of and facility with popular mediums extend beyond newspapers to include an unusual mixing of the classes. In Chapter Two, I gave an example of Brooke's awareness of middle-class and working-class signifiers and how that awareness gave her the needed clue in the case; she could tell from the arrangement of the room what type of occupant lived there. However, while that clue was based on knowledge of the proper management of a middle- or upper-class household, something Brooke might be expected to know because of her upbringing, the knowledge she exhibited in this case, the "lower-class amusement" of penny readings, is an element outside the typical realm of middle-class femininity. In addition, she recognizes the slang that a cabby uses, the "sweet stuffshop," meaning the office, to help solve a crime. Here she crosses not only gender lines but class lines as well, and yet her femininity, her middle-class values, have not altered. Pirkis seems to question the gender and class boundaries which enclosed her and other women of her upbringing, showing through this characterization a clear example of a woman who is middle-class, feminine, conservative and who has a job. Yet to get her job done, she is also knowledgeable of and willing to mix with the working classes without fear of impunity.

4. See Showalter, A Literature of Their Own, chapter VI. Robert Lee Wolff, Sensational Victorian: The Life and Fiction of Mary Elizabeth Braddon (New York: Garland, 1979) is a very thorough account of Braddon's life, and he discusses throughout the business-like attitude Braddon had toward her writing, editing, and publishing activities.

5. Wolff 353.

6. Kestner, though he argues convincingly that in this novel Braddon "transform[s] female sensation into female detection" (71), stretches his theory a bit too thin for my taste, arguing that even Braddon's use of diary-keeping shows indebtedness to Holmes' The Sign of Four! He also makes the case that Sibyl Penrith is the true female detective of the story, believing that Cora does nothing but record events: "it is difficult to see how she is a detective in any genuine sense" (60). Yet Sibyl does no "genuine" detecting either, and he gives us no textual examples to support this point.

7. For a still-definitive discussion of these types of "features," see John Cawelti, Adventure, Mystery, and Romance: Formula Stories as Art and Popular Culture (Chicago: University of Chicago Press, 1976). He discusses in detail the myths of a culture and how they infiltrate the formulas which appear in pop-

ular fictions. The success of detective fiction, for instance, a genre which relied on certain myths but had to continually evolve to be exciting, was predicated on following a formula while simultaneously expanding it; it always had to strike a balance between, as Cawelti says, "convention and invention."

Perhaps one reason why women were so successful in the genre was because they understood the compromises that such a stance required, since they continually practiced this balancing act in their own lives when trying to establish professional authority: they did not wish to break completely with the conventions of separate spheres for men and women but at the same time sought to expand what woman's sphere could contain.

8. The fact that Christie received money from a newspaper to serialize this story as "Anna the Adventuress" adds another layer to women detective fiction writer's reliance on and increased use of newspapers. Anne, within the plotline, becomes a reporter, makes money and supports herself; and Christie, having written a story which stars a young writer-detective, has sold it to a newspaper and thus makes money and supports herself.

9. See, for example, Teresa Chris' book, *Georgette Heyer's Regency England* (London: Sidgwick & Jackson, 1989), in which the reader can be taken on a "step-by-step" tour of London according to Heyer's novels.

10. See Christie's *Autobiography* for a sample of her in the act of creating, 259.

CHAPTER FIVE

1. Like Gayle Wald, in "Strong Poison: Love and the Novelistic in Dorothy Sayers," I am intentionally excluding *Busman's Honeymoon* from this analysis, though it is indeed the "fourth" novel in the Wimsey-Vane series. Wald's reasons for exclusion are sufficient: "originally, it was a play written in collaboration with Muriel St. Clare Byrne; the conflicts of the love interest between Harriet and Lord Peter are essentially resolved with their embrace at the conclusion of *Gaudy Night*; and Sayers herself refers only once, briefly, to *Busman's Honeymoon* in 'Gaudy Night,' her account of the writing of the Wimsey-Vane story." See Gayle Wald in Ronald G. Walker and June M. Frazer, eds., *The Cunning Craft: Original Essays on Detective*

Fiction and Contemporary Literary Theory, Essays in Literature (Macomb, Ill: Western Illinois University, 1990) 108, fn1.

I would only add as further explanation that the probable reason Sayers mentions *Busman's Honeymoon* only once in "Gaudy Night" is that she herself did not think of this novel as necessary for resolving the problems she sets out for herself and completes in the novel *Gaudy Night*; nor does she really consider *Busman's Honeymoon* a "detective" novel, as her subtitle to it—"A Love Story with Detective Interruptions"—makes clear.

2. See Janet Hitchman, *Such a Strange Lady: A Biography of Dorothy L. Sayers*, New York: Harper & Row, 1975, Chapter 1, for an account of this time.

3. Biographers have given various reasons for this early departure: Reynolds says she may have caught scarlet fever, which was going around the school at the time and to which Sayers' letters from the school allude, but that there is no record of this; (64) Hitchman says she suffered nervous breakdown and had to be sent to a nursing home in Salisbury to convalesce (15); Dale combines the two accounts and writes that Sayers "became sick again and had to be sent to a nursing home in Salisbury" (24). See Barbara Reynolds, ed., *The Letters of Dorothy L. Sayers, 1899-1936: The Making of a Detective Novelist*, New York : St. Martin's Press, 1996; and Alzina Stone Dale, *Maker and Craftsman: The Story of Dorothy L. Sayers*, Grand Rapids: Eerdmans, 1978.

4. Sayers did not actually get a degree, however, until 1920, as Oxford did not confer degrees upon women until then. Sayers was among the first group of women to get her degree at this time.

5. Michele Slung says that Sayers' introduction and footnotes in this volume alone are "worth many another writer's entire career." In John Reilly, ed., *Twentieth Century Crime and Mystery Writers* 792. Haycraft calls it indispensable in his introduction to it in *The Art of the Mystery Story*, his collection of the finest essays on the genre, 71.

6. Harriet's situation here resembles another incident in Sayers' life, which she transforms in this novel—another close similarity between the two. The love of Sayers' adult life was a Russian Jewish émigré, John Cournos, who asked Sayers to enter into a sexual relationship with him and use birth control, on the grounds that he did not believe in marriage and did not want chil-

dren. Sayers refused and ended the relationship, and Cournos left for America. Yet he returned two years later, married to a woman writer of detective fiction who had two children. Sayers did resume contact with him, and the letters to him that Reynolds includes in her volume are very pained and show a very emotional and passionate side to Sayers. It is probably more than coincidence that in the next Harriet Vane novel, *Have His Carcase*, the murdered man is a Russian émigré, found by Harriet with his throat slit. See Reynolds 215–16; 217–31; 232–33; 236–42.

7. Kathleen Gregory Klein, in her chapter on Sayers in Bargannier's *Ten Women of Mystery*, gets to the meat of this conflict in one sentence; according to her, Harriet is "accused of the murder of her lover because he had offered to marry her" (22). Indeed, when reading over the judge's speech, it is hard to imagine any other interpretation.

8. It may be hard to imagine today that these detective fiction writers considered their work realistic. Slung notes that Golden Age fiction has "drawn fire from today's critics for its artificiality and lack of touch with reality," but points out that "ironically," these were the same qualities "with which the Golden Age authors thought they were dispensing" (xxiii).

9. Christie in her *Autobiography* writes: "I myself always found the love interest a terrible bore in detective stories. Love, I felt, belonged to romantic stories. To force a love motif into what should be a scientific process went much against the grain. However, at that period detective stories always had to have a love interest—so there it was" (259–260).

10. In yet another instance of doubling, Templeton is the alias Sayers provided for Peter Wimsey in the earlier *Unnatural Death* (1926); it could simply be that Sayers forgot that she had previously used this name when she gives it to Harriet as *her* detective, but its interesting nonetheless.

11. In *Adventure, Mystery and Romance: Formula Stories as Art and Popular Culture*. Chicago: University of Chicago Press, 1976.

12. Sayers, in her foreward to *Unpopular Opinions*, writes that the BBC said this about "Living to Work," a different essay in the collection. Hitchman thus appears to be wrong—and other critics have repeated this information—but it is not known from where Hitchman got his information.

13. In *Maker and Craftsman* 63–64. She states further that it was not until 1925 that women were allowed to be legal guardians of their own children.

14. This is her only non-Wimsey novel, done in collaboration with Dr. Robert Eustace (by no coincidence, the same Eustace who collaborated with L.T. Meade). Since this novel revolved around a medical problem, she began a correspondence with Eustace to ask questions and get scientific answers. She was quite upset, therefore, when a reader wrote to her that the solution to *Documents* was impossible, because of the specific properties of that specific type of deadly mushroom. Though she made a humorous reference to it during a radio address later that year, she never forgot this episode. Trevor Hall, in *Nine Literary Studies* (Hamden, CT: Archon Books, 1980), writes: "This mistake must have seemed a great nuisance to Miss Sayers, who prided herself on the accuracy of the details of her books, as was natural to a scholar of her standard" (73). Hall says that she wasn't necessarily upset with Eustace, but she blamed herself for "her reliance upon Robert Eustace in his choice of the experts who were consulted" (73). A small distinction, but one which shows the level of perfection she demanded from herself, though not necessarily from other people.

15. This is another example of an overlap between women detective fiction writers and the use of newspapers—writers use them to help construct their works of crime fiction.

16. She did manage to publish *Tristan in Brittany* around this time (1927), the translation of which she began when a student at Somerville.

17. See Denise Marie Marshall, "Who Is Harriet Vane? And Where Does She Live? Dorothy L. Sayers and Women's Search for Self in British Culture, 1930–1937," MA thesis, Bowling Green State U, 1976, 88–95.

18. As I find this one of the best novels of any sort that I've ever read, I take a rather childish pleasure in noting that Robin Winks, the editor of the volume in which this essay appears, adds a footnote at this point in the text, saying, "As editor, I cannot forbear to remark that no one today, reading *Gaudy Night*, would consider the penultimate scene, which clearly deals with a feminist issue, 'repellent.' This is another excellent indication of how Miss Sayers moved ahead of her readers" (100). Grella's essay first appeared in 1976. Unfortunately, I think

Winks is wrong and that there are many who would still dismiss the novel.

19. Several critics have written on the historical accuracy of Sayers' books. See for example, P.L. Scowcroft, "The Detective Fiction of Dorothy L. Sayers: A Source for the Social Historian?" *Seven* 5 (1984): 70–83. Even better is the book length study by Terrance L. Lewis, *Dorothy L. Sayers' Wimsey and Interwar British Society*, Lewiston: E. Mellen Press, 1994, which has chapters not only on the way that topical concerns like women's struggles and class struggles are seen in Sayers' novels, but more "vital" social concerns as well: "Politics and the Changing World" and "The Effects of the Great War" are two such chapters.

Bibliography

PRIMARY SOURCES

Bentley, E.C. *Trent's Last Case*. 1914. Fifty Classics of Crime Fiction, 1900–1950. New York: Garland Publishing, 1976.

Braddon, Mary E. *Aurora Floyd*. 1863. London: Virago Press, 1984.

_____. *Lady Audley's Secret*. 1862. New York: Dover, 1974.

_____. *Thou Art the Man*. 3 vols. London: Simpkin, Marshall, Hamilton, Kent and Co., 1895.

Brittain, Vera. *Testament of Youth*. 1933. New York: Seaview Books, 1980.

Christie, Agatha. *Cards on the Table*. 1936. New York: Berkley Books, 1984.

_____. *The Man in the Brown Suit*. 1924. New York: Berkley Books, 1984.

_____. *The Murder at the Vicarage*. 1930. New York: G.P. Putnam's Sons, 1995.

_____. *The Mystery of the Blue Train*. 1928. New York: Berkley Books, 1984.

_____. *N or M?* 1941. New York: G.P. Putnam's Sons, 1995.

_____. *Partners in Crime*. 1929. New York: Dell, 1981.

_____. *Parker Pyne Investigates*. 1934. New York: Berkley Books, 1984.

_____. *The Secret Adversary*. 1922. New York: Bantam, 1970.

_____. *The Secret of Chimneys*. 1925. New York: Berkley Books, 1984.

_____. *The Seven Dials Mystery*. 1929. New York: Berkley Books, 1984.

_____. *The Tuesday Club Murders*. 1933. New York: Berkley Books, 1984.

Cole, G.D.H. and Margaret. *Mrs. Warrender's Profession*. New York: Macmillan, 1939.

Collins, Wilkie. *The Law and the Lady*. New York: Harper & Brothers,1875.

"The Detection Club Oath." In Haycraft, *Art* 209–211.

Franklin, Miles. *Bring the Monkey*. 1933. Introduction by Bronwen Levy. St. Lucia: U of Queensland P, 1984.

Forrester, Andrew, Jr. *The Female Detective*. in *Three Victorian Detective Novels*. Ed. by E. L. Bleiler. New York: Dover, 1978.

Green, Anna Katherine. *The Leavenworth Case: A Lawyer's Story*. 1878. New York: A.L. Burt, 1906.

Heron-Maxwell, Beatrice. *The Adventures of a Lady Pearl-Broker*. London: New Century, 1899.

Heyer, Georgette. *A Blunt Instrument*. 1938. Fifty Classics of Crime Fiction, 1900–1950. New York: Garland Publishing, 1976.

Leighton, Marie Connor. *Joan Mar, Detective*. London: Ward & Lock, 1910.

_____. *Lucille Dare, Detective*. London: Ward & Lock, 1919.

_____, and Robert Leighton. *Michael Dred, Detective*. 1899. Literature of Mystery and Detection. New York: Arno Press, 1976.

Lowndes, Marie Belloc. *The Lodger*. New York: Charles Scribner's Sons, 1914.

Meade, L.T. *Polly: A New-Fashioned Girl*. New York: A.L. Burt, 18 [ ].

_____, and Clifford Halifax. *Stories from the Diary of a Doctor*. 1894. New York: Arno Press, 1976.

_____, and Robert Eustace. "The Arrest of Captain Vandaleur." *The Harmsworth Magazine* 2 (1899): 545–54.

_____. "Mr. Bovey's Unexpected Will." *The Harmsworth Magazine* 2 (1899): 259–268.

_____. "Mrs. Reid's Terror." *The Harmsworth Magazine* 6 (1901): 121–128.

_____. "The Outside Ledge." *The Harmsworth Magazine* 5 (1901): 201–207.

_____. "A Terrible Railway Ride." *The Harmsworth Magazine* 4 (1900): 559–567.

Miller, Elizabeth York. "Valeska, Woman Detective: The Matter of the Savoy Thefts." *The London Magazine* 20 (1908): 291–301.

_____. "Valeska, Woman Detective: The Murder of Lawrence Drummond." *The London Magazine* 21 (1908/9): 666–672.

Mitchell, Gladys. *Mystery of a Butcher Shop*. 1929. New York: Mason, 1934.

_____. *The Saltmarsh Murders*. 1933. Introduction Patricia Craig and Mary Cadogan. London: Hogarth, 1984.

_____. *Speedy Death*. 1929. New York: Mason, 1932.

Orczy, Baroness. *Lady Molly of Scotland Yard*. 1910. Literature of Mystery and Detection. New York: Arno Press, 1976.

_____. *The Old Man in the Corner*. 1909. Introduction E.F. Bleiler. New York: Dover, 1980.

Pirkis, C.L. "The Experiences of Loveday Brooke, Lady Detective: A Princess's Revenge." *The Ludgate Monthly* 5 (1893): 5–16.

_____. "The Experiences of Loveday Brooke, Lady Detective: Drawn Daggers." *The Ludgate Monthly* 7 (1893): 131–144.

_____. "The Experiences of Loveday Brooke, Lady Detective: The Black Bag Left on a Doorstep." *The Ludgate Monthly* 2 (1893): 401–414.

_____. "The Experiences of Loveday Brooke, Lady Detective: The Murder at Troyte's Hill." *The Ludgate Monthly* 3 (1893): 528–543.

_____. "The Experiences of Loveday Brooke, Lady Detective: The Redhill Sisterhood." *The Ludgate Monthly* 4 (1893): 581–595.

_____. "The Ghost of Fountain Lane." *The Experiences of Loveday Brooke, Lady Detective*. 1894. Ed. Michelle Slung. New York: Dover Publications, 1986. 72–84.

_____. "Missing!" *The Experiences of Loveday Brooke, Lady Detective*. 1894. Ed. Michelle Slung. New York: Dover Publications, 1986. 85–96.

Sayers, Dorothy L. "Aristotle on Detective Fiction." In Winks 25–34.

_____. *Busman's Honeymoon*. 1937. New York: Harper Paperbacks, 1995.

_____. *Gaudy Night*. 1935. New York: Harper Paperbacks, 1995.

_____. "Gaudy Night." Haycraft, Art 208–221.

_____. *Have His Carcase*. 1932. New York: Harper Paperbacks, 1995.

_____. "The Present Status of the Mystery Story." *The London Mercury* (Nov 1930): 47–52.

_____. "Review." *Sunday Times*. 3 November 1933.

_____. *Strong Poison*. 1930. New York: Harper Paperbacks, 1995.

_____. *Unnatural Death*. 1927. New York: Harper Paperbacks, 1995.

_____. *Unpopular Opinions: Twenty-one essays*. New York: Harcourt, Brace, 1947.

Sayers, Dorothy L., ed. *The Omnibus of Crime*. New York: Payson and Clarke, 1929.

Wentworth, Patricia. *The Case Is Closed*. Philadelphia: Lippincott, 1937.

_____. *Dead or Alive*. Philadelphia: Lippincott, 1936.

_____. *Grey Mask*. 1928. New York: Berkley, 1972.

_____. *Lonesome Road*. 1939. New York: HarperPerennial, 1993.

SECONDARY SOURCES

Abel, Elizabeth, Marianne Hirsh, and Elizabeth Langland. *The Voyage In: Fictions of Female Development*. Hanover: UP of New England, 1983.

Adams, Donald, ed. *The Mystery and Detection Annual*. Pasadena, CA: Castle Press, 1974.

Adams, Gail. "Double Jeopardy: Husband and Wife Teams in Detective Fiction." *The Armchair Detective* 8 (1975): 251–256.

Adrian, Jack. *Detective Stories from The Strand*. Oxford: Oxford UP, 1991.

Allen, Mary Sophia. *The Pioneer Policewoman*. Arr. and Ed. Julie Helen Heyneman. London: Chatto and Windus, 1925.

Appignanesi, Lisa, and John Forrester. *Freud's Women*. New York: BasicBooks, 1992.

Ardis, Ann. *New Women, New Novels: Feminism and Early Modernism*. New Brunswick: Rutgers UP, 1990.

Armstrong, Nancy. *Desire and Domestic Fiction: A Political History of the Novel*. Oxford: Oxford UP, 1987.

Ashley, Bob, ed. *The Study of Popular Fiction: A Source Book*. Philadelphia: U of Pennsylvania P, 1989.

Auerbach, Nina. Foreword. *Old Maids and Radical Spinsters: Unmarried Women in the Twentieth Century Novel*. Ed. Laura Doan. Urbana: U of Illinois P, 1991.

_____. *Woman and the Demon: The Life of a Victorian Myth*. Cambridge: Harvard UP, 1982.

Bander, Elaine. "The English Detective Novel Between the Wars: 1919–1939." *Armchair Detective* 11 (1979): 262–273.

Bargainnier, Earl F., ed. *Comic Crime*. Bowling Green: Bowling Green University Popular Press, 1987.

_____. *Ten Women of Mystery*. Bowling Green: BGSU Popular Press, 1981.

Barry, W. "The Strike of a Sex." *Quarterly Review* 179 (1894): 289–318.

Barzun, Jacques, and Wedell Hertig Taylor, eds. Preface. *A Blunt Instrument*. By Georgette Heyer. *Fifty Classics of Crime Fiction, 1900–1950*. New York: Garland Publishing, 1976.

_____, and _____. Preface. *Strong Poison*. By Dorothy L. Sayers. *Fifty Classics of Crime Fiction, 1900–1950*. New York: Garland Publishing, 1976.

_____, and _____. Preface. *Trent's Last Case*. By E.C. Bentley. *Fifty Classics of Crime Fiction, 1900–1950*. New York: Garland Publishing, 1976.

Beach, Sarah. "Harriet in Rehearsal: Hilary Thorpe in 'The Nine Tailors.'" *Mythlore* 19.3 (Summer 1993): 37–39, 65.

Beauman, Nicola. *A Very Great Profession: The Woman's Novel 1914–39*. London: Virago, 1983.

Bedell, Jeanne F. "Melodrama and Manners: Changing Attitudes toward Class Distinctions in English Detective Fiction, 1868–1939." *Clues* 1.1 (1980): 15–24.

Bennett, E. A. *Fame and Fiction: An Enquiry into Certain Popularities*. 1901. Plainview, NY: Books for Libraries Press, 1975.

_____. *Journalism for Women: A Practical Guide*. London: John Lane, 1898.

Benstock, Bernard, ed. *Art in Crime Writing: Essays on Detective Fiction*. New York: St. Martin's, 1983.

Bevan, David. *University Fiction*. Rodopi Perspectives on Modern Literature 5. Amsterdam: Rodopi, 1990.

Binyon, T.J. *"Murder Will Out": The Detective in Fiction*. Oxford: Oxford UP, 1989.

Birns, Nicholas, and Margaret Boe Birns. "Agatha Christie: Modern and Modernist."
   Walker and Frazer 120–134.
Black, Helen C. *Notable Women Authors of the Day.* 1893. Hollandale, FL: New World
   Book Manufacturing Co, 1972.
Blake, Fay. "Lady Sleuths and Women Detectives." *Turn of the Century Women* 3.1 (Sum-
   mer 1986): 29–42.
Bland, Lucy. "In the Name of Protection: The Policing of Women in the First World
   War." *Women-in-law: Explorations in Law, Family, and Sexuality.* Eds. Julia Brophy and
   Carol Smart. London: Routledge & Kegan Paul, 1985 23–49.
Bloom, Clive, ed. *Twentieth-Century Suspense: The Thriller Comes of Age.* New York: St. Mar-
   tin's, 1990.
Bloom, Harold, ed. *British Women Fiction Writers, 1900–1960.* Women Writers of English
   and Their Works. Philadelphia: Chelsea House, 1997.
Boufis, Christina. "'Of Home Birth and Breeding': Eliza Lynn Linton and the Girl of
   the Period." Nelson and Vallone 98–123.
Bowers, Bege K. and Barbara Brothers, eds. *Reading and Writing Women's Lives: A Study
   of the Novel of Manners.* Ann Arbor: UMI Research Press, 1990.
Brooks, Marie. *Alternative Identities: The Self in Literature, History, Theory.* Wellesley
   Studies in Critical Theory, Literary History, and Culture 7. New York: Garland,
   1995.
Brown, Penny. *Poison at the Source: The Female Novel of Self-Development in the Early Twen-
   tieth Century.* New York: St. Martin's, 1992.
Buchanan, R. "Society's Looking Glass." *Temple Bar* 6 (1862): 129–137.
Cadogan, Mary, and Patricia Craig. *You're a Brick Angela!: A New Look at Girls' Fiction
   from 1839–1975.* London: Gollancz, 1976.
Caine, Barbara. *Victorian Feminists.* Oxford: Oxford UP, 1992.
Campbell, SueEllen. "The Detective Heroine and the Death of Her Hero: Dorothy Say-
   ers to P.D. James." Irons, *Feminism* 12–28.
Candee, Helen Churchill. *How Women May Earn a Living.* New York: Macmillan, 1900.
Cawelti, John G. *Adventure, Mystery, and Romance: Formula Stories as Art and Popular Cul-
   ture.* Chicago: U of Chicago P, 1976.
_____. "Artistic Failures and Success: Christie and Sayers." Winks 188–199.
Chandler, Raymond. "The Simple Art of Murder." Haycraft, *Art* 222–237.
Charney, Hannah. *The Detective Novel of Manners: Hedonism, Morality, and the Life of Rea-
   son.* Rutherford, NJ: Fairleigh Dickenson, 1981.
Chesterton, G.K. "A Defence of Detective Stories." Haycraft, *Art.* 3–6.
Christopher, Joe R. "The Mystery of Robert Eustace." *Armchair Detective* 13 (1980):
   365–366.
_____. "Three 'Unknown' Stories—Two of Them Unpublished—By Dorothy L. Sayers."
   The Mystery Fancier 11 (1989): 15–21.
Clark, Anna. "The Politics of Seduction in English Popular Culture, 1748–1848. Rad-
   ford, 1986 47–70.
Colby, Vineta. *Yesterday's Woman: Domestic Realism in the English Novel.* Princeton: Prince-
   ton UP, 1974.
Corbett, Mary Jean. "Feminine Authorship and Spiritual Authority in Victorian Women
   Writers' Autobiographies." *Women's Studies* 18.1 (1990): 13–29.
Cornillon, John. "The Case for Violet Strange." Koppelman Cornillon 206–215.
Cornillon, Susan Koppelman, ed. *Images of Women in Fiction: Feminist Perspectives.* Bowl-
   ing Green: BGSU Popular Press, 1972.
Coward, Rosalind, and Linda Semple. "Tracking Down the Past: Women and Detective
   Fiction." *From My Guy to Sci-Fi: Genre and Women's Writing in the Postmodern World.* Ed.
   Helen Carr. London: Pandora Press, 1989. 39–57.

Cox, Michael, ed. *Victorian Tales of Mystery and Detection: An Oxford Anthology.* Oxford: Oxford UP, 1992.

Craig, Patricia and Mary Cadogan. *The Lady Investigates: Women Detectives and Spies in Fiction.* London: Gollancz, 1981.

Crosthwait, Elizabeth. "'The Girl Behind the Man Behind the Gun': The Women's Army Auxiliary Corps, 1914–1918." Davidoff and Westover 161–181.

Cummings, J.C. "Inside Views of Fiction: Detective Stories." *The Bookman* 30 (1910): 499–500.

"Current Literary Topics: The Girl in the Newspaper Office." *The Writer* 14.2 (February 1901): 30.

Cutter, Martha. *Unruly Tongue: Identity and Voice in American Women's Writing.* Jackson: UP of Mississippi, 1999.

Cvetkovich, Ann. *Mixed Feelings: Feminism, Mass Culture, and Victorian Sensationalism.* New Brunswick: Rutgers UP, 1992.

Dale, Alzina Stone. *Maker and Craftsman: The Story of Dorothy L. Sayers.* Wheaton, Ill: Harold Shaw Publishers, 1992.

_____. "Wimsey Lost and Found." *The Armchair Detective* 23.2 (Spring 1990): 142–151.

Davidoff, Leonore, and Belinda Westover. "'From Queen Victoria to the Jazz Age': Women's World in England, 1880–1939." Davidoff and Westover 1–35.

_____, and _____, eds. *Our Work, Our Lives, Our Words: Women's History and Women's Work.* Totowa, NJ: Barnes & Noble, 1986.

Davy, Teresa. "'A Cissy Job for Men; A Nice Job for Girls': Women Shorthand Typists in London, 1900–1939." Davidoff and Westover 124–144.

DeMarr, Mary Jean, ed. *In the Beginning: First Novels in a Mystery Series.* Bowling Green: BGSU Popular Press, 1995.

Depaolo, Rosemary. "From Howtoits to Whodunits: Jane Austen to Agatha Christie." *Clues* 2.2 (Fall/Winter 1981): 8–14.

Dickerson, Vanessa D., ed. *Keeping the Victorian House: A Collection of Essays.* New York: Garland, 1995.

Dickie, Margaret. "The Maternal Gaze: Women Modernists and Poetic Authority." *Alternative Identities: The Self in Literature, History, Theory.* Ed. Marie Brooks. Wellesley Studies in Critical Theory, Literary History, and Culture. New York: Garland, 1995.

Doan, Laura, ed. *Old Maids and Radical Spinsters: Unmarried Women in the Twentieth Century Novel.* foreword by Nina Auerbach. Urbana: U of Illinois P, 1991.

Drotner, Kirsten. "Intensities of Feeling: Emotion, Reception and Gender in Popular Culture." *Dolphin* 17 (1989): 76–100.

_____. "The Modern Girl and Mass Culture." *Ethnologia Scandinavia* (1988): 95–101.

Dyhouse, Carol. *No Distinction of Sex? Women in British Universities 1870–1939.* London: UCL Press, 1995.

Eco, Umberto. "Narrative Structures in Fleming." Irons, *Gender* 157–182.

Edmondson, Belinda. *Making Men: Gender, Literary Authority, and Women's Writing in Caribbean Narrative.* Durham: Duke UP, 1999.

Edwards, Lee. "Love and Work: Fantasies of Resolution." *Frontiers* 2.3 (1977): 31–38.

Emsley, Clive. "The English Bobby: An Indulgent Tradition." *Myths of the English.* Ed. Roy Porter. Cambridge, MA: Polity Press, 1992, 114–135.

Erisman, Fred. "Crime Fiction: Some Varieties of Historical Experience." *Clues* 1.1 (1980): 1–8.

Erkkila, Betsy. *The Wicked Sisters: Women Poets, Literary History and Discord.* Oxford: Oxford UP, 1992.

Fasick, Laura. "God's House, Women's Place." Dickerson 75–104.

_____. *Vessels of Meaning: Women's Bodies, Gender Norms, and Class Bias from Richardson to Lawrence.* Dekalb: Northern Illinois UP, 1997.

Figes, Eva, ed. *Women's Letter's in Wartime 1450-1945*. London: Pandora, 1993.

Forrester, Wendy. *Great-Grandmama's Weekly: A Celebration of The Girl's Own Paper 1880-1901*. Guildford and London: Lutterworth, 1980.

Fraiman, Susan. *Unbecoming Women: British Women Writers and the Novel of Development*. New York: Columbia UP, 1993.

Fraser, Helen. *Women And War Work*. New York: G. Arnold Shaw, 1918.

Freeman, R. Austin. "The Art of the Detective Story." Haycraft, *Art* 7-17.

Gallagher, Catherine. *Nobody's Story: The Vanishing Acts of Women Writers in the Marketplace, 1670-1820*. Berkeley: U of California P, 1994.

Gamman, Lorraine. "Watching the Detectives: The Enigma of the Female Gaze." Gamman and Marshment 8-26.

_____, and Margaret Marshment, eds. *The Female Gaze: Women as Viewers of Popular Culture*. Seattle: The Real Comet Press, 1989.

Gerard, Jessica. "The Chatelaine: Women of the Victorian Landed Classes and the Country House." Dickerson 175-206.

Gilbert, Sandra M., and Susan Gubar. *The Madwoman in the Attic*. New Haven: Yale UP, 1979.

_____, and _____. *No Man's Land*. 3 vols. New Haven: Yale UP, 1988, 1989, 1994.

Goldsmith, Elizabeth C, ed. *Writing the Female Voice: Essays on Epistolary Literature*. Boston: Northeastern UP, 1989.

Graves, Robert, and Alan Hodge. *The Long Weekend: A Social History of Great Britain, 1918-1939*. New York: Macmillan, 1941.

Green, Jen, ed. *Reader, I Murdered Him: Original Crime Stories By Women*. New York: St. Martin's, 1989.

Greene, Sir Hugh, ed. *The Further Rivals of Sherlock Holmes*. New York: Pantheon Books, 1973.

_____. *The Rivals of Sherlock Holmes*. New York: Pantheon Books, 1970.

Grella, George. "Dorothy Sayers and Peter Wimsey." *University of Rochester Library Bulletin* 28 (Summer 1974): 33-42.

_____. "The Formal Detective Novel." Winks 84-102.

Grossberg, Lawrence, Cary Nelson, and Paula A. Treichler, eds. *Cultural Studies*. New York: Routledge, 1992.

Grossvogel, David I. "Death Deferred: The Long Life, Splendid Afterlife and Mysterious Workings of Agatha Christie." Benstock 1-17.

Haining, Peter, ed. *The Shilling Shockers: Stories of Terror from the Gothic Bluebooks*. New York: St. Martins, 1978.

Hall, Trevor H. *Dorothy L. Sayers: Nine Literary Studies*. Hamden, CT: Archon Books, 1980.

Hamilton, Mary E. *The Policewoman: Her Service and Ideals*. New York: Frederick A. Stoles, 1924.

Hannay, Margaret P., ed. "Harriet's Influence on the Characterization of Lord Peter Wimsey." *As Her Whimsey Took Her: Critical Essays on the Work of Dorothy Sayers*. Ed. Margaret P. Hannay. Kent, OH: Kent State UP, 1979.

Haycraft, Howard. *Murder for Pleasure: The Life and Times of the Detective Story*. New York: Appleton-Century, 1941.

_____, ed. *The Art of the Mystery Story: A Collection of Critical Essays*. New York: Simon and Schuster, 1946.

Hearnshaw, L. S. *A Short History of British Psychology, 1840-1940*. Methuen's Manuals of Modern Psychology. New York: Barnes & Noble, 1964.

Heilbrun, Carolyn. "The Detective Novel of Manners." in Bege and Brothers 187-197.

_____. *Writing a Woman's Life*. New York: W. W. Norton & Company, 1988.

Heldreth, Lillian M. "Breaking the Rules of the Game: Shattered Patterns in Dorothy L. Sayers' 'Gaudy Night.'" *Clues* 3.1 (Spring 1982): 120-127.

Hellerstein, Erna Olafson, Leslie Parker Hume, and Karen M. Offen, eds. *Victorian Women: A Documentary Account of Women's Lives in Nineteenth-Century England, France, and the United States.* Stanford: Stanford UP, 1981.

Helsinger, Elizabeth K., Robin Lauterbach Sheets, and William Veeder. *The Woman Question: Society and Literature in Britain and America, 1837-1883.* 3 vols. New York: Garland, 1983.

Holcombe, Lee. *Victorian Ladies at Work.* Hamden, CT: Archon Books, 1973.

Hone, Ralph E. *Dorothy L. Sayers: A Literary Biography.* Kent, OH: Kent State UP, 1979.

____. "Dorothy L. Sayers: Critic of Detective Fiction." *Seven* 6 (1985): 45–71.

Hughes, Winifred. *The Maniac in the Cellar: Sensation Novels of the 1860s.* Princeton: Princeton UP, 1980.

Humm, Maggie. "Feminist Detective Fiction." Bloom, *Twentieth* 237–254.

Humphreys, Anne. "Locating the Popular Text." *Victorian Literature and Culture* 19 (1991): 351–359.

Hutter, Albert D., and Mary W. Miller. "'Who Can Be Trusted?': 'The Detective,' An Early Journal of Detection." Adams 167–192.

Ingman, Heather. *Women's Fiction Between the Wars: Mothers, Daughters and Writing.* New York: St. Martin's, 1998.

Irons, Glenwood. "New Women Detectives: G Is for Gender-Bending." Irons, *Gender* 127–141.

____, ed. *Feminism in Women's Detective Fiction.* Toronto: U of Toronto P, 1995.

____, ed. *Gender, Language and Myth: Essays on Popular Narrative.* Toronto: U of Toronto P, 1992.

Irons, Glenwood, and Joan Warthling Roberts. "From Spinster to Hipster: The 'Suitability' of Miss Marple and Anna Lee." Irons, *Feminism* 64–73.

Jeffreys, Sheila. *The Spinster and Her Enemies: Feminism and Sexuality 1880-1930.* London: Pandora, 1985.

John, Angela V., ed. *Unequal Opportunities. Women's Employment in England 1800-1918.* Oxford: Basil Blackwell, 1986.

Jones, Suzanne W., ed. *Writing the Woman Artist: Essays on Poetics, Politics, and Portraitures.* Philadelphia: U of Philadelphia P, 1991.

Kalikoff, Beth. *Murder and Moral Decay in Victorian Popular Literature.* Nineteenth Century Studies. Ann Arbor: UMI Research Press, 1986.

Kaplan, Sydney Janet. *Feminine Consciousness in the Modern British Novel.* Urbana: U of Illinois P, 1975.

Keating, H.R.F. "Comedy and the British Crime Novel." Bargainnier, *Comic* 7–22.

____, ed. *Agatha Christie: First Lady of Crime.* London: Weidenfeld and Nicolson, 1977.

Kenny, Catherine. "Detecting a Novel Use for Spinsters in Sayers' Fiction." Doan 123–138.

Kestner, Joseph, A. *Sherlock's Sisters: The British Female Detective, 1864-1913.* The Nineteenth Century. Hants, England: Ashgate, 2003.

Klein, Kathleen Gregory. "Dorothy Sayers." Bargainnier, *Ten* 8–39.

____. "Dorothy Sayers: From First to Last." DeMarr 5–18.

____. "*Habeas Corpus*: Feminism and Detective Fiction." Irons, *Feminism* 171–190.

____. *The Woman Detective: Gender and Genre.* 2nd ed. Urbana: U of Illinois Press, 1995.

Klein, Kathleen Gregory, ed. *Great Women Mystery Writers: Classic to Contemporary.* Westport: Greenwood Press, 1994.

____, ed. *Women Times Three: Writers, Detectives, Readers.* Bowling Green: BGSU Popular Press, 1995.

Knepper, Marty S. "Agatha Christie, Feminist." *The Armchair Detective* 16.4 (1983): 398–406.

____. Reading Agatha Christie's Miss Marple Series: The Thirteen Problems." DeMarr 33–58.

Knox, Ronald A. "Detective Story Decalogue." Haycraft, Art 194–196.

Koppelman, Susan, ed. Old Maids: Short Stories by Nineteenth-Century U.S. Women Writers. Boston: Pandora Press, 1984.

Lane, Thomas D. "Dignity in the Detective Novel." Clues 1.1 (Spring 1980): 119–122.

Langland, Elizabeth. Nobody's Angels: Middle-Class Women and Domestic Ideology in Victorian Culture. Ithaca: Cornell UP, 1995.

Lanser, Susan Sniader. Fictions of Authority: Women Writers and Narrative Voice. Ithaca: Cornell UP, 1992.

Lawrence, Barbara. "Female Detectives: The Feminist–Anti-Feminist Debate." Clues 3.1 (Spring 1982): 38–48.

Leonardi, Susan J. Dangerous by Degrees: Women at Oxford and the Somerville College Novelists. New Brunswick: Rutgers UP, 1989.

Levine, Philippa. Feminist Lives in Victorian England. Oxford: Basil Blackwell, 1990.

____. Victorian Feminism 1850–1900. London: Hutchinson, 1987.

____. "'Walking the Streets in a Way No Decent Woman Should': Women Police in World War I." Journal of Modern History 66 (1994): 34–78.

Lewis, Terrance L. Dorothy L. Sayers' Wimsey and Interwar British Society. Lewiston, NY: The Edwin Mellen Press, 1994.

Light, Alison. Forever England: Femininity, Literature and Conservatism Between the Wars. London: Routledge, 1991.

Linkon, Sherry Lee, ed. In Her Own Voice: Nineteenth Century American Women Essayists. New York: Garland, 1997.

Linton, Elizabeth Lynn. "The Wild Woman as Social Insurgent." The Nineteenth Century 30 (1891): 596–605.

Lock, Joan. The British Policewoman: Her Story. London: Robert Hale, 1979.

Lougnan, Naomi. "Munition Work." in Stone 25–45.

Lovitt, Carl R. "Controlling Discourse in Detective Fiction, or Caring Very Much Who Killed Roger Ackroyd." Walker and Frazer 68–85.

MacDonald, Ross. "The Writer As Detective Hero." Winks 179–187.

Mackinnon, Alison. Love and Freedom: Professional Women and the Reshaping of Personal Life. Cambridge: Cambridge UP, 1997.

Maida, Patricia D. and Nicholas B. Spornick. Murder She Wrote: A Study of Agatha Christie's Detective Fiction. Bowling Green: BGSU Popular Press, 1982.

Maio, Kathleen L. "'A Strange and Fierce Delight': The Early Days of Women's Mystery Fiction." Chrysalis 10: 94–105.

Mann, Jessica. Deadlier Than the Male: An Investigation into Feminine Crime Writing. London: David & Charles, 1981.

Manos, Nikki Lee, and Meri-Jane Rochelson, eds. Transforming Genres: New Approaches to British Fiction of the 1890s. New York: St. Martin's, 1994.

Marcus, Laura, ed. Twelve Women Detective Stories. Oxford: Oxford UP, 1997.

Marshall, Denise Marie. "Who Is Harriet Vane? And Where Does She Live? Dorothy L. Sayers and Women's Search for Self in British Culture, 1930–1937." Master's Thesis, Bowling Green State U, 1976.

Marshall, Donald G. "'Gaudy Night': An Investigation of Truth." Seven 4 (1983): 98–114.

Marwick, Arthur. Women at War, 1914–1918. Fontana Paperbacks in Association with The Imperial War Museum, 1977.

Mason, Bobbie Ann. The Girl Sleuth: A Feminist Guide. New York: The Feminist Press, 1975.

McDiarmid, John. "The Quality of Play: Agatha Christie Among British Mystery Writers." Mid-Hudson Language Review 5 (1982): 91–105.

McLaren, Barbara. Women of the War. London: Hodder & Stoughton, 1917.

Melman, Billie. Women and the Popular Imagination in the Twenties. New York: St. Martin's, 1988.

Merry, Bruce. "Dorothy L. Sayers: Mystery and Demystification." Benstock 18–32.

Michie, Elsie B. *Outside the Pale: Cultural Exclusion, Gender Difference, and the Victorian Woman Writer.* Ithaca: Cornell UP, 1993.

Miller, Nancy K. *Subject to Change: Reading Feminist Writing.* Gender and Culture. New York: Columbia UP, 1988.

Mitchell, David. *Monstrous Regiment: The Story of the Women of the First World War.* New York: Macmillan, 1965.

Mitchell, Sally. "The Forgotten Woman of the Period: Penny Weekly Family Magazines of the 1840s and 1850s." Vicinus, *Widening* 29–51.

_____. "Girl's Culture: At Work." Nelson and Vallone 243–258.

_____. *The New Girl: Girl's Culture in England 1880–1915.* New York: Columbia, 1995.

Modleski, Tania. *Loving with a Vengeance: Mass-Produced Fantasies for Women.* New York: Methuen, 1984.

Morantz-Sanchez, Regina Markell. *Sympathy and Science: Women Physicians in American Medicine.* New York: Oxford UP, 1985.

Morley, Edith J. "Women at the Universities and University Teaching as a Profession." Morley 11–24

_____, ed. *Women Workers in Seven Professions: A Survey of their Economic Conditions and Prospects.* (edited for the Studies Committee of the Fabian Women's Group) London: George Routledge & Sons, 1914.

Moulder, Priscilla. "England's Girls and the Women Police." *Life and Labor* (May 1919): 121–123.

Moylan, J.F., C.B., C.B.E. *Scotland Yard and the Metropolitan Police.* London: G.P. Putnam's Sons, 1929.

"Mrs. L.T. Meade." *The Writer.* 14.2 (Feburary 1901): 28–30.

Mukerji, Chandra, and Michael Schudson. *Rethinking Popular Culture: Contemporary Perspectives in Cultural Studies.* Berkeley: U of California P, 1991.

Munt, Sally R. *Murder By the Book? Feminism and the Crime Novel.* Narrative Forms and Social Formations. New York: Routledge, 1994.

Murch, A. E. *The Development of the Detective Novel.* New York: Philosophical Library, Inc., 1958.

Nead, Lynda. *Myths of Sexuality: Representations of Women in Victorian Britain.* Oxford: Basil Blackwell, 1990.

Nelson, Carolyn Christensen. *British Women Fiction Writers of the 1890s.* Twanye's English Authors Series. New York: Twayne Publishers, 1996.

Nelson, Claudia, and Lynne Vallone, eds. *The Girls Own: Cultural Histories of the Anglo-American Girl, 1830–1915.* Athens: U of Georgia P, 1994.

Nichols, Victoria, and Susan Thompson. *Silk Stalkings: When Women Write of Murder.* Berkeley: Black Lizard Books, 1988.

Nicholson, Marjorie. "The Professor and the Detective." Haycraft, *Art* 110–127.

Nicolay, Theresa Freda. *Gender Roles, Literary Authority, and Three American Women Writers.* The Age of Revolution and Romanticism Interdisciplinary Studies. New York: Peter Lang, 1995.

Nollen, Elizabeth Mahn. "Female Detective Figures in British Fiction: Coping With Madness and Imprisonment." *Clues* 15.2 (Fall/Winter 1994): 39–49.

O'Brien, Catherine. *Women's Fictional Responses to the First World War: A Comparative Study of Selected Texts by French and German Writers.* Studies in Modern German Literature. New York: Peter Lang, 1997.

Oldfield, Sybil, ed. *This Working-Day World: Women's Life and Culture(s) in Britain 1914–1945.* London: Taylor & Francis, 1994.

Oliphant, Margaret. "Novels." Blackwood's *Edinburgh Magazine* 102.623 (Sept. 1867): 257–281.

Ousby, Ian. *Bloodhounds of Heaven: The Detective in Fiction from Godwin to Doyle*. Cambridge: Harvard UP, 1976.

Owings, Chloe. *Women Police*. New York: Frederick H. Hitchcock, 1925.

Panek, LeRoy Lad. *An Introduction to the Detective Story*. Bowling Green: BGSU Popular Press, 1987.

_____. *Watteau's Shepherds: The Detective Novel in Britain 1914–1940*. Bowling Green: BGSU Popular Press, 1979.

Patterson, Sylvia. "Agatha Christie's Alter Ego: Ariadne Oliver." *The Armchair Detective* 14.3 (1981): 221–227.

Paul, Robert S. *Whatever Happened to Sherlock Holmes? Detective Fiction, Popular Theology, and Society*. Carbondale: Southern Illinois UP, 1991.

Penderson, Joyce Senders. "Life's Lessons: Liberal Feminist Ideals of Family, School, and Community in Victorian England." Nelson and Vallone 194–215.

Perkin, Joan. *Victorian Women*. New York: New York UP, 1995.

Peters, Margot, and Agate Nesaule Krouse. "Women and Crime: Sexism in Allingham, Sayers, and Christie." *Southwest Review* (Spring 1974): 144–152.

Peto, Dorothy. "Policewomen: The Making of a Type." *The Englishwoman* (September 1920): 169–176.

_____. "Policewomen's Conditions of Service." *The Englishwoman* (Dec 1919): 170–176.

_____. "The Training of Women Police and Woman Patrols." *The Englishwoman* (Oct 1916): 22–27.

Pike, B.A. "In Praise of Gladys Mitchell." *The Armchair Detective* 9 (1976): 250–260.

Pitt, Valerie. "Dorothy Sayers: The Predicaments of Women." *Literature and History* 14.2 (Autumn 1988): 172–180.

_____. "The Masks of Lord Peter." Bloom, *Twentieth* 97–113.

Plain, Gill. *Women's Fiction of the Second World War: Gender, Power, and Resistance*. New York: St. Martin's Press, 1996.

Pollock, Griselda. *Vision and Difference: Femininity, Feminism, and Histories of Art*. New York: Routledge, 1988.

Potter, Jane. "'A Great Purifier': The Great War in Women's Romances and Memoirs." Raitt and Tate 85–106.

Poovey, Mary. *The Proper Lady and the Woman Writer: Ideology as Style in the Works of Mary Wollstonecraft, Mary Shelley, and Jane Austen*. Chicago: U of Chicago P, 1984.

_____. *Uneven Developments*. Chicago: U of Chicago P, 1988.

Pound, Reginald. *Mirror of the Century: The Strand Magazine 1891–1950*. New York: A. S. Barnes and Co., 1966.

Pykett, Lyn. *The 'Improper' Feminine: The Women's Sensation Novel and the New Woman Writing*. New York: Routledge, 1992.

Queen, Ellery. *The Female of the Species: The Great Women Detectives and Criminals*. Boston: Little, Brown, 1944.

Rader, Barbara, and Howard G. Zettler, eds. *The Sleuth and the Scholar*. New York: Greenwood Press, 1988.

Radford, Jean, ed. *The Progress of Romance: The Politics of Popular Fiction*. London: Routledge & Kegan Paul, 1986.

Rado, Lisa, ed. *Rereading Modernism: New Directions in Feminist Criticism*. Wellesley Studies in Critical Theory, Literary History, and Culture. New York: Garland, 1994.

Rahn, B.J. "Seeley Regester: America's First Detective Novel." Rader and Zettler 47–62.

Raitt, Suzanne, and Trudi Tate, eds. *Women's Fiction and the Great War*. Oxford: Clarendon Press, 1997.

Ray, Laura Krugman. "The Mysteries of 'Gaudy Night': Feminism, Faith, and the Depths of Character." Adams 272–285.

Reddy, Maureen T. "The Feminist Counter-Tradition in Crime: Cross, Grafton, Paretsky, and Wilson." Walker and Frazer 174–190.

_____. *Sisters in Crime: Feminism and the Crime Novel.* New York: Continuum, 1988.

Reid, Robin Anne. "The Centenary Caper: Casing the Two Competing Schools of Detective Fiction." *Rocky Mountain Modern Language Association* 46.2 (1992): 55–62.

Reilly, John M., ed. *Twentieth Century Crime and Mystery Writers.* 2nd ed. New York: St. Martin's, 1985.

Repplier, Agnes. *Compromises.* Boston: Houghton, Mifflin and Co., 1904.

Reynolds, Kimberly. *Girls Only? Gender and Popular Children's Fiction in Britain, 1880–1910.* Philadelphia: Temple UP, 1990.

_____, and Nicola Humble. *Victorian Heroines: Representations of Femininity in Nineteenth-Century Literature and Art.* New York: New York UP, 1993.

Reynolds, William. "Dorothy L. Sayers' 'Busman's Honeymoon' and the Mind of Its Maker." *Clues* 10.2 (Fall/Winter 1989): 65–80.

_____. "Literature, Latin, and Love: Dorothy L. Sayers' 'Gaudy Night.'" *Clues* 6.1 (Spring 1985): 67–78.

Ritchie, John. "Agatha Christie's England, 1918–39." *ANU Historical Society* (December 1972): 3–9.

Robbins, Joan Hammerman. "A Redefined Sensibility: Raising Consciousness about Women's Issues in Maud Silver's World." *Armchair Detective* 29.4 (Fall 1996): 430–435.

Roberts, Joan Warthling. "Amelia Butterworth: The Spinster Detective." Irons, *Feminism* 3–11.

Ross, Helaine. "A Woman's Intuition: Wives and Lovers in British Golden Age Detective Novels." *Clues* 2.1 (1981): 17–25.

Rossen, Janice. "Oxford *in loco parentis*: The College as Mother in Dorothy Sayers' *Gaudy Night.*" in Bevan 139–156.

Ross-Wagaman, Cheri Louise. "Anna Katharine Green's Experiment With Feminism in the Detective Novel." *The Mid-Atlantic Almanack* 3 (1994): 40–54.

Roth, Mary. *Foul and Fair Play: Reading Genre in Classic Detective Fiction.* Athens: U of Georgia P, 1995.

Rowbotham, Judith. *Good Girls Make Good Wives: Guidance for Girls in Victorian Fiction.* Oxford: Basil Blackwell, 1989.

Rowbotham, Sheila. *A Century of Women: A History of Women in Britain and the United States.* New York: Viking, 1997.

Rubinstein, David. *Before the Suffragettes: Women's Emancipation in the 1890s.* New York, St. Martin's, 1986.

Russ, Joanna. "What Can a Heroine Do? or Why Women Can't Write." Koppelman Cornillon 3–20.

Salmonson, Jessica Amanda, Isabelle D. Waugh, and Charles Waugh. *Wife or Spinster: Stories by Nineteenth-Century Women.* Camden, ME, 1991.

Sanders, Dennis, and Len Lovallo. *The Agatha Christie Companion.* New York: Delacorte Press, 1984.

Sarjeant, William A. "The Last of the 'Golden Age' Writers: Gladys Mitchell, 1901–1983." *The Armchair Detective* 18.4 (1983): 351–360.

Scheick, William J. *Authority and Female Authorship in Colonial America.* Lexington: UP of Kentucky, 1998

_____. "Ethical Romance and the Detecting Reader: The Example of Chesterton's 'The Club of Queer Trades.'" Walker and Frazer 86–97.

Schor, Hilary M. *Scheherezade in the Marketplace: Elizabeth Gaskell and the Victorian Novel.* Oxford: Oxford UP, 1992.

Scott, Mrs. Elspeth Keith Robinson. "Women Clerks and Secretaries." in Morley 280–297.

Scott-Giles, C.W. *The Wimsey Family: A Fragmentary History Compiled from Correspondence with Dorothy L. Sayers*. New York: Harper & Row, 1977.

Scowcroft, P. L. "The Detective Fiction of Dorothy L. Sayers: A Source for the Social Historian?" *Seven* 5 (1984): 70–83.

Shaw, Marian, and Sabine Vanacker. *Reflecting on Miss Marple (Heroines?)*. New York: Routledge, 1991.

Shires, Linda M., ed. *Rewriting the Victorians: Theory, History, and the Politics of Gender*. New York: Routledge, 1992.

Showalter, Elaine. *A Literature of Their Own*. Princeton: Princeton UP, 1977.

_____. *Sexual Anarchy*. New York: Penguin, 1990.

_____, ed. *Daughters of Decadence: Women Writers of the Fin-de-Siecle*. New Brunswick: Rutgers UP, 1993.

Simpson, Bob. "Amazing Grace." *The Mystery Fancier*. 6.4 (July /August 1982): 23–29.

Slung Michelle. Introduction. *The Experiences of Loveday Brooke, Lady Detective*. By C.L. Pirkis. 1894. New York: Dover Publications, 1986.

_____. "Let's Hear it for Agatha Christie: A Feminist Appreciation." Rader and Zettler 63–68.

_____, ed. *Crime on Her Mind: Fifteen Stories of Female Sleuths from the Victorian Era to the Forties*. New York: Pantheon, 1975.

Smith, Harold L. "British Feminism in the Twentieth Century." Harold L. Smith, ed. *British Feminism in the Twentieth Century*. Amherst: U of Massachusetts P, 1990. 47–65.

Smith, Wilbur Jordan. "Mystery Fiction in the Nineteenth Century." Adams 193–203.

Smith-Rosenberg, Carroll. *Disorderly Conduct: Visions of Gender in Victorian America*. New York: Knopf, 1985.

Stallybrass, Peter, and Allon White. *The Politics and Poetics of Transgression*. Ithaca: Cornell UP, 1986.

Steinbrunner, Chris, and Otto Penzler, eds. *Encyclopedia of Mystery and Detection*. 1976. New York: Harvest, HBJ, 1984.

Stetz, Margaret Diane. "Anita Brookner: Woman Writer as Reluctant Feminist." in Jones 96–112.

Stewart, Clare. "'Weird Fascination': The Response to Victorian Women's Ghost Stories." *Feminist Readings of Victorian Popular Texts: Divergent Femininities. The Nineteenth Century*. Ed. Emma Liggins and Daniel Duffy. Hants, England: Ashgate, 1988.

Stone, Gilbert, ed. *Women War Workers*. New York: Thomas Y. Crowell Company, 1917.

Summers, Anne. *Angels and Citizens: British Women as Military Nurses 1854-1914*. London: Routledge & Kegan Paul, 1987.

Swanson, Jean, and Dean James. *By a Woman's Hand: A Guide to Mystery Fiction by Women*. New York: Berkley Books, 1994.

Symons, Julian. *Bloody Murder: From the Detective Story to the Crime Novel: A History*. 1972. New York: Viking, 1985.

Thomas, Ronald R. "Minding the Body Politic: The Romance of Science and the Revision of History in Victorian Detective Fiction." *Victorian Literature and Culture* 19 (1991): 233–254.

Thompson, Allison. "The Reflective Eye: Agatha Christie's View of British Society." *British Heritage* 9.5 (August-September 1988): 58–64.

Thompson, Nicola Diane. *Reviewing Sex: Gender and the Reception of Victorian Novels*. New York: New York UP, 1996.

Thorton, Tamara Plakins. *Handwriting in America: A Cultural History*. New Haven: Yale, 1996.

Todorov, Tzvetan. *The Poetics of Prose*. Trans. Richard Howard. Oxford: Basil Blackwell, 1977.

Trodd, Anthea. *Domestic Crime in the Victorian Novel*. New York: St. Martin's, 1989.

Tweedie, Mrs. Alec. *Women and Soldiers*. London: John Lane, The Bodley Head, 1918.

Van Dine, S. S. "Twenty Rules for Writing Detective Stories." Haycraft, *Art* 189–193.

Vicinus, Martha. *Independent Women: Work and Community for Single Women, 1850–1920*. Chicago: University of Chicago Press, 1985.

_____, ed. Introduction. *A Widening Sphere: Changing Roles of Victorian Women*. Bloomington: Indiana UP, 1977. ix-xix.

_____, ed. *Suffer and Be Still: Women in the Victorian Age*. Bloomington: Indiana UP, 1972.

Vipond, M. "Agatha Christie's Women." *International Fiction Review* 8.2 (1981): 119–123.

Vrettos, Athena. *Somatic Fictions: Imagining Illness in Victorian Culture*. Stanford UP, 1995.

Wald, Gayle F. "Strong Poison: Love and the Novelistic in Dorothy Sayers." Walker and Frazer 98–108,

Walker, Ronald G. and June M. Frazer, eds. *The Cunning Craft: Original Essays on Detective Fiction and Contemporary Literary Theory*. Essays in Literature. Macomb, Ill: Western Illinois University, 1990.

Wall, Wendy. *The Imprint of Gender: Authorship and Publication in the English Renaissance*. Ithaca: Cornell UP, 1993.

Watson, Colin. *Snobbery With Violence: Crime Stories and Their Audience*. London: Eye & Spottiswoode Ltd., 1971.

Watts, Joyce Lammon. "The Androgynous Aspects of Sayers in Harriet and Peter." *The Sayers Review* 4.2 (January 1981): 1–11.

West, Katharine. *Chapter of Governesses: A Study of the Governess in English Fiction 1800–1949*. London: Cohen & West, 1949.

Widdowson, Frances. "'Educating Teacher': Women and Elementary Teaching in London, 1900–1914." in Davidoff and Westover 99–123.

Williams, Gwen. "Fear's Keen Knife: Suspense and the Female Detective, 1890–1920." Bloom, *Twentieth* 37–50.

Williams, H.J. "The Germ of the Detective Novel." *Book Buyer* 3:24.4 (November 1900): 268–274.

Wilson, Edmund. "Who Cares Who Killed Roger Ackroyd?" Haycraft, *Art* 390–397.

Winks, Robin, ed. *Detective Fiction: A Collection of Critical Essays*. 2nd ed. Woodstock, VT: The Countryman Press, 1988.

Winn, Dilys, ed. *Murder Ink: The Mystery Reader's Companion*. 2nd ed. New York: Workman, 1984.

Wisker, Gina, ed. *It's My Party: Reading Twentieth Century Women's Writing*. London: Pluto Press, 1994.

Wolff, Robert Lee. *Sensational Victorian: The Life and Fiction of Mary Elizabeth Braddon*. New York: Garland, 1979.

Woodmansee, Martha. *The Author, Art, and the Market: Rereading the History of Aesthetics*. New York: Columbia UP, 1994.

Woods, Robin. "'His Appearance Is Against Him': The Emergence of the Detective." Walker and Frazer 15–24.

Woollacott, Angela. "From Moral to Professional Authority: Secularism, Social Work, and Middle-Class Women's Self-Construction in World War I Britain." *Journal of Women's History* 10.2 (Summer 1998): 85–111.

_____. "'Khaki Fever' and Its Control: Gender, Class, Age and Sexual Morality on the British Homefront in the First World War." *Journal of Contemporary History* 29 (1994): 325–347.

_____. *"On Her Their Lives Depend": Munitions Workers in the Great World War*. Berkeley: U of California P, 1994.

Wright, Willard Huntington. "The Great Detective Stories." Haycraft, Art 33–70.
Wrong, E.M. "Crime and Detection." Haycraft, Art 18–32.
Wynne, Nancy Blue. "Patricia Wentworth Revisited." Armchair Detective 14.1 (Winter 1981): 90–92.

Index